Bloom's Classic Critical Views

JONATHAN SWIFT

Bloom's Classic Critical Views

JONATHAN SWIFT

Edited and with an Introduction by
Harold Bloom
Sterling Professor of the Humanities
Yale University

BLOOM'S
LITERARY CRITICISM
An imprint of Infobase Publishing

Bloom's Classic Critical Views: Jonathan Swift

Copyright © 2009 Infobase Publishing

Introduction © 2009 by Harold Bloom

All rights reserved. No part of this publication may be reproduced or utilized in any form or by any means, electronic or mechanical, including photocopying, recording, or by any information storage or retrieval systems, without permission in writing from the publisher. For more information contact:

Bloom's Literary Criticism
An imprint of Infobase Publishing
132 West 31st Street
New York NY 10001

Library of Congress Cataloging-in-Publication Data
Jonathan Swift / edited and with an introduction by Harold Bloom ; Daniel Cook, volume editor.
     p. cm. — (Bloom's classic critical views)
   Includes bibliographical references and index.
   ISBN 978-1-60413-434-6 (hardcover)
  1. Swift, Jonathan, 1667–1745—Criticism and interpretation.   I. Bloom, Harold.
II. Cook, Daniel, 1981– III. Title.   IV. Series.
   PR3727.J6265 2009
   828'.509—dc22   2009001610

Bloom's Literary Criticism books are available at special discounts when purchased in bulk quantities for businesses, associations, institutions, or sales promotions. Please call our Special Sales Department in New York at (212) 967-8800 or (800) 322-8755.

You can find Bloom's Literary Criticism on the World Wide Web at
http://www.chelseahouse.com

Volume editor: Daniel Cook
Series design by Erika K. Arroyo
Cover designed by Takeshi Takahashi
Printed in the United States of America
IBT IBT 10 9 8 7 6 5 4 3 2 1

This book is printed on acid-free paper.

All links and Web addresses were checked and verified to be correct at the time of publication. Because of the dynamic nature of the Web, some addresses and links may have changed since publication and may no longer be valid.

Contents

Contents

Series Introduction

Bloom's Classic Critical Views is a new series presenting a selection of the most important older literary criticism on the greatest authors commonly read in high school and college classes today. Unlike the Bloom's Modern Critical Views series, which for more than 20 years has provided the best contemporary criticism on great authors, Bloom's Classic Critical Views attempts to present the authors in the context of their time and to provide criticism that has proved over the years to be the most valuable to readers and writers. Selections range from contemporary reviews in popular magazines, which demonstrate how a work was received in its own era, to profound essays by some of the strongest critics in the British and American tradition, including Henry James, G.K. Chesterton, Matthew Arnold, and many more.

Some of the critical essays and extracts presented here have appeared previously in other titles edited by Harold Bloom, such as the New Moulton's Library of Literary Criticism. Other selections appear here for the first time in any book by this publisher. All were selected under Harold Bloom's guidance.

In addition, each volume in this series contains a series of essays by a contemporary expert, who comments on the most important critical selections, putting them in context and suggesting how they might be used by a student writer to influence his or her own writing. This series is intended above all for students, to help them think more deeply and write more powerfully about great writers and their works.

Introduction by Harold Bloom

The greatest ironist in Western literature, the Anglo-Irish Jonathan Swift perpetually writes one thing while meaning another. Other major ironists write in his praise, from his contemporaries Henry Fielding, Alexander Pope, and Voltaire on through Byron in Regency England to twentieth-century luminaries such as W.B. Yeats, James Joyce, and Samuel Beckett.

Irony is a dangerous mode, an invitation to misunderstanding. Voltaire, Carlyle in *Sartor Resartus*, Kierkegaard, Nietzsche, and Freud risk weak misreadings, as did Swift, particularly in his masterwork, *A Tale of a Tub*. Martin Price, Swift's best modern critic, catches the irony of Swift's reception by unwary readers:

> . . . he has as a result been accused of all the malevolence and blindness that resentment can invent. He does not allow man much comfort or dignity, and he cruelly reduces grand pretensions to systematic follies and mechanized brutality.

I regularly reread *A Tale of a Tub* every year to admonish myself against the corruptions of learning and the madness of solipsism. Swift's *Tale* teaches several modes of madness including disgressiveness, to which I myself am prone, whether talking, teaching, or writing. And so I wince, yet profit by reading the *Tale*'s great "Digression Concerning . . . Madness":

> But when a man's fancy gets astride of his reason, when imagination is at cuffs with the senses, and common understanding as well as common sense is kicked out of doors; the first proselyte he makes is himself; and when that is once compassed, the difficulty is not so great in bringing over others; a strong delusion always operating from without as vigorously as from within. For cant and vision are to the ear and the eye the same that tickling is to the touch. Those entertainments and pleasures we most value in life are such as dupe and play the wag with the senses. For,

if we take an examination of what is generally understood by happiness as it has respect either to the understanding or the senses, we shall find all its properties and adjuncts will herd under this short definition, that it is a perpetual possession of being well deceived.

Swift is a therapeutic ironist, strangely akin to Hamlet. Like the prince of Denmark, the Anglo-Irish wit intends our good, if he can persuade us to self-recognition. Swift went mad; Hamlet feigned madness and perhaps achieved it.

The line between irony and satire always wavers, but Swift is a satirist only in the highest style. There he stands with Rabelais, William Blake, and Byron. He matches them in exuberance and in wisdom, though unlike them he wars against spiritual enthusiasm.

BIOGRAPHY

Jonathan Swift
(1667–1745)

Jonathan Swift was born in Dublin on November 30, 1667, seven months after his father's death. He was the son of Jonathan Swift and Abigail Erick (or Herrick); since both parents were from England, Swift, though born and educated in Ireland, did not think of himself as Irish. He attended Kilkenny Grammar School and Trinity College, Dublin, where, because of disciplinary problems, he obtained his B.A. degree only by "special grace" (*ex speciali gratia*).

In 1689, Swift left for England, becoming secretary to Sir William Temple, through whom he apparently hoped to achieve some advancement in political affairs. Nothing came of this association, however, and, having received his M.A. degree in 1692 from Hart Hall, Oxford, Swift took orders as a priest of the Anglican Church of Ireland early in 1695, more to achieve independence than out of any particular religious fervor.

After spending an unhappy year as prebendary of Kilroot, Swift returned to England and remained with Temple at Moor Park until 1699. It was during this period that he began his literary career, writing pindarics and, in 1697, *The Battle of the Books*, which was inspired by Temple's involvement in the "Phalaris" controversy.

Temple died in 1699, leaving Swift without a patron. He returned to Ireland, settling this time in Dublin as the chaplain to Lord Berkeley, the new lord justice of Ireland. In 1704, Swift published *A Tale of a Tub* (along with *The Battle of the Books*), which was primarily an attack on various religious abuses. Swift's outspokenness, manifested also in a number of pamphlets on religious questions, such as *An Argument Against Abolishing Christianity* (1708), made it harder for Swift to gain the preferment that would have enabled him to leave Ireland. He was, however, a frequent visitor to England, where he gained a literary reputation; became acquainted with Addison, Steele, Pope, and Congreve; and was briefly, in 1714, a member of the Scriblerus Club with Pope, Gay, Arbuthnot, and others. In 1710, he switched his political allegiance to the Tories and was active as a political journalist, writing poems and tracts in support of the Tory ministry and editing *The Examiner* for four years. Events in Swift's personal life are reflected in *Journal to Stella* (1710–13) and in the poem *Cadenus and Vanessa* (1713).

In 1713, Swift became dean of St. Patrick's Cathedral in Dublin, the highest position he was to achieve. The death of Queen Anne in 1714 put an end to his political career and ensured that he would remain in Ireland for most of the rest of his life. He wrote several pamphlets in defense of Irish rights, most notably *The Drapier's Letters* (1724), which frustrated an attempt to circulate debased currency in Ireland.

Swift published *Gulliver's Travels* in 1726; it satirized contemporary politics and the conventions of both philosophical and "factual" tales of exploration. *The Grand Question Debated* and *A Modest Proposal* were published in 1729, and *Verses on the Death of Dr. Swift* appeared in 1731. Having suffered since his twenty-third year from a condition now called Meniere's disease, which causes nausea and loss of equilibrium, Swift developed a brain tumor late in life; in 1742, he lapsed into dementia and died on October 19, 1745.

PERSONAL

The following extracts present various views of Jonathan Swift's character from the perspectives of friends, allies, and, in some cases, enemies and jealous rivals. What the extracts have in common is just how difficult it was, and remains for critics today, to justify absolute statements about Swift's personal qualities. Almost every extract's author feels that he or she has some insight into the character of the dean of St. Patrick, but those impressions are always specific to a particular meeting and a momentary appreciation of the man at a single point in time.

The first extract is from a private letter sent to Sir Robert Southwell by Sir William Temple, who had welcomed the young Swift into his home as a valued personal secretary. Brief as it is, we can gain some insight into the kind of aide he sought and evidently received. The second is a poem on the dean's birthday by Thomas Parnell, who prophesizes the eternal fame awaiting his friend. As a way of contrast, the third extract offers some dismissive thoughts on the rise of Swift. For White Kennett, the bishop of Peterborough, Swift was proving to be an unwelcome distraction. The next extract is taken from a 1755 essay on Swift by a relative, Deane Swift, in which we find a vivid autobiographical fragment of the "Family of Swift." Biographies and biographical commentaries on Swift abounded in the period, so much so that it proved increasingly difficult to dissociate the author from his works.

Other extracts include the controversial "Judas-biography" by Lord Orrery, John Boyle, which elicited a number of furrowed responses from Swift's friends and well-wishers. One close friend of Swift's, Patrick Delany, produced his own biographical study largely in order to refute specific charges made by Orrery. Samuel Richardson, an astute observer, is quick to deflate Orrery's reliance on an acquaintanceship with Swift as a form of critical authority. In addition to this, we have an notice from the novelist Henry Fielding and anecdotes from Swift's friends Alexander Pope and Laetitia Pilkington, as well as more casual acquaintances such as Thomas Amory. Together these anecdotes offer a perspective different from that of the formal biographies, even if both present us with an affable if difficult man.

The section concludes with extracts from two Irishmen of a much later period, the late nineteenth century. The inclusion of this commentary helps illustrate the longevity and endurance of a peculiarly personal approach to Swift's life and works. The mind of Edward Dowden's Swift is "eminently practical and positive," clear and clean, though manifesting itself in indignant rage at humanity. *Gulliver's Travels*, Swift's best-known work, is interpreted as a message of "reconciliation, not of revolt." Dowden, it must be said, is not the first, nor the last, reader to glean character insights from the works of the author; but he does so in especially graphic terms. Augustine Birrell, a decade or so later, pursues further the commonly held view that "No fouler pen than Swift's has soiled our literature." The venality of his writing is mirrored in his personal habits for Birrell, who gleefully recounts the story of an exchange of words between Swift and an innkeeper, Mrs. Seneca of Drogheda. "'[Y]ou are the last man, doctor,' she exclaims, 'that should complain of dirty sheets.'" The suggestion here is that "dirty" literature, penned on once-clean white paper, is emblematically matched by the unkempt room of the inn. Horace Walpole felt he knew the inner workings of the author well enough to inform his correspondent Sir Horace Mann in 1780 that "Swift was a wild beast." Wild perhaps he was, but what can we truly know about the man and his works?

WILLIAM TEMPLE "LETTER TO SIR ROBERT SOUTHWELL" (1690)

In 1689, Jonathan Swift moved to the English household of Sir William Temple, the son of Sir John Temple, the Swifts' benefactor in Ireland. Over a ten-year period, with extended breaks, Swift acted as secretary and amanuensis to the baronet. In addition, he acted as Temple's emissary to the court of William III, although it is unclear whether he operated as a learned informer or a glorified mailman. Although valuing Swift highly, Temple often treated him as duty-bound. Swift, for his part, felt Temple was not as supportive of his advancement as he would have hoped. Nonetheless, they aided each other's publications, and in Temple's circle Swift met a number of useful political contacts. As for Temple, he died in 1699, barely a decade after hiring the young Swift. From this short, rather matter-of-fact statement from Temple we can infer a lot about the values he favored in his aide.

Hee has latine and greek, some french, writes a very good and current hand, is very honest and diligent.

—WILLIAM TEMPLE, letter to
Sir Robert Southwell, May 29, 1690

THOMAS PARNELL "TO DR. SWIFT, ON HIS BIRTHDAY, NOVEMBER 30TH, 1713" (1713)

A fellow Dubliner, Thomas Parnell met Jonathan Swift at St. Patrick's Cathedral on August 16, 1704, and evidently they formed a strong friendship. The death of Parnell's wife in August 1711 led to a long period of grief, and he became a regular visitor to London. Studying at the University of Dublin he became doctor of divinity in 1712, but he moved away from his low Anglican, Whig background and supported the Tories, just as Swift had done. After Swift had been offered the deanery of St. Patrick's, he successfully requested, on April 30, 1713, that Parnell become prebend of Dunlavin. Parnell, however, was absorbed by the Scriblerus Club, which emerged from the intellectual companionship that developed among Swift, Alexander Pope, John Gay, John Arbuthnot, Robert Harley, and others. The death of Queen Anne on August 1, 1714, accelerated the dissolution of the Scriblerian commune, and Parnell returned to Ireland in 1714. He made a brief return to London in the summer of 1718 for a reunion with some of the Scriblerians, but he died suddenly on his journey home to

Ireland. This version of the poem is taken from a 1787 collection of Swift's
works, which has some accidental and a few substantive variants.

Urg'd by the warmth of friendship's sacred flame,
But more by all the glories of thy fame;
By all those offsprings of thy learned mind,
In judgment solid, as in wit refin'd,
Resolv'd I sing, tho' lab'ring up the way
To reach my theme, O Swift! accept my lay.
    Rapt by the force of thought, and rais'd above,
Through Contemplation's airy fields I rove,
Where pow'rful Fancy purifies my eye,
And lights the beauties of a brighter sky,
Fresh paints the meadows, bids green shades ascend,
Clear rivers wind, and op'ning plains extend;
Then fills its landscape thro' the vary'd parts
With Virtues, Graces, Sciences, and Arts;
Superior forms, of more than mortal air,
More large than mortals, more serenely fair.
Of these two Chiefs, the guardians of thy name,
Conspire to raise thee to the point of fame.
Ye future Times! I heard the silver sound,
I saw the Graces form a circle round;
Each where she fix'd attentive seem'd to root,
And all, but Eloquence herself was mute.
High o'er the rest I see the goddess rise,
Loose to the breeze her upper garment flies:
By turns within her eyes the passions burn,
And softer passions languish in their turn:
Upon her tongue persuasion or command,
And decent Action dwells upon her hand.
    From out her breast ('twas there the treasure lay)
She drew thy Labours to the blaze of day;
Then gaz'd, and read the charms she could inspire,
And taught the list'ning audience to admire.
How strong thy flight, how large thy grasp of thought,
How just thy schemes, how regularly wrought!
How sure you wound when Ironies deride,
Which must be seen, and feign to turn aside!

'Twas thus exploring she rejoic'd to see
Her brightest features drawn so near by thee:
Then here, she cries, let future ages dwell,
And learn to copy where they can't excell.
  She spake; applause attended on the close:
Then Poesy, her sister-art, arose;
Her fairer sister, born in deeper ease,
Not made so much for bus'ness, more to please.
Upon her cheek sits Beauty, ever young;
The soul of Music warbles on her tongue;
Bright in her eyes a pleasing ardour glows,
And from her heart the sweetest temper flows;
A laurel-wreath adorns her curls of hair,
And binds their order to the dancing air:
She shakes the colours of her radiant wing,
And from the spheres she takes a pitch to sing.
  Thrice happy genius his! whose Works have hit
The lucky point of bus'ness and of wit:
They seem like show'rs, which April months prepare
To call their flow'ry glories up to air;
The drops, descending, take the painted bow,
And dress with sunshine, while for good they flow:
To me retiring oft', he finds relief
In slowly-wasting care, and biting grief:
From me retreating oft', he gives to view
What eases care and grief in others too.
Ye fondly grave! be wise enough to know,
"Life ne'er unbent, were but a life of woe".
Some full in stretch for greatness, some for gain,
On his own rack each puts himself to pain.
I'll gently steal you from your toils away,
Where balmy winds with scents ambrosial play;
Where on the banks, as crystal rivers flow,
They teach immortal amaranths to grow;
Then from the mild indulgence of the scene
Restore your tempers strong for toils again.
  She ceas'd; soft music trembled in the wind,
And sweet delight diffus'd thro' ev'ry mind:
The little Smiles, which still the goddess grace,
Sportive arose, and ran from face to face.

But chief (and in that place the Virtues bless)
A gentle band their eager joy express:
Here Friendship asks, and Love of Merit longs
To hear the goddesses renew their songs;
Here great Benevolence to Man is pleas'd;
These own their Swift, and grateful hear him prais'd.
You gentle band! you well may bear your part,
You reign superior graces in his heart.
O Swift! if fame be life (as well we know
That bards and heroes have esteem'd it so)
Thou canst not wholly die; thy Works will shine
To future times, and life in fame be thine.

—THOMAS PARNELL, "To Dr. Swift, On His Birthday,
November 30th, 1713" (1713), *The Poetical Works of
Dr. Jonathan Swift, Dean of St. Patrick's, Dublin.
In Four Volumes. With the Life of the Author*, 1787,
vol. 1, pp. cxlix–clii

WHITE KENNETT (1713)

The bishop of Peterborough, White Kennett, was a ferocious religious historian who, among other things, used extensive research to argue for the validity of lay baptism in the face of charges laid against it by the high-church party. In 1711, Kennett contributed to the *Medley*, a Whig publication, in response to Swift's claims in the *Examiner* that the bishops of the low-church party sought to subvert the church. Kennett was evidently preoccupied with Swift's celebrity in religious circles, as he refers to the distraction caused by Swift's attendance at his sermon "against Popery and Profaneness" of November 1713, as well as in the following diary extract.

Swift came into the coffee-house, and had a bow from everybody but me. When I came to the antechamber to wait before prayers Dr. Swift was the principal man of talk and business, and acted as Minister of Requests. He was soliciting the Earl of Arran to speak to his brother, the Duke of Ormond, to get a chaplain's place established in the garrison of Hull for Mr. Fiddes, a clergyman in that neighborhood, who had lately been in jail, and published sermons to pay fees. He was promising Mr. Thorold to undertake with my Lord Treasurer that according to his petition he should obtain a salary of 200 *l.* per annum, as minister of the English Church at Rotterdam. He stopped F. Gwynne, Esq., going in with the red bag to the Queen, and told him aloud he had something to say to him from my Lord Treasurer. He talked with the son of Dr. Davenant to be sent abroad, and took out his pocket-book and wrote down several things as *memoranda* to do for him. He turned to the fire, and took out his gold watch, and telling him the time of day, complained it was very late. A gentleman said, "it was too fast." "How can I help it," says the Doctor, "if the courtiers give me a watch that won't go right?" Then he instructed a young nobleman that the best poet in England was Mr. Pope (a Papist), who had begun a translation of Homer into English verse for which, he said, he must have them all subscribe. "For," says he, "the author *shall not* begin to print till I *have* a thousand guineas for him." Lord Treasurer, after leaving the Queen, came through the room, beckoning Dr. Swift to follow him; both went off just before prayers.

—WHITE KENNETT, *Diary,* 1713

JONATHAN SWIFT "FAMILY OF SWIFT" (1727)

This autobiographical fragment appeared as an appendix to Deane Swift's essay on Swift in 1755. In the beginning of the book, Deane Swift asserts that "Family of Swift" was written "about six or eight and twenty Years ago" and that the manuscript, which came to the editor by way of his familial connections, was deposited by him in the university library of Trinity College, Dublin. Deane Swift's edited version removes a number of archaic spellings and, more substantially, amends details in part. The student might wish to consider the status of autobiography here. Why does Jonathan Swift wish to highlight certain aspects of his life? Which parts does he omit or rewrite? How reliable are his accounts of events and people such as Sir William Temple? Is this a work of fiction or a historical document?

J.S. D.D., and D. of St. P— was the only Son of JONATHAN SWIFT, who was the seventh or eighth Son of Mr. THOMAS SWIFT abovementioned, so eminent for his Loyalty and his Sufferings.

His Father died young, about two Years after his Marriage: He had some Employments and Agencies; his Death was much lamented on Account of his Reputation, for Integrity, with a tolerable good Understanding.

He married Mrs. ABIGAIL ERICK of *Leicestershire,* descended from the most antient Family of ERICKS, who derive their Lineage from ERICK the Forester, a great Commander, who raised an Army to oppose the Invasion of WILLIAM the Conqueror, by whom he was vanquished, but afterwards employed to command that Prince's Forces, and in his old Age retired to his House in

Leicestershire, where his Family hath continued ever since, but declining every Age, and are now in the Condition of very private Gentlemen.

This Marriage was on both Sides very indiscreet, for his Wife brought her Husband little or no Fortune; and his Death happening so suddenly, before he could make a sufficient Establishment for his Family, his son (not then born) hath often been heard to say, that he felt the Consequences of that Marriage, not only through the whole Course of his Education, but during the greatest Part of his Life.

He was born in *Dublin*, on St. ANDREW's day; and when he was a Year old, an Event happened to him that seems very unusual; for his Nurse, who was a woman of *Whitehaven*, being under an absolute Necessity of seeing one of her Relations, who was then extremely sick, and from whom she expected a Legacy; and being at the same time extremely fond of the Infant, she stole him on Shipboard unknown to his Mother and Uncle, and carried him with her to *Whitehaven*, where he continued for almost three Years. For, when the Matter was discovered, his Mother sent Orders by all Means not to hazard a second Voyage, till he could be better able to bear it. The Nurse was so careful of him, that before he returned he had learnt to spell; and by the Time that he was three Years old, he could read any Chapter in the Bible.

After his Return to *Ireland*, he was sent at six Years old to the School of *Kilkenny*, from whence at fourteen he was admitted into the University of *Dublin*; where by the ill Treatment of his nearest Relations, he was so discouraged and sunk in his Spirits, that he too much neglected some Parts of his Academick Studies: For which he had no great Relish by Nature, and turned himself to reading History and Poetry; so that when the Time came for taking his Degree of Batchelor, although he had lived with great Regularity and due Observance of the Statutes, he was stopped of his Degree for Dulness and Insufficiency; and at last hardly admitted in a Manner, little to his Credit, which is called in that College, *Speciali gratia*. And this discreditable Mark, as I am told, stands upon Record in their College Registry.

The Troubles then breaking out, he went to his Mother, who lived in *Leicester*; and after continuing there some Months, he was received by Sir WILLIAM TEMPLE, whose Father had been a great Friend to the Family, and who was now retired to his House called *Moor-park*, near *Farnham* in *Surry*, where he continued for about two Years: For he happened before twenty Years old, by a Surfeit of Fruit to contract a Giddiness and Coldness of Stomach, that almost brought him to his Grave; and this Disorder pursued him with Intermissions of two or three Years to the End of his Life. Upon this Occasion he returned to *Ireland*, by Advice of Physicians, who weakly imagined that his native Air might be of some Use to recover his Health:

But growing worse, he soon went back to Sir WILLIAM TEMPLE; with whom growing into some Confidence, he was often trusted with Matters of great Importance. King WILLIAM had a high Esteem for Sir WILLIAM TEMPLE by a long Acquaintance, while that Gentleman was Ambassador and Mediator of a General Peace at *Nimeguen*. The King soon after his Expedition to *England*, visited his old Friend often at *Sheen*, and took his Advice in Affairs of greatest Consequence. But Sir WILLIAM TEMPLE, weary of living so near *London*, and resolving to retire to a more private Scene, bought an Estate near *Farnham* in *Surry*, of about 100 *l.* a Year, where Mr. SWIFT accompanied him.

About that Time a Bill was brought in to the House of Commons for triennial Parliaments; against which, the King, who was a Stranger to our Constitution, was very averse, by the Advice of some weak People, who persuaded the Earl of PORTLAND, that King CHARLES the first lost his Crown and Life by consenting to pass such a bill. The Earl who was a weak Man, came down to *Moor-park*, by his Majesty's Orders, to have Sir WILLIAM TEMPLE's Advice, who said much to shew him the Mistake. But he continued still to advise the King against passing the Bill. Whereupon Mr. SWIFT was sent to *Kensington* with the whole Account of that Matter in writing, to convince the King and the Earl how ill they were informed. He told the Earl, to whom he was referred by his Majesty (and gave it in Writing) that the Ruin of King CHARLES the first was not owing to his passing the triennial Bill, which did not hinder him from dissolving any Parlmt, but to the passing another bill, which put it out of his power to dissolve the Parliament then in Being, without the Consent of the House. Mr. SWIFT, who was well versed in *English* History, although he were then under twenty-one Years old, gave the King a short Account of the Matter, but a more large one to the Earl of PORTLAND; but all in vain; For the King by ill Advisers was prevailed upon to refuse passing the Bill. This was the first Time that Mr. SWIFT had ever any Converse with Courts, and he told his Friends it was the first Incident that helped to cure him of Vanity. The Consequence of this wrong Step in his Majesty was very unhappy; for it put that Prince under a Necessity of introducing those People called Whigs into Power and Employments, in order to pacify them. For, although it be held a Part of the King's Prerogative to refuse passing a Bill, yet the learned in the Law think otherwise, from that Expression used at the Coronation, wherein the Prince obligeth himself to consent to all Laws, *quas vulgus elegerit.*

Mr. SWIFT lived with him (Sir W. TEMPLE) some Time, but resolving to settle himself in some Way of living, was inclined to take orders. However, although his Fortune was very small, he had a Scruple of entering into the Church merely for Support, and Sir W. TEMPLE then being Master of the Rolls in

Ireland, offered him an Employ of about 120 *l.* a Year in that Office; whereupon Mr. SWIFT told him, that since he had now an Opportunity of living without being driven into the Church for a Maintenance, he was resolved to go to *Ireland* and take Holy Orders. He was recommended to the Lord CAPEL, then Lord Deputy, who gave him a Prebend in the North, worth about 100 *l.* a Year, of which growing weary in a few Months, he returned to *England*, resigned his Living in Favour of a Friend, and continued in Sir WILLIAM TEMPLE's house till the Death of that great Man, who besides a Legacy, left him the Care, and Trust and Advantage of publishing his posthumous Writings.

Upon this Event Mr. SWIFT removed to *London*, and applied by Petition to King WILLIAM, upon the Claim of a Promise his Majesty had made to Sir W. TEMPLE, that he would give Mr. SWIFT a Prebend of *Canterbury* or *Westminster*. The Earl of RUMNEY, who professed much Friendship for him, promised to second his Petition; but as he was an old, vicious, illiterate Rake, without any Sense of Truth or Honour, said not a Word to the King. And Mr. SWIFT, after long Attendance in vain, thought it better to comply with an Invitation given him by the Earl of BERKLEY to attend him to *Ireland*, as his Chaplain and private Secretary; his Lordship having been appointed one of the Lords Justices of that Kingdom. He attended his Lordship, who landed near *Waterford*, and Mr. SWIFT acted as Secretary the whole Journey to *Dublin*. But another Person had so far insinuated himself into the Earls favour, by telling him, that the Post of Secretary was not proper for a Clergyman, nor would be of any Advantage to one who aimed only at Church Preferments; that his Lordship, after a poor Apology, gave that Office to the other.

In some Months the Deanery of *Derry* fell vacant, and it was the Earl of BERKLEY's turn to dispose of it. Yet Things were so ordered, that the Secretary having received a Bribe, the Deanery was disposed of to another, and Mr. SWIFT was put off with some other Church Livings not worth above a third Part of that rich Deanery; and at this present time not a sixth. The Excuse pretended was his being too young, although he were then thirty Years old.

—JONATHAN SWIFT, "Family of Swift," circa 1727,
in Deane Swift, *An Essay upon the Life, Writings,
and Character, of Dr. Jonathan Swift*,
1755, pp. xxxvii–liii

ALEXANDER POPE (1728–30)

Alongside Swift, the renowned poet Alexander Pope was a prominent member of the Scriblerus Club, an informal grouping of satirists that also included John Gay (mentioned below), John Arbuthnot, and Thomas Parnell (whose poem was included at the beginning of this section). Although the history of the group remains unclear, due to its informal nature, by 1714 it had acquired a distinctly Tory viewpoint. This suited Swift, who had left his Whig associations largely behind him, and Pope, who sought to dissociate himself from Joseph Addison's Whig circle. Nonetheless, Swift fled to Ireland around this time, so it is difficult to position him securely in the club. But his influence on the group can be attested to by the fact that Pope explicitly refers to a partial reunion of the club in 1726 and links this to the renewed creative energy manifested in Gay's masterpiece, *The Beggar's Opera*. During this period, Swift produced his most famous work, *Gulliver's Travels*, which Pope again explicitly links to the Scriblerian commune. In this extract, Pope offers some personal insights into the character of his friend, specifically the "odd blunt way" that was often misunderstood by strangers. This anecdotal account, taken from Joseph Spence's collection, is also valuable for the insight it gives into Swift's generosity, here manifested in his aggressive insistence that his friends should not spare him the expenses associated with good hospitality. In the second of Pope's extracts given here, again taken from Spence's collection, we get an insight into Swift's discomfort with praise.

Dr. Swift has an odd blunt way, that is mistaken, by strangers, for ill-nature.—'Tis so odd that there's no describing it but by facts.—I'll tell you one that just comes into my head. One evening Gay and I went to see him: you know how intimately we were all acquainted. On our coming in; "Hey-day, gentlemen," says the Doctor, "what's the meaning of this visit? How come you to leave all the great lords, that you are so fond of, to come hither to see a poor Dean?"—Because we would rather see you than any of them.—"Ay, any one that did not know you so well as I do, might believe you. But, since you are come, I must get some supper for you, I suppose?"—No, Doctor, we have supped already.—"Supped already! that's impossible: why, 'tis not eight o'clock yet."—Indeed we have.—"That's very strange: but if you had not supped, I must have got something for you.—Let me see, what should I have had? a couple of lobsters? ay, that would have done very well;—two shillings: tarts; a shilling. But you will drink a glass of wine with me, though you supped so much before your usual time, only to spare my pocket?"—No, we had rather talk with you, than drink with you.—"But if you had supped with me, as in all reason you ought to have done, you must have drank with me.—A bottle of wine; two shillings.—Two and two, is four; and one is five: just two and sixpence a piece. There, Pope, there's half-a-crown for you; and there's another for you, sir: for I won't save any thing by you I am determined." This was all said and done with his usual seriousness on such occasions; and in spite of every thing we could say to the contrary, he actually obliged us to take the money.

—ALEXANDER POPE (1728–30), cited in Joseph Spence,
*Anecdotes, Observations, and Characters, of Books
and Men,* ed. Samuel Weller Singer, 1820, pp. 19–20

ALEXANDER POPE (1742–43)

Rollin has written a letter very full of compliments to Dr. Swift.—"Has not he affronted him by it?"—No:—the doctor does not hate praise, he only dislikes it when 'tis extravagant or coarse.—When B— told him he loved him more than all his friends and relations; the dean made him no manner of answer; but said afterwards: "the man's a fool!"—I once said to him, "There's a lady, doctor, that longs to see you, and admires you above all things."—"Then I despise her heartily!" said he.

—ALEXANDER POPE (1742–43), cited in Joseph Spence,
*Anecdotes, Observations, and Characters, of Books
and Men,* ed. Samuel Weller Singer, 1820, p. 256

HENRY FIELDING (1745)

This early notice on the death of Swift from Henry Fielding, a contemporary novelist, is a useful indication of the esteem in which Swift was held by fellow writers. The presence of numerous typographical and grammatical errors indicates that this small piece was rushed through the press—as it was—barely a fortnight after the death of Swift. In this notice, we have the familiar comparisons made with Rabelais and Cervantes, but Fielding is sure to go beyond this, focusing in particular on Swift's political bite and personal character.

A few Days since died in Ireland, Dr. Jonathan Swift, Dean of St. Patrick's in Dublin. A Genius who deserves to be ranked among the first whom the World ever saw. He possessed the Talents of a Lucian, a Rabelais, and a Cervantes, and in his Works exceeded them all. He employed his Wit to the noblest Purposes, in ridiculing as well Superstition in Religion as Infidelity, and several Errors and Immortalities which sprung up from time to time in his Age; and lastly, in the Defence of his Country, against several pernicious

Schemes of wicked Politicians. Nor was he only a Genius and a Patriot: he was in private Life a good and charitable Man, and frequently lent Sums of Money without Interest to the Poor and Industrious; by which means many Families were preserved from Destruction. The Loss of so excellent a Person would have been more to be lamented, had not a Disease that affected his Understanding, long since deprived him of the Enjoyment of Life, and his Country of the Benefit of his great Talents; But we hope this short and hasty Character will not be the last Piece of Gratitude paid by his Contemporaries to such eminent Merit.

—HENRY FIELDING, obituary of Swift,
The True Patriot (No. 1), November 5, 1745

LAETITIA PILKINGTON (1748)

Taken from the *Memoirs* of the Anglo-Irish poet Laetitia Pilkington, this poem was presented to Swift by his biographer Patrick Delany, who had attended university with Pilkington's father. In her version of events, Pilkington describes in vivid detail how she had long held an ambition to meet Swift. As Delany and his friends were to meet with her idol the next day, on his birthday, she passed him this commemorative poem. A few days later, she and her husband, Reverend Matthew Pilkington, dined with Swift, much to her delight. She talks fondly of their conversations, including a witty episode in the author's library in which he shows her the income he had earned from the ruling political party: empty drawers! The *Memoirs* were much admired, and no doubt such anecdotes as this one attracted much attention. Modern scholars tend to draw on Pilkington's various accounts of Swift in their vain attempts to understand his complex attitudes toward women. From Pilkington we learn of his cruel mockery of her diminutiveness, of his literal attempts to brand her, and of his infamously saucy innuendo. Despite this, she often spoke highly of Swift and remained an avid reader of his works, often in unpublished manuscripts.

While I the God-like Men of Old,
In Admiration wrapt, behold!
Rever'd Antiquity explore,
And turn the long-liv'd Volumes o'er,
Where *Cato, Plutarch, Flaccus* shine
In ev'ry Excellence divine;
I grieve that our degen'rate Days,
Produce no mighty Souls like these;

Patriot, philosopher and Bard,
Are Names unknown, and seldom heard.
Spare your Reflection, *Phoebus* cries,
'Tis as ungrateful as unwise;
Can you complain this sacred Day,
That Virtues, or that Arts decay?
Behold in SWIFT reviv'd appears
The Virtues of unnumbered Years,
Behold in Him with new Delight,
The Patriot, Bard and Sage unite;
And know *Ierne* in that Name
Shall rival *Greece* and *Rome* in Fame.

—LAETITIA PILKINGTON, *Memoirs of Mrs. Laetitia*
Pilkington, Wife to the Rev. Mr. Matthew Pilkington.
Written by herself, 1748, vol. 1, pp. 50–51

LORD ORRERY (1752)

Fifth earl of Cork and fifth earl of Orrery, the biographer John Boyle was an intimate acquaintance of both Pope and Swift from the early 1730s until their deaths. He is perhaps best remembered for his malignant "Judas-biography" on Swift: *Remarks on the Life and Writings of Dr. Jonathan Swift* (1752). This book incited a number of outraged responses, largely from Dublin, such as Patrick Delany's important *Observations upon Lord Orrery's Remarks* (1754), and in private correspondence (see Samuel Richardson's entry). In particular, Orrery introduced and popularized a number of stories that have remained with us, including the suggestion that Swift had secretly married his Stella. Indeed, Orrery routinely highlights his close acquaintance with Swift in order to lend credence to his words. The biographer also writes in an often underhanded way, emphasizing the strengths he gleaned from the mistakes made by his subject, such as in the extract here. Students might examine Orrery's presentation of Swift's sincerity. This might be seen as a recurrent theme among Swift's commentators, who, on the whole, insist on the sincerity and honesty of Swift the man as much as Swift the writer. Is Orrery here, as elsewhere in his book, permanently undermining the grounds of Swift's sincerity as much as he promotes it as one of Swift's more admirable qualities?

He was in the decline of life when I knew him. His friendship was an honour to me, and to say the truth, I have even drawn advantage from his errors. I have beheld him in all humours and dispositions, and I have formed various speculations from the several weaknesses, to which I observed him liable. His capacity and strength of mind were undoubtedly equal to any task whatever. His pride, his spirit, or his ambition, call it by what name you please, was boundless: but, his views were checked in his younger years, and the anxiety of that disappointment had a visible effect upon all his actions. He was sour and severe, but not absolutely ill-natured. He was sociable only to particular friends, and to them only at particular hours. He knew politeness more than he practised it. He was a mixture of avarice, and generosity: the former, was frequently prevalent, the latter, seldom appeared, unless excited by compassion. He was open to adulation, and could not, or would not distinguish between low flattery, and just applause. His abilities rendered him superiour to envy. He was undisguised and perfectly sincere. I am induced to think, that he entered into orders, more from some private and fixed resolution, than from absolute choice: be that as it may, he performed the duties of the church with great punctuality, and a decent degree of devotion. He read prayers rather in a strong nervous voice, than in a graceful manner: and altho' he has often been accused of irreligion, nothing of that kind appeared in his conversation or behaviour. His cast of mind induced him to think, and speak more of politics than of religion. His perpetual views were directed towards power: and his chief aim was to be removed into *England:* but when he found himself entirely disappointed, he turned his thoughts to opposition, and became the patron of *Ireland,* in which country he was born.

—JOHN BOYLE, EARL OF ORRERY, *Remarks on the Life and Writings of Dr. Jonathan Swift, Dean of St. Patrick's, Dublin,* 1752, pp. 4–6

SAMUEL RICHARDSON (1752)

I really think my Lord Orrery, in his *Life of Swift,* has intended to be laudably impartial. I have no notion of that friendship which makes a man think himself obliged to gloss over the faults of a man whom he wishes not to have great ones. Is it not a strong proof of the sacred authority of the Scriptures, that the histories of David, Solomon, and its other heros, are handed down to us with their mixture of vices and virtues? Lord Orrery says very high and very great things of Swift. The bad ones we knew, in part, before. Had he attempted to whiten them over, would it not have weakened the credibility of what he says in his favour? I am told, that my Lord is mistaken in some of his facts: for instance, in that, wherein he asserts that Swift's learning was a late acquirement.

I am very well warranted by the son of an eminent divine, a prelate, who was for three years what is called his *chum,* in the following account of that fact: Dr. Swift made as great a progress in his learning, at the University of Dublin, in his youth, as any of his cotemporaries; but was so very ill-natured and troublesome, that he was made *Terrae-filius,* (Sir Roger will explain what that means, if your Ladyship is unacquainted with the University term) on purpose to have a pretence to expel him. He raked up all the scandal against the Heads of that University that a severe inquirer, and a still severer temper, could get together into his harangue. He was expelled in consequence of his abuse, and, having his *decessit,* afterwards got admitted, at Oxford, to his degrees.

I cannot find that my Lord was very intimate with him. As from a man of quality, and the son of a nobleman who had been obnoxious to ministers, no doubt but the Dean might countenance those professions of friendship which the young Lord might be forward to make to a man who was looked upon as the genius of Ireland and the fashion. But he could be only acquainted with him in the decline of the Dean's genius.

My Lord, I think, has partly drawn censure upon himself, by a little piece of affectation. My *friends* will, he says, by way of preface to some of the things that the friends of Swift think the severest. I was a little disgusted, as I read it, at these ill-placed assumptions of friendship in words. I thought these affectations below Lord Orrery, as it seemed, by them, as if he was proud of being thought of, as a friend, by the man, who, whatever his head was, had not, I am afraid, near so good a heart as his own.

Mr. Temple, nephew to Sir William Temple, and brother to Lord Palmerston, who lately died at Bath, declared, to a friend of mine, that Sir William hired Swift, at his first entrance into the world, to read to him, and sometimes to be his amanuensis, at the rate of 20£ a year and his board, which was then high preferment to him; but that Sir William never favoured him with his conversation, because of his ill qualities, nor allowed him to sit down at table with him. Swift, your Ladyship will easily see by his writings, had bitterness, satire, moroseness, that must make him insufferable both to equals and inferiors, and unsafe for his superiors to countenance. Sir William Temple was a wise and discerning man. He could easily see through a young fellow taken into a low office, and inclined to forget himself. Probably, too, the Dean was always unpolite, and never could be a man of breeding. Sir William Temple was one of the politest men of his time.

Whoever the lady be, who is so severe upon Lord Orrery, I cannot but think that she is too severe. The story of Swift's marriage, and behaviour to a worthy, very worthy wife, I have been told long before Lord Orrery's history of him came out. It was not, as the angry lady charges, a chimera, but a certain truth. And this I was informed of by a lady of goodness, and no enemy, but to what was bad in Swift. Surely this lady, who calls my Lord to account for his unchristian-like usage of a dead friend, should have shewn a little more of the Christian in her invectives. Near twenty years ago I heard from a gentleman now living, with whom Vanessa lived, or lodged, in England, an account of the Dean's behaviour to the unhappy woman, much less to his reputation than the account my Lord gives of that affair. According to this gentleman's account, she was not the creature that she became when she was in Ireland, whither she followed him, and, in hopes to make herself an interest with his vanity, threw herself into glare and expense; and, at last, by disappointment, into a habit of drinking, till grief and the effects of that vice destroyed her. You may gather from that really pretty piece of his, *Cadenus and Vanessa,* how much he flattered her, and that he took great pains to gloss over that affair. I remember once to have seen a little collection of letters and poetical scraps of Swift's, which passed between him and Mrs. Van Homrigh, this same Vanessa, which the bookseller then told me were sent him to be published, from the originals, by this lady, in resentment of his perfidy . . .

—SAMUEL RICHARDSON, letter to
Lady Bradshaigh, April 22, 1752

PATRICK DELANY (1754)

Patrick Delany, the Church of Ireland dean of Down, formed so close a bond with Swift late in the writer's life that, in 1754, he felt obliged to refute Lord Orrery's recent scandal-mongering biography. The friendship between the two deans was based in large part on their shared beliefs. In his own sermons, Delany denounced republican ideas, which to his mind led to popery and arbitrary power, in favor of unstinting support for the ruling monarch. Swift admired this refusal to compromise and his unostentatious ideals. For his own part, Delany expressly admired Swift's unswerving faith in what he perceived to be true religion and liberty. But, above all, Delany admired his friend's patriotism, a quality questioned throughout the Orrery account. Students might wish to pursue further the contrasts set up by these two opposed biographical studies. Whereas Orrery presents an anti-Irish Swift, one who supposedly exclaimed that "I am not of this vile country," Delany insists that Swift was an honor to his native land.

To sum up all—he lived long an honour to the powers of the human mind: and died (as he had lived for some few later years) a sad monument of the infirmities incident to it in this house of clay: and a melancholly mortifying memento to the vanity of the pride of parts. His little power and fortune, whilst he enjoyed them, were in miniature, a resemblance of that great tree which shadowed out the grandeur, might, magnificence and munificence of NEBUCHADNEZZAR: it protected, as far as it could, all those that resorted to it for shade and shelter: and supported those that fled to it, for relief and sustenance; and this was cut down as that was, when God *had purposed to stain the pride of all glory.*

My Lord, when you consider SWIFT's singular, peculiar, and most variegated vein of wit, always rightly intended (although not always so rightly directed) delightful in many instances, and salutary, even where it is most offensive; when you consider his strict truth, his fortitude in resisting oppression, and arbitrary power; his fidelity in friendship; his sincere love and zeal for religion; his uprightness in making right resolutions, and his steadiness in adhering to them: his care of his church, its choir, its œconomy, and its income: his attention to all those that preached in his cathedral, in order to their amendment in pronunciation and style; as also his remarkable attention to the interest of his successors, preferably to his own present emoluments; his invincible patriotism, even to a country which he did not love; his very various, well devised, well judged, and extensive charities, throughout his life; and his whole fortune (to say nothing of his wife's) conveyed to the same Christian purposes at his death: charities from which he could enjoy no honour, advantage, or satisfaction of any kind, in this world.

When you consider his ironical and humorous, as well as his serious schemes for the promotion of true religion and virtue; his success in solliciting for the first fruits and twentieths, to the unspeakable benefit of the established church of *Ireland;* and his felicity (to rate it no higher) in giving occasion to the building of fifty new churches in *London.*

All this considered, the character of his life will appear like that of his writings; they will both bear to be re-considered and re-examined with the utmost attention; and will always discover new beauties and excellencies, upon every examination.

They will bear to be considered as the sun, in which the brightness will hide the blemishes; and whenever petulant ignorance, pride, malice, malignity, or envy interposes, to cloud, or sully his fame, I will take upon me to pronounce, that the eclipse will not last long.

To conclude,—no man ever deserved better of any country than SWIFT did of his. A steady, persevering, inflexible friend; a wise, a watchful, and a faithful counsellor under many severe trials, and bitter persecutions, to the manifest hazard, both of his liberty and fortune!

He lived a blessing, he died a benefactor, and his name will ever live an honour to *Ireland*.

—PATRICK DELANY, *Observations upon
Lord Orrery's "Remarks on the Life and Writings of
Dr. Jonathan Swift,"* 1754, pp. 288–291

THOMAS AMORY "THE HISTORY OF THESE MEMOIRS" (1755)

I knew him well, tho I never was within side of his house, because I could not flatter, cringe, or meanly humour the extravagances of any man. I am sure I knew him better than any of those friends he entertained twice a-week at the Deanery; *Stella* excepted. I had him often to myself in his rides, and walks, and have studied his soul when he little thought what I was about. As I lodged for a year within a few doors of him, I knew his times of going out to a minute, and generally nicked the opportunity. He was fond of company upon these occasions, and glad to have any rational to talk to: for, whatever was the meaning of it, he rarely had any of his friends attending him at his exercises. One servant only, and no companion, he had with him, as often as I have met him, or came up with him. What gave me the easier access to him, was my being tolerably well acquainted with our politics and history, and knowing many places, things, people, and parties, civil and religious, of his beloved England. Upon this account he was glad I joined him. We talked generally of factions and religion, states, revolutions, leaders, and pieties. Sometimes we had other subjects. Who I was he never knew: nor did I seem to know he was the Dean for a long time; not till one Sunday evening that his Verger put me into his seat at St. Patrick's prayers; without my knowing the Doctor sat there. Then I was obliged to recognize the great man, and seemed in a very great surprize. This pretended ignorance of mine as to the person of the Dean, had given me an opportunity of discoursing more freely with, and of receiving more information from the Doctor, than otherwise I could have enjoyed. The Dean was proud beyond all other mortals that I have seen, and quite another man when he was known.

—THOMAS AMORY, "The History of These Memoirs,"
Memoirs of Several Ladies of Great Britain,
1755, pp. xxviii–xxix

DEANE SWIFT (1755)

Chiefly remembered for *An Essay upon the life, writings, and character of Dr. Jonathan Swift* (1755), from which this extract is taken, Deane Swift was also responsible for a number of volumes of John Hawkesworth's compendious 1769 edition of Swift's works. A relative of Swift, Deane Swift had ready access to his materials and so was eager to offer an authoritative view on his subject. Much of the *Essay* is given to deflating myths about Swift's character as much as it is to addressing the works. It might be reasonably argued that Deane Swift's intentions were more honorable than those of the controversial Orrery, but a reader might ask: What role did he play in the shaping of Swift's reception in the eighteenth century and beyond? In particular, Deane Swift offers some insights into Swift's private conduct. Like Shakespeare's Falstaff, he is both a source of wit and an inciter of wit in others, a congenial companion.

SWIFT in his private Character was a Man of fine Address, and perfectly well bred: He knew to a Point all the Modes and Variations of Complaisance and Politeness. And yet his Manners were not framed like the Manners of any other Mortal: But, corrected by general Observation, and adapted to his own peculiar Turn of Genius, they shone forth, always enlivened more or less with some Spirit of Dominion, in a Blaze of Politeness, so inimitably, and so determinately his own, that in Effect they seemed to be the Result of pure Nature, uncopied from any the brightest, or the fairest Original.

SWIFT talked a great deal in all Companies, without engrossing the Conversation to himself. His Rule of Politeness in this Case was, that every Man had a Right to speak for a Minute; and when that Minute was out, if nobody else took up the Discourse, after a short Pause of two or three Moments, the same Person had an equal Right with any of the rest of the Company, to speak again, and again, and again, and so on during the whole Evening. His chief Delight, however, was to entertain, and be entertained, in small Circles; which he liked the better, if two or three Women of good Understanding happened to be of the Party, the Delicacy of their Sentiments, like the Delicacy of their Frame, being in all Likelihood providentially designed, to embellish and refine our Conversation, as well as to smooth and polish the Roughness of our Nature: Which indeed is remarked by SWIFT himself, in his Letter to my Lord Treasurer OXFORD. "Since the Women (saith he) have been left out of all Meetings, except Parties of Play, or where worse Designs are carried on, our Conversation hath very much degenerated." But, in the Character of a *tete à tete* Companion, according to the best Judgment that I can form of his great Abilities, if I may be allowed the Expression, he rather excelled himself. Few that are equal to him in that Respect, perhaps none that are his Superiors, can be found upon Earth. He was by no Means in the Class with those, who pour down their Eloquence like a Torrent, driving all before it. Far from any Desires of that Sort, he equally loved to speak, and loved to hearken: Like FALSTAFF, he not only had Wit himself, but frequently was the Cause of Wit in others. However indeed, that universal Reverence which was paid to his great Abilities, frequently struck a Damp on the Spirits of those who were not perfectly well acquainted with him; an Effect of Modesty, which however did not always happen to be construed to their Advantage, unless it were in the Case of very young People. For, when such Persons were gone, if none but his Intimates were present, he would express himself with some Degree of Emotion; and cry, Such a one, I have heard, is a very great Man; or such a one, they say, has Abundance of Learning; or, such a one, I have been told, has an excellent Understanding; but GOD deliver me from such companions!

—DEANE SWIFT, *An Essay upon the Life, Writings, and Character, of Dr. Jonathan Swift,* 1755, pp. 386–388

HORACE WALPOLE (1780)

A leading man of letters in his own right, Walpole was the son of Sir Robert Walpole, the country's first prime minister in effect. Swift had an uneasy relationship with the Walpole administration, which he famously attacked in *An Epistle to a Lady*. As for Horace Walpole, he was a prolific letter writer. Almost 1,800 letters to and from Sir Horace Mann alone are known to have been written. The relationship existed almost exclusively through letters as Mann, a diplomat, rarely, if ever, left Florence. Mann, it should be noted, largely owed his rapid success to Robert Walpole, to whom he was distantly related.

Swift was a wild beast, who baited and worried all mankind almost, because his intolerable arrogance, vanity, pride, and ambition were disappointed—he abused Lady Suffolk who tried and wished to raise him, only because she had not power to do so; and one is sure that a man who could deify that silly woman Queen Anne, would have been more profuse of incense to Queen Caroline, who had sense, if the court he paid to her had been crowned with success.

—HORACE WALPOLE, letter to Sir Horace Mann, January 13, 1780

EDWARD DOWDEN (1882)

Edward Dowden was an Irish literary scholar and poet. Although he wrote about a wide number of themes, he was especially fond of Shakespeare and the younger romantics, most notably Percy Bysshe Shelley, and he was an early admirer of Walt Whitman. He visited the United States and Canada on occasion but spent almost his entire life in Dublin. This parochialism aside, Dowden opposed the idea of a national body of Anglo-Irish litera-ture and did not wish to be considered an Irish writer, something for which he was later criticized by the nationalist poet W.B. Yeats. In this extract, Dowden discusses the temper of Swift, a topic of great interest to seem-ingly all but a handful of Swift scholars. In particular, students may wish to contrast Dowden's account with that of his Irish contemporary Augustine Birrell, which follows it.

It is a wonder that, in these days of scientific criticism, the melancholy ocean (ocean, the very reverse of melancholy, breather of health, bringer of food) has not been summoned to account for the dark and tempestuous temper of Swift. The stage-manager of the world's tragi-comedy doubtless needed his pessimism and despair as a foil to the amiable ethics of Addison and the smooth optimism of Pope. What gives his rage against life its peculiar character is that Swift's genius was not speculative, nor in a high sense imaginative, but was eminently practical and positive. He is not confounded by the thought of man's mingled greatness and misery—"how noble in reason! how infinite in faculty!" and yet "the quintessence of dust." "Le silence éternel de ces espaces infinis m'effraie," exclaimed Pascal; but if the eternal silence drives us in from the outposts of creation upon our central self it also invites us to escape from self, and be at rest. Swift never reached out to the eternal silence; the din of this world clattered upon his ears perpetually. He did not expect infinite things from life—infinite love, boundless knowledge, absolute beauty. But he thought men and women might at least be clean, healthy, industrious, quiet, comfortable, honest, friendly, temperate, rational. Was it a too ambitious programme? And he found, or thought he found, them nasty, slothful, diseased, malicious, vain—creatures by so much more hateful than the Yahoo as corrupted reason is worse than brutality itself. Yet his last word in *Gulliver* is one of reconciliation, not of revolt. The sometime pupil of the noble Houyhnhyms will try to apply their lessons of virtue; he will try to enjoy his own speculations in his little garden at Redriff; he will instruct the Yahoos of his own family so far as they are docible animals; he will behold his figure often in a glass, and thus, if possible, habituate himself by time to tolerate the sight of a human creature. Only the pride of a Yahoo drives him mad.

And yet what contradictions! What Titanic pride to strive to see things as a god; to dwarf man's glory or aggrandise his vices with planetary magnifying or diminishing glasses; to distort his features in the concave mirror of the heavens! The Houyhnhyms—Swift's ideals of moral excellence—are calm, rational, benevolent creatures, devoid of passions: and he himself is devoured by scorn and hate. They have not learnt to say the thing that is not: and Swift does not scruple to print monstrous falsehoods for a party purpose. They are modest and cleanly: and Swift flings ordure in the faces of women and of little children. They have tranquil deaths, towards which they move with resignation: and he makes his exit in a rage.

—EDWARD DOWDEN, *The Academy*,
September 30, 1882, p. 233

AUGUSTINE BIRRELL (1894)

No fouler pen than Swift's has soiled our literature. His language is horrible from first to last. He is full of odious images, of base and abominable allusions. It would be a labour of Hercules to cleanse his pages. His love-letters are defaced by his incurable coarseness. This habit of his is so inveterate that it seems a miracle he kept his sermons free from his blackguard phrases. It is a question not of morality, but of decency, whether it is becoming to sit in the same room with the works of this divine. How the good Sir Walter [Scott] ever managed to see him through the press is amazing. In this matter Swift is inexcusable.

Then his unfeeling temper, his domineering brutality—the tears he drew, the discomfort he occasioned. . . . One is glad to know he sometimes met his match. He slept one night at an inn kept by a widow lady of very respectable family, Mrs. Seneca, of Drogheda. In the morning he made a violent complaint of the sheets being dirty.

'Dirty, indeed!' exclaimed Mrs. Seneca; 'you are the last man, doctor, that should complain of dirty sheets.'

And so, indeed, he was, for he had just published the 'Lady's Dressing-room', a very dirty sheet indeed.

Honour to Mrs. Seneca, of Drogheda! . . .

I only know of one good-humoured anecdote of Swift; it is very slight, but it is fair to tell it. He dined one day in the company of the Lord Keeper, his son, and their two ladies, with Mr. Caesar, Treasurer of the Navy, at his house in the City. They happened to talk of Brutus, and Swift said something in his praise, and then, as it were, suddenly recollecting himself, said:

'Mr. Caesar, I beg your pardon.'

One can fancy this occasioning a pleasant ripple of laughter.

There is another story I cannot lay my hands on to verify, but it is to this effect: Faulkner, Swift's Dublin publisher, years after the Dean's death, was dining with some friends, who rallied him upon his odd way of eating some dish—I think, asparagus. He confessed Swift had told him it was the right way; therefore, they laughed the louder, until Faulkner, growing a little angry, exclaimed:

'I tell you what it is, gentlemen: if you had ever dined with the Dean, you would have eaten your asparagus as he bade you.'

Truly a wonderful man—imperious, masterful. Yet his state is not kingly like Johnson's—it is tyrannical, sinister, forbidding.

—AUGUSTINE BIRRELL, *Essays about Men, Women, and Books*, 2nd edition, 1894, pp. 2–10

GENERAL

Although the selection here, as in the other sections of this book, is far from exhaustive, by placing extracts side by side and in close proximity, we can hope to gain some insight into the general remarks made about Swift in the eighteenth and nineteenth centuries. Included here are comments made by a wide range of people from the 1700s up to 1900, taken from public lecturers, poets, philosophers, novelists; from the United States, Great Britain, Ireland, and France; from aristocrats to civil servants.

In the commentary of this period, it is possible to trace the recurrence of themes, comparisons, and contrasts. One such repetition is the name of Rabelais, the sixteenth-century French satirist with whom Swift is frequently compared. For Voltaire, one of the leading French intellectuals of his day, Swift's honorific title—"the *English Rabelais*"—is only partially appropriate, insofar as both men wrote in an irreverent style. Voltaire goes so far as to say that such a comparison is "highly derogatory" to Swift's genius. Where Rabelais lacks delicacy and justness, Swift's claims to such qualities give "true Humour" to his masterly prose and verse. By contrast, Lady Mary Wortley Montagu and Samuel Taylor Coleridge believe that no distinction should be drawn between the satirists. Swift was, to Coleridge's mind, "the soul of Rabelais dwelling in a dry place." Less poetically, perhaps, Lady Montagu is of the opinion that Swift had "stolen all his humour" from not only Rabelais but also Cervantes. William Hazlitt, in the course of his 1818 lecture series on English poets, revisits Voltaire's denunciation of the comparison with Rabelais. Swift "hated absurdity," Hazlitt exclaims, whereas the Frenchman "rioted in nonsense."

Tangential to this debate, numerous commentators have focused on the inimitable qualities of Swift. For W.E.H. Lecky, Swift is "unrivalled." For David Masson, he had one of the most "robust minds of his age." From the vantage point of the 1830s, Thomas Carlyle insists that Swift was "[b]y far the greatest man of that time." "He saw himself in a world of confusion and falsehood," and, accordingly, delivered works eminently suitable to that world. From a different perspective, Swift began to appear grossly outdated as an intellectual and artistic figure by some observers among the generations that followed. In William Makepeace Thackeray's novel *The History of Henry Esmond, Esq.* (1852), which is set in the time of Swift, we find the satirist on the periphery, a bully of diminished powers in his twilight years. Even in the late nineteenth century, commentators were struggling to overcome the imposition of Swift's perceived crudity in his writings. For Sir Leslie Stephen, Edmund Gosse, and others, it was an inconceivable task to bypass the author's "morbid interest in the physically disgusting," in Stephen's words. Even Swift's admirers could not discount the "dirty language, and the noisome jest" (Lord Byron), even if his preeminent wit had partially obfuscated such "faults." Yet, as Gosse is quick to point out, even Swift's "frivolities of a compromising humour" could be eclipsed by his sudden thunderbolts. For all his technical faults and personal vices, it is the matchless wit of Swift that made him so celebrated a figure. The duchess of Marlborough was so captivated by his charm that she could "easily forgive him all the slaps he has given me and the Duke of Marlborough."

Yet, this is not to discount Swift's literary skills. Many commentators praised Swift's "simple style," the plainness and clarity of his artistic expression. The rhetorician Hugh Blair, to take an esteemed example, considers him to be "one of the most useful models." Thomas De Quincey, a number of years later, debates the qualities that rendered Swift's style "a model of excellence," principally his *"vernacularity"* and unadorned clarity. Henry Craik, an influential Swift scholar in the late nineteenth century, suggests that Swift's simplicity was offset against his flexibility. Paradoxically, that is, Swift's so-called artlessness owed much to the "perfection of his art." By adhering to the rules of the English language so assiduously, he knew when to break them. For other observers, though, this "inartistic" simplicity was more straightforwardly a weakness. Ralph Waldo Emerson posits that Swift's writings are supremely realistic, rather than artistic, because he draws his characters as though he were doing so "for the police." This reflects Dr. Johnson's famous characterization of Swift as merely a literal writer: "[Swift] had to count ten, and he has counted it right."

Many other commentators emphasize the vast universe of Swift's imagination. Alexander Chalmers was not alone in his suggestion that Swift's voluminous writings "place him among the most illustrious ornaments of literature, as an author of incomparable ability, of multiform talent, and inexhaustible fancy." In this way, many of the general remarks included here extemporize on Swift's talents as a writer. But they also maintain the importance of Swift's life story in appreciations of his works. The latter part of this section includes a subsection on John Forster, who edited a collection of Swift in the 1870s. The inclusion of this commentary provides a useful illustration of how two trends operated. First, a consistent faith in the practice of reading Swift's works biographically remains, as does, second, an enduring belief that statements made about Swift could be taken for granted by subsequent commentators. Like John Hawkesworth in 1755, Thomas Roscoe in 1841, and any number of Swift editors throughout the ages, Forster insists that "[Swift's] writings and his life are connected so closely, that to judge of either fairly with an imperfect knowledge of the other is not possible." In his review of the Forster edition, the American poet James Russell Lowell concurs that, in order to "properly understand Swift's cynicism," one must take "his whole life into account."

WILLIAM WARBURTON (1727)

But there is a Sect of Anti Moralists, who have *our Hobbes*, and the *French Duke de la Rochfoucault* for their Leaders, that, give it but Encouragement, would soon rid our Hands of this Inconvenience, and most effectually prevent all Return from that Quarter: For whereas it was the Business of ancient Philosophy, to give us a due Veneration for the Dignity of *human Nature*; they described it as it really was, beneficent, brave, and *a Lover of its Species*; a Principle, become Sacred since our divine Master made it the Foundation of his Religion: These Men, for what Ends we shall see presently, endeavouring to create a Contempt and Horror for it, have *painted* it base, cowardly, envious, and *a Lover of its self.* A *View* so senseless and shocking to the common Notices of Humanity, that I affirm him no honest Man. . . . Thy Pride, perhaps, won't suffer thee *to degrade thy Species*; nor thy Partiality to thy country, *to abuse thy Governors.* Your Masters, *the Ancients*, said it, and you, alas! believed it, that Mankind was more free from Malignity than Weakness; and less able, than dispos'd to mend: But hearken to better Instructors, and learn to efface those silly Prejudices.

The *religious Author of the Tale of a Tub* will tell you, *Religion* is but a Reservoir of Fools and Madmen; and *the virtuous Lemuel Gulliver* will answer for the *State*, that it is a Den of Savages and Cut-throats. What think you, Reader; is not the System round and great? And now the Fig-leaf is so cleanly plucked off, what remains but bravely to strike away the rotten Staff, that yet keeps our old doting Parents on their last Legs?

Seriously let it be as they say, that Ridicule and Satire are the Supplement of publick Laws; should not then, the Ends of both be the same; the Benefit of Mankind? But where is the sense of a general Satire, if the whole Species be degenerated? And where is the Justice of it, if it be not? The Punishment of Lunaticks is as wise as the one; and a general Execution as honest as the other. In short, a general Satire, the Work only of ill Men or little Genius's, was proscribed of Old, both by the *Critic* and the *Magistrate*, as an Offence equally against Justice and common Sense.

—WILLIAM WARBURTON, *A Critical and Philosophical Enquiry into the Causes of Prodigies and Miracles, as Related by Historians. With an Essay Towards Restoring a Method and Purity in History,* 1727, pp. 26–33

VOLTAIRE (FRANÇOIS-MARIE AROUET) "LETTER XXII: ON MR. POPE AND SOME OTHER FAMOUS POETS" (1733)

An aristocratic Parisian, Voltaire was a writer and philosopher of esteemed standing among his contemporaries. A frequent visitor to and sometime traveler in England, Voltaire was intimately acquainted with a number of its writers, including Swift. Swift was himself a great admirer of Voltaire and is listed among the large group of Voltaire's eighteenth-century translators and editors. While Voltaire was not the first to liken Swift to Rabelais, the bawdy sixteenth-century satirist, Voltaire's comments are still revealing in their candor. In this extract, he suggests that Swift "will never be well understood in *France*" because his works, by which he means his poems, "are of a singular and almost inimitable Taste." One "must visit the Island in which he was born," he surmises, perhaps deliberately invoking the recent publication of *Gulliver's Travels* (1726). This extract is taken from a rather loose translation of Voltaire's controversial *Lettres écrites de Londres sur les Anglois et autres sujets*, which is based on his exile in England in the mid-1720s. Throughout the eighteenth century and beyond, Voltaire's views on Swift were revisited by a number of commentators, not just on the continent but in Great Britain too.

. . . the Works of the ingenious Dean *Swift*, who has been call'd the *English Rabelais*, will never be well understood in *France*. This Gentleman has the Honour (in common with *Rabelais*) of being a Priest, and like him laughs at every Thing. But in my humble Opinion, the title of the *English Rabelais* which is given the Dean, is highly derogatory to his Genius. The former has interspers'd his unaccountably-fantastic and unintelligible Book, with the most gay Strokes of Humour, but which at the same Time has a greater Proportion of Impertinence. He has been vastly lavish of Erudition, of Smut, of insipid Raillery. An agreeable Tale of two Pages is purchas'd at the Expense of whole Volumes of Nonsense. There are but few Persons, and those of a grotesque Taste, who pretend to Understand, and to esteem this Work; for as to the rest of the Nation, they laugh at the pleasant and diverting Touches which are found in *Rabelais* and despise his Book. He is look'd upon as the Prince of Buffoons. The Readers are vex'd to think that a Man who was Master of so much Wit should have made so wtched a Use of it. He is an intoxicated philosopher, who never writ but when he was in Liquor.

DEAN *Swift* is *Rabelais* in his Senses, and frequenting the politest Company. The former indeed is not so gay as the latter, but then he possesses all the Delicacy, the Justness, the Choice, the good Taste, in all which Particulars our giggling rural Vicar *Rabelais* is wanting. The poetical Numbers of Dean Swift are of a singular and almost inimitable Taste; true Humour whether in Prose or Verse, seems to be his particular Talent, but whoever is desirous of understanding him perfectly, must visit the Island in which he was born.

—Voltaire (François-Marie Arouet),
"Letter XXII: On Mr. Pope and Some Other
Famous Poets," *Letters Concerning the English Nation*,
translated by John Lockman, 1733, pp. 213–215

ALEXANDER POPE (1734–36)

When Swift and I were once in the country for some time together, I happened one day to be saying, "that if a man was to take notice of the reflections that came into his mind on a sudden as he was walking in the fields, or sauntering in his study, there might be several of them perhaps as good as his most deliberate thoughts."—On this hint, we both agreed to write down all the volunteer reflections that should thus come into our heads, all the time we staid there. We did so: and this was what afterwards furnished out the maxims published in our miscellanies. Those at the end of one volume are mine; and those in the other Dr. Swift's.

—Alexander Pope, 1734–36, cited in Joseph Spence,
*Anecdotes, Observations, and Characters, of Books
and Men,* ed. Samuel Weller Singer, 1820, p. 158

THE DUCHESS OF MARLBOROUGH (1736)

Dean Swift gives the most exact account of Kings, Ministers, Bishops, and the Courts of Justice, that is possible to be writ. He has certainly a vast deal of wit; and since he could contribute so much to the pulling down of the most honest and best intentioned Ministry that ever I knew, with the help only of Abigail and one or two more; and has certainly stopt the finishing stroke to ruin the Irish in the project of the half-pence, in spite of all the Ministry could do;—I could not [cannot] help wishing, that we had had his assistance in the opposition;—for I could easily forgive him all the slaps he has given me and the Duke of Marlborough, and have thanked him heartily, whenever he would please to do good.

—Sarah Churchill, The Duchess of
Marlborough, 1736, *The Opinions of
Sarah Duchess-Dowager of Marlborough.
Published from Original MSS.,* ed. Sir
David Dalrymple, Lord Hailes, 1788, p. 79

Mary Wortley Montagu (1740–41)

Swift has stolen all his humour from Cervantes and Rabelais.

—Mary Wortley Montagu, 1740–41, cited in
Joseph Spence, *Anecdotes, Observations, and Characters,
of Books and Men,* ed. Samuel Weller Singer, 1820, p. 234

John Hawkesworth (1755)

In the mid-eighteenth century, John Hawkesworth produced the first truly complete works of Swift. In this extract we have an emphatic example of his insistence that it is Swift's life, as much as his works, that holds such great appeal. A number of Swift scholars of the period were of the opinion that the two cannot be divided. Hawkesworth, it must be noted, introduced and popularized a number of stories about Swift and edited his works with a heavy hand. All in all, however, he insists that Swift's influence as a man and writer remains a positive one.

It will readily be admitted that every man has some appetite, affection, or disposition, which either in kind or in degree is irregular, and which it is the province of reason to order and restrain. As it will always happen that in some circumstances passion will predominate and reason in others, it follows that there must be some dissimilitude in every character, from which *Swift's* could not therefore be exempt; but upon the whole it will be found uncommonly steady and uniform, though some, to screen their own scattered and inconsistent representations of it from censure, have pretended that it was capricious, various, and contradictory.

Swift appears to have been naturally temperate and chaste, it was therefore easy for him to be frugal; but he was also naturally high-spirited, and therefore, as wealth is the pledge of independence, it is not strange his frugality should verge towards excess. However, as he acted upon principles, not only of general virtue, but of the noblest moral system of *Christianity,* he did not deliver himself up to natural propensities, when they were contrary to his duty, and therefore his love of money did not contract his charity to the poor, or defraud his successors to inrich himself. The same spirit which secured his integrity by disdaining the meanness of a lye, produced that dread of hypocrisy which concealed his piety, and betrayed him into appearances of evil; and the same want of natural tenderness which made him appear obdurate and austere, transferred the distribution of his liberality from instinct to religion, and made that, which in others is an exercise of self-love, in him an act of obedience to God.

Such was Dr. *Jonathan Swift*, whose writings either stimulate mankind to sustain their dignity as rational and moral beings, by shewing how low they stand in mere animal nature, or fright them from indecency by holding up its picture before them in its native deformity: and whose life, with all the advantages of genius and learning, was a scale of infelicity gradually ascending till pain and anguish destroyed the faculties by which they were felt; while he was viewed at a distance with envy, he became a burden to himself; he was forsaken by his friends, and his memory has been loaded with unmerited reproach: his life therefore does not afford less instruction than his writings, since to the wise it may teach humility, and to the simple content.

—JOHN HAWKESWORTH, *The Works of*
Jonathan Swift, D.D., Dean of St Patrick's,
Dublin, 1755, vol. 1, pp. 39–40

SAMUEL JOHNSON "SWIFT" (1779–81)

The influence of Samuel Johnson on Swift studies can never be under-estimated. Many commentators hark back to Johnson in their own writings on Swift, often setting up a contrast with another literary giant, Sir Walter Scott. While Scott is often depicted as too generous in his praise of Swift at times, Johnson can be seen as the leader of an opposing camp, those who relentlessly attack Swift. Among other failings, Swift, to Johnson's mind, lacked artistry. His "few metaphors," he states, "seem to be received rather by necessity than choice. . . . His style was well suited to his thoughts, which are never subtilised by nice disquisitions, decorated by sparkling conceits, elevated by ambitious sentences, or variegated by far-sought learning." Johnson acknowledges that Swift sought purity in his style and, to this effect, he ought to be judged properly on those terms: *"proper words in proper places."* But Johnson seemed unconvinced, prefer-ring literature to be intellectually vigorous (to his mind) and ambitiously ornate. Swift's poetical works, for instance, are too light to warrant a critical response, since "there is not much upon which the critick can exercise his powers. They are often humorous, almost always light, and have the quali-ties which recommend such compositions, easiness and gaiety."

When Swift is considered as an author, it is just to estimate his powers by their effects. In the reign of Queen Anne he turned the stream of popularity against the Whigs, and must be confessed to have dictated for a time the political opinions of the English nation. In the succeeding reign he delivered Ireland from plunder and oppression; and shewed that wit, confederated with truth, had such force as authority was unable to resist. He said truly of himself, that Ireland *was his debtor*. It was from the time when he first began to patronize the Irish, that they may date their riches and prosperity. He taught them first to know their own interest, their weight, and their strength, and gave them spirit to assert that equality with their fellow-subjects to which they have ever since been making vigorous advances, and to claim those rights which they have at last established. Nor can they be charged with ingratitude to their benefactor; for they reverenced him as a guardian, and obeyed him as a dictator.

In his works, he has given very different specimens both of sentiment and expression. His *Tale of a Tub* has little resemblance to his other pieces. It exhibits a vehemence and rapidity of mind, a copiousness of images, and vivacity of diction, such as he afterwards never possessed, or never exerted. It is of a mode so distinct and peculiar, that it must be considered by itself; what is true of that, is not true of any thing else which he has written.

In his other works is found an equable tenour of easy language, which rather trickles than flows. His delight was in simplicity. That he has in his works no metaphor, as has been said, is not true; but his few metaphors seem to be received rather by necessity than choice. He studied purity; and though perhaps all his strictures are not exact, yet it is not often that solecisms can be found; and whoever depends on his authority may generally conclude himself safe. His sentences are never too much dilated or contracted; and it will not be easy to find any embarrassment in the complication of his clauses, and inconsequence in his connections, or abruptness in his transitions.

His style was well suited to his thoughts, which are never subtilised by nice disquisitions, decorated by sparkling conceits, elevated by ambitious sentences, or variegated by far-sought learning. He pays no court to the passions; he excites neither surprise nor admiration; he always understands himself: and his reader always understands him: the peruser of Swift wants little previous knowledge: it will be sufficient that he is acquainted with common words and common things; he is neither required to mount elevations, nor to explore profundities; his passage is always on a level, along solid ground, without asperities, without obstruction.

This easy and safe conveyance of meaning it was Swift's desire to attain, and for having attained he deserves praise, though perhaps not the highest praise. For purposes merely didactick, when something is to be told that was not known before, it is the best mode, but against that inattention by which known truths are suffered to lie neglected, it makes no provision; it instructs, but does not persuade.

By his political education he was associated with the Whigs; but he deserted them when they deserted their principles, yet without running into the contrary extreme; he continued throughout his life to retain the disposition which he assigns to the *Church-of-England Man,* of thinking commonly with the Whigs of the State, and with the Tories of the Church.

He was a churchman rationally zealous; he desired the prosperity, and maintained the honour of the Clergy; of the Dissenters he did not wish to infringe the toleration, but he opposed their encroachments.

To his duty as Dean he was very attentive. He managed the revenues of his church with exact œconomy; and it is said by Delany, that more money was, under his direction, laid out in repairs than had ever been in the same time since its first erection. Of his choir he was eminently careful; and, though he neither loved nor understood musick, took care that all the singers were well qualified, admitting none without the testimony of skilful judges.

In his church he restored the practice of weekly communion, and distributed the sacramental elements in the most solemn and devout manner with his own hand. He came to church every morning, preached commonly in his turn, and attended the evening anthem, that it might not be negligently performed.

He read the service *rather with a strong nervous voice than in a graceful manner; his voice was sharp and high-toned, rather than harmonious.*

He entered upon the clerical state with hope to excel in preaching; but complained, that, from the time of his political controversies, *he could only preach pamphlets.* This censure of himself, if judgement be made from those sermons which have been published, was unreasonably severe.

The suspicions of his irreligion proceeded in a great measure from his dread of hypocrisy; instead of wishing to seem better, he delighted in seeming worse than he was. He went in London to early prayers, lest he should be seen at church; he read prayers to his servants every morning with such dexterous secrecy, that Dr. Delany was six months in his house before he knew it. He was not only careful to hide the good which he did, but willingly incurred the suspicion of evil which he did not. He forgot what himself had formerly asserted, that hypocrisy is less mischievous than open impiety. Dr. Delany, with all his zeal for his honour, has justly condemned this part of his character.

The person of Swift had not many recommendations. He had a kind of muddy complexion, which, though he washed himself with oriental scrupulosity, did not look clear. He had a countenance sour and severe, which he seldom softened by any appearance of gaiety. He stubbornly resisted any tendency to laughter.

To his domesticks he was naturally rough; and a man of a rigorous temper, with that vigilance of minute attention which his works discover, must have been a master that few could bear. That he was disposed to do his servants good, on important occasions, is no great mitigation; benefaction can be but rare, and tyrannick peevishness is perpetual. He did not spare the servants of others. Once, when he dined alone with the Earl of Orrery, he said of one that waited in the room, *That man has, since we sat to the table, committed fifteen faults.* What the faults were, Lord Orrery, from whom I heard the story, had not been attentive enough to discover. My number may perhaps not be exact.

In his œconomy he practised a peculiar and offensive parsimony, without disguise or apology. The practice of saving being once necessary became habitual, and grew first ridiculous, and at last detestable. But his avarice, though it might exclude pleasure, was never suffered to encroach upon his virtue. He was frugal by inclination, but liberal by principle; and if the purpose to which he destined his little accumulations be remembered, with his distribution of occasional charity, it will perhaps appear that he only liked one mode of expence better than another, and saved merely that he might have something to give. He did not grow rich by injuring his successors, but left both Laracor and the Deanery more valuable than he found them.—With all this talk of his covetousness and generosity, it should be remembered that he was never rich. The revenue of his Deanery was not much more than seven hundred a year.

His beneficence was not graced with tenderness or civility; he relieved without pity, and assisted without kindness, so that those who were fed by him could hardly love him.

He made a rule to himself to give but one piece at a time, and therefore always stored his pocket with coins of different value.

Whatever he did, he seemed willing to do in a manner peculiar to himself, without sufficiently considering that singularity, as it implies a contempt of the general practice, is a kind of defiance which justly provokes the hostility of ridicule; he therefore who indulges peculiar habits is worse than others, if he be not better. . . .

In the intercourse of familiar life, he indulged his disposition to petulance and sarcasm, and thought himself injured if the licentiousness of his raillery, the freedom of his censures, or the petulance of his frolicks, was resented or repressed. He predominated over his companions with very high ascendency, and probably would bear none over whom he could not predominate. To give him advice was, in the style of his friend Delany, *to venture to speak to him.* This customary superiority soon grew too delicate for truth; and Swift, with all his penetration, allowed himself to be delighted with low flattery.

On all common occasions, he habitually affects a style of arrogance, and dictates rather than persuades. This authoritative and magisterial language he expected to be received as his peculiar mode of jocularity; but he apparently flattered his own arrogance by an assumed imperiousness, in which he was ironical only to the resentful, and to the submissive sufficiently serious.

He told stories with great felicity, and delighted in doing what he knew himself to do well. He was therefore captivated by the respective silence of a steady listener, and told the same tales too often.

He did not, however, claim the right of talking alone; for it was his rule, when he had spoken a minute, to give room by a pause for any other speaker. Of time, on all occasions, he was an exact computer, and knew the minutes required to every common operation.

It may be justly supposed that there was in his conversation, what appears so frequently in his Letters, an affectation of familiarity with the Great, an ambition of momentary equality sought and enjoyed by the neglect of those ceremonies which custom has established as the barriers between one order of society and another. This transgression of regularity was by himself and his admirers termed greatness of soul. But a great mind disdains to hold any thing by courtesy, and therefore never usurps what a lawful claimant may take away. He that encroaches on another's dignity, puts himself in his power; he is either repelled with helpless indignity, or endured by clemency and condescension.

Of Swift's general habits of thinking, if his Letters can be supposed to afford any evidence, he was not a man to be either loved or envied. He seems to have wasted life in discontent, by the rage of neglected pride, and the languishment of unsatisfied desire. He is querulous and fastidious, arrogant and malignant; he scarcely speaks of himself but with indignant lamentations, or of others but with insolent superiority when he is gay, and with angry contempt when he is gloomy. From the Letters that pass between him and Pope it might be inferred that they, with Arbuthnot and Gay, had engrossed all the understanding and virtue of mankind, that their merits filled the world; or that there was no hope of more. They shew the age involved in darkness, and shade the picture with sullen emulation.

When the Queen's death drove him into Ireland, he might be allowed to regret for a time the interception of his views, the extinction of his hopes, and his ejection from gay scenes, important employment, and splendid friendships; but when time had enabled reason to prevail over vexation, the complaints, which at first were natural, became ridiculous because they were useless. But querulousness was now grown habitual, and he cried out when he probably had ceased to feel. His reiterated wailings persuaded Bolingbroke that he was really willing to quit his deanery for an English parish; and Bolingbroke procured an exchange, which was rejected, and Swift still retained the pleasure of complaining.

The greatest difficulty that occurs, in analysing his character, is to discover by what depravity of intellect he took delight in revolting ideas, from which almost every other mind shrinks with disgust. The ideas of pleasure, even when criminal, may solicit the imagination; but what has disease, deformity, and filth, upon which the thoughts can be allured to dwell? Delany is willing to think that Swift's mind was not much tainted with this gross corruption before his long visit to Pope. He does not consider how he degrades his hero, by making him at fifty-nine the pupil of turpitude, and liable to the malignant influence of an ascendant mind. But the truth is, that Gulliver had described his *Yahoos* before the visit, and he that had formed those images had nothing filthy to learn.

I have here given the character of Swift as he exhibits himself to my perception; but now let another be heard, who knew him better; Dr. Delany, after long acquaintance, describes him to Lord Orrery in these terms:

"My Lord, when you consider Swift's singular, peculiar, and most variegated vein of wit, always rightly intended (although not always so rightly directed), delightful in many instances, and salutary, even where it is most offensive; when you consider his strict truth, his fortitude in resisting oppression and arbitrary power; his fidelity in friendship, his sincere love and zeal for religion, his uprightness in making right resolutions, and his steadiness in adhering to them; his care of his church, its choir, its œconomy, and its income; his attention to all those that preached in his cathedral, in order to their amendment in pronunciation and style; as also his remarkable attention to the interest of his successors, preferably to his own present emoluments; invincible patriotism, even to a country which he did not love; his very various, well-devised, well-judged, and extensive charities, throughout his life, and his whole fortune (to say nothing of his wife's) conveyed to the same Christian purposes at his death; charities from which he could enjoy no honour, advantage or satisfaction of any kind in this world. When you consider his ironical and humorous, as well as his serious schemes, for the promotion of true religion and virtue; his success in soliciting for the First Fruits and Twentieths, to the unspeakable benefit of the established Church of Ireland; and his felicity (to rate it no higher) in giving occasion to the building of fifty new churches in London.

All this considered, the character of his life will appear like that of his writings; they will both bear to be re-considered and re-examined with the utmost attention, and always discover new beauties and excellences upon every examination.

They will bear to be considered as the sun, in which the brightness will hide the blemishes; and whenever petulant ignorance, pride, malice, malignity, or envy, interposes to cloud or sully his fame, I will take upon me to pronounce that the eclipse will not last long.

To conclude—No man ever deserved better of any country than Swift did of his. A steady, persevering, inflexible friend; a wise, a watchful, and a faithful counsellor, under many severe trials and bitter persecutions, to the manifest hazard both of his liberty and fortune.

He lived a blessing, he died a benefactor, and his name will ever live an honour to Ireland."

In the Poetical Works of Dr. Swift there is not much upon which the critick can exercise his powers. They are often humorous, almost always light, and have the qualities which recommend such compositions, easiness and gaiety. They are, for the most part, what their author intended. The diction is correct, the numbers are smooth, and the rhymes exact. There seldom occurs a hard-laboured expression, or a redundant epithet; all his verses exemplify his own definition of a good style, they consist of *proper words in proper places.*

To divide this Collection into classes, and shew how some pieces are gross, and some are trifling, would be to tell the reader what he knows already, and to find faults of which the author could not be ignorant, who certainly wrote not often to his judgement, but his humour.

It was said, in a Preface to one of the Irish editions, that Swift had never been known to take a single thought from any writer, ancient or modern. This is not literally true; but perhaps no writer can easily be found that has borrowed so little, or that in all his excellences and all his defects has so well maintained his claim to be considered as original.

—SAMUEL JOHNSON, "Swift," *Prefaces, Biographical and Critical, to the Works of the English Poets,* 1779–81, vol. 8, pp. 83–112

WILLIAM HAYLEY (1781)

Although often derided in contemporary reviews for what was sometimes characterized as tinselly rhymes, William Hayley was a relatively accomplished poet. This extract here is taken from his most successful poem, *The Triumphs of Temper* (1781), a long work in six cantos that ran to fourteen editions. This allegorical poem sought to teach young women the virtues of a pleasant nature, and evidently, judging by a number of letters he received, his intentions were realized. In this section of the third canto, Hayley addresses the "strange" spirit of Jonathan Swift.

"Now mark, SERENA!" (the mild Guide began)
The proudest Phantom of the gloomy clan,

Appointed, by this surly Monarch's grace,
High-priest of all his Misanthropic race!
See o'er the crowd a throne of vapours lift
That strange and motley form, the shade of SWIFT!
Now shalt thou view" (the guardian Sprite pursues)
"His horrid pennance, that each day renews:
Perchance its terrors may o'erwhelm thy sense,
But trust my care to bear thee safely hence!"
As thus she spoke, above the gazing throng,
High in a sailing cloud the Spectre swept along.
Vain of his power, of elocution proud,
In mystic language he harangu'd the crowd;
The bounds he mark'd, with measure so precise,
Of Equine virtue, and of Human vice,
That, cursing Nature's gifts, without remorse,
Each sullen hearer wish'd himself a Horse.
Pleas'd with the pure effect his sermon wrought,
Th' ambitious Priest a rich Tiara caught,
Which, hovering o'er his high-aspiring head,
Sarcastic Humour dangled by a thread.
The rich Tiara, for his temples fit,
Blaz'd with each polish'd gem of brilliant wit;
And sharp-fac'd Irony, his darling Sprite,
Who rais'd her patron to this giddy height,
Fast on his brow the dangerous honour bound,
But, in the moment that her Priest was crown'd,
His airy throne dissolv'd, and thunder rent the ground.
Forth from the yawning earth, with lightning's speed,
Sprung the fierce phantom of a fiery Steed,
Spurring his sides, whence bloody poison flow'd,
The ghastly-grinning Fiend, Derision, rode.
In her right-hand a horrid whip she shakes,
Whose sounding lash was form'd of knotted snakes:
An uncouth bugle her left-hand display'd,
From a grey monkey's skull by Malice made;
As her distorted lips this whistle blew,
Forth rush'd the Spectre of a wild Yahoo.
See the poor Wit in hasty terror spring,
And fly for succour to his grisly King!
In vain his piercing cries that succour court:

The grizzly King enjoys the cruel sport.
Behold the fierce Yahoo, her victim caught,
Drive her sharp talons thro' the seat of thought!
That copious fountain, which too well supplied
Perverted Ridicule's malignant tide.
Quick from her steed the grinning Fiend descends,
From the pierc'd skull the spleenful brain she rends,
To black Misanthropy, her ghastly King,
See the keen Hag this horrid present bring!
Her daily gift! for, as each day arrives,
Her destin'd victim for new death revives.
The Huntress now, this direst pageant past,
On her wild bugle blew so dread a blast,
The sharp sound pierc'd thro' all the depths of Hell;
The Fiends all answer'd in one hideous yell,
And in a fearful trance the soft SERENA fell.
Hence from the lovely Nymph her senses fled,
Till, thro' the parted curtains of her bed,
The amorous Sun, who now began to rise,
Kist, with a sportive beam, her opening eyes.

—WILLIAM HAYLEY, *The Triumphs of Temper*,
1781, canto 3, ll. 587–648

WILLIAM COWPER "TABLE TALK" (1782)

Nature imparting her satyric gift,
Her serious mirth, to Arbuthnot and Swift,
With droll sobriety they rais'd a smile
At folly's cost, themselves unmov'd the while.
That constellation set, the world in vain
Must hope to look upon their like again.

—WILLIAM COWPER, "Table Talk," *Poems by
William Cowper, of the Inner Temple, Esq.*, 1782, p. 34

HUGH BLAIR (1783)

A Church of Scotland minister and university professor, Hugh Blair was a leading intellectual of the Scottish Enlightenment. His *Lectures on Rhetoric and Belles Lettres* (1783) in two quarto volumes was a text of particular importance, in which Blair analyzes the faculties of taste and criticism, the development of language and style, and, tangentially, English litera- ture. In this extract, Blair discusses the merits of Swift's "plain style" as a rhetorical model.

Dean Swift . . . may be placed at the head of those that have employed the Plain Style. Few writers have discovered more capacity. He treats every subject which he handles, whether serious or ludicrous, in a masterly manner. He knew, almost beyond any man, the Purity, the Extent, the Precision of the English Language; and, therefore, to such as wish to attain a pure and correct Style, he is one of the most useful models. But we must not look for much ornament and grace in his Language. His haughty and morose genius, made him despise any embellishment of this kind as beneath his dignity. He delivers his sentiments in a plain, downright, positive manner, like one who is sure he is in the right; and is very indifferent whether you be pleased or not. His sentences are commonly negligently arranged; distinctly enough as to the sense; but, without any regard to smoothness of sound; often without much regard to compactness, or elegance. If a metaphor, or any other figure, chanced to render his satire more poignant, he would, perhaps, vouchsafe to adopt it, when it came in his way; but if it tended only to embellish and illustrate, he would rather throw it aside. Hence, in his serious pieces, his style often borders upon the dry and unpleasing; in his humorous ones, the plainness of his manner gives his wit a singular edge, and sets it off to the highest advantage. There is no froth, nor affectation in it; it flows without any studied preparation; and while he hardly appears to smile himself, he makes his reader laugh heartily. To a writer of such a genius as Dean Swift, the Plain Style was most admirably fitted.

—Hugh Blair, *Lectures on Rhetoric and Belles Lettres*, 1783, Lecture XVIII, pp. 381–382

James Boswell (1791)

Chiefly remembered as the attentive biographer of the great Dr. Johnson, James Boswell is assuredly a vivid storyteller. In this extract, he gives an account of Johnson's nonplussed view of Swift's literary merits. Swift, to Johnson's mind, is a matter-of-fact writer: "He had to count ten, and he has counted it right." In addition to his occasional references to Swift, Johnson wrote a lengthy biographical study of the writer, excerpted in this volume, as part of his compendious *Lives of the Poets* series. Students are strongly encouraged to consult this work in more detail, even if only for its numerous putdowns.

Swift having been mentioned, Johnson, as usual, treated him with little respect as an authour. Some of us endeavoured to support the Dean of St. Patrick's, by various arguments. One in particular praised his "Conduct of the Allies." JOHNSON. 'Sir, his "Conduct of the Allies" is a performance of very little ability.' 'Surely, Sir, (said Dr. Douglas,) you must allow it has strong facts.' JOHNSON. 'Why yes, Sir; but what is that to the merit of the composition? In the Sessions-paper of the Old Bailey there are strong facts. Housebreaking is a strong fact; robbery is a strong fact; and murder is a *mighty* strong fact: but is great praise due to the historian of those strong facts? No, Sir. Swift has told what he had to tell distinctly enough, but that is all. He had to count ten, and he has counted it right.'

—JAMES BOSWELL, *The Life of Samuel Johnson, LL.D.*
Comprehending an Account of his Studies and
Numerous Works, 1791, vol. 1, pp. 306–307

ALEXANDER CHALMERS (1803)

Those who wish to appreciate SWIFT's character with justice, must derive their information from his voluminous writings, which undoubtedly place him among the most illustrious ornaments of literature, as an author of incomparable ability, of multiform talent, and inexhaustible fancy. But the most charitable conclusion that can be formed of his private life, or the general tendency of his writings, will not, I fear, differ much from the opinion of a celebrated writer who, with the truest relish for wit and humour, never loses sight of more important considerations.

—ALEXANDER CHALMERS, *The British Essayists:*
With Prefaces, Historical and Biographical,
1803, vol. 1, p. lxv

GEORGE GORDON, LORD BYRON (1811)

Lord Byron admired the eighteenth-century satirists, especially Pope. Like Swift, Byron translated Horace, the eminent Roman lyric poet and satirist during the time of Augustus. In this piece Byron sets up a lively contrast between modern politeness and the "dirty language, and the noisome jest" of Swift's generation. Capitalizing on a commonly held notion that

Swift was technically inferior to Pope, to take a pertinent example, Byron
asserts that Swift's wit sees him through his faults.

A vulgar scribbler, certes, stands disgraced
In this nice age, when all aspire to taste;
The dirty language, and the noisome jest,
Which pleased in Swift of yore, we now detest;
Proscribed not only in the world polite,
But even too nasty for a city knight!
Peace to Swift's faults! his wit hath made them pass,
Unmatch'd by all, save matchless Hudibras!
Whose author is perhaps the first we meet,
Who from our couplet lopp'd two final feet;
Nor less in merit than the longer line,
This measure moves a favourite of the Nine.

—GEORGE GORDON, LORD BYRON,
"Hints from Horace," 1811, *The Works of Lord
Byron. In Six Volumes*, 1831, vol. 5, pp. 297–298

WILLIAM HAZLITT (1818)

William Hazlitt was a ubiquitous commentator who wrote exhaustively on a
wide range of topics and intellectual disciplines in the romantic period. He
held a particular interest in the history of literature and, in 1818, gave a popular lecture series on the history of English poets. This extract is taken from
a lecture "On Swift, Young, Gray, Collins, &c." Here Swift is placed alongside
his fellow wits Pope, Matthew Prior, and John Gay as the "most eminent
of our poets" of the age of Queen Anne. After some detailed discussion of
other poets of the age—including Swift's friends Parnell and Arbuthnot,
as well as Dr. Johnson, Prior, and Gay—Hazlitt insists on focusing on Swift
the poet as opposed to Swift the prose writer. The latter, Hazlitt argues, has
obscured the merits of the former; nonetheless, Hazlitt proceeds to focus
on the major prose works. Hazlitt keenly deflates the comparisons of Swift
to Rabelais and Voltaire, as made by the critic's contemporary Coleridge,
since he "was not a Frenchman" in his style or outlook. After all, Rabelais
reveled in the absurd, whereas Swift, we are told, hated it.

Swift's reputation as a poet has been in a manner obscured by the greater
splendour, by the natural force and inventive genius of his prose writings;

but if he had never written either the Tale of a Tub or Gulliver's Travels, his name merely as a poet would have come down to us, and have gone down to posterity with well-earned honours. His Imitations of Horace, and still more his Verses on his own Death, place him in the first rank of agreeable moralists in verse. There is not only a dry humour, an exquisite tone of irony, in these productions of his pen; but there is a touching, unpretending pathos, mixed up with the most whimsical and eccentric strokes of pleasantry and satire. His Description of the Morning in London, and of a City Shower, which were first published in the Tatler, are among the most delightful of the contents of that very delightful work. Swift shone as one of the most sensible of the poets; he is also distinguished as one of the most nonsensical of them. No man has written so many lack-a-daisical, slip-shod, tedious, trifling, foolish, fantastical verses as he, which are so little an imputation on the wisdom of the writer; and which, in fact, only show his readiness to oblige others, and to forget himself. He has gone so far as to invent a new stanza of fourteen and sixteen syllable lines for Mary the cookmaid to vent her budget of nothings, and for Mrs. Harris to gossip with the deaf old housekeeper. Oh, when shall we have such another Rector of Laracor!—The Tale of a Tub is one of the most masterly compositions in the language, whether for thought, wit, or style. It is so capital and undeniable a proof of the author's talents, that Dr. Johnson, who did not like Swift, would not allow that he wrote it. It is hard that the same performance should stand in the way of a man's promotion to a bishopric, as wanting gravity, and at the same time be denied to be his, as having too much wit. It is a pity the Doctor did not find out some graver author, for whom he felt a critical kindness, on whom to father this splendid but unacknowledged production. Dr. Johnson could not deny that Gulliver's Travels were his; he therefore disputed their merits, and said that after the first idea of them was conceived, they were easy to execute; all the rest followed mechanically. I do not know how that may be; but the mechanism employed is something very different from any that the author of Rasselas was in the habit of bringing to bear on such occasions. There is nothing more futile, as well as invidious, than this mode of criticising a work of original genius. Its greatest merit is supposed to be in the invention; and you say, very wisely, that it is not *in the execution*. You might as well take away the merit of the invention of the telescope, by saying that, after its uses were explained and understood, any ordinary eyesight could look through it. Whether the excellence of Gulliver's Travels is in the conception or the execution, is of little consequence; the power is somewhere, and it is a power that has moved the world. The power is not that of big words and vaunting common places. Swift left these to those who wanted them; and has done what his acuteness and intensity of mind alone could enable any one to conceive or to perform. His object was to strip empty pride and grandeur of the imposing air which external circumstances throw around them; and for this purpose he has cheated the imagination of the illusions which the prejudices of sense and of the world put upon it, by reducing every thing to the abstract predicament of size. He enlarges or diminishes the scale, as he wishes to show the insignificance or the grossness of our overweening self-love. That he has done this with mathematical precision, with complete presence of mind and perfect keeping, in a manner that comes equally home to the understanding of the man and of the child, does not take away from the merit of the work or the genius of the author. He has taken a new view of human nature, such as a being of a higher sphere might take of it; he has torn the scales from off his moral vision; he has tried an experiment upon human life, and gifted its pretensions from the alloy of circumstances; he has measured it with a rule, has weighed it in a balance, and found it, for the most part, wanting and worthless—in substance and in show. Nothing solid, nothing valuable is left in his system but virtue and wisdom. What a libel is this upon mankind! What a convincing proof of misanthropy! What presumption and what *malice prepense,* to show men what they are, and to teach them what they ought to be! What a mortifying stroke aimed at national glory, is that unlucky incident of Gulliver's wading across the channel and carrying off the whole fleet of Blefuscu! After that, we have only to consider which of the contending parties was in the right. What a shock to personal vanity is given in the account of Gulliver's nurse Glumdalclitch! Still, notwithstanding the disparagement to her personal charms, her good-nature remains the same amiable quality as before. I cannot see the harm, the misanthropy, the immoral and degrading tendency of this. The moral lesson is as fine as the intellectual exhibition is amusing. It is an attempt to tear off the mask of imposture from the world; and nothing but imposture has a right to complain of it. It is, indeed, the way with our quacks in morality to preach up the dignity of human nature, to pamper pride and hypocrisy with the idle mockeries of the virtues they pretend to, and which they have not: but it was not Swift's way to cant morality, or any thing else; nor did his genius prompt him to write unmeaning panegyrics on mankind!

I do not, therefore, agree with the estimate of Swift's moral or intellectual character, given by an eminent critic, who does not seem to have forgotten the party politics of Swift. I do not carry my political resentments so far back: I can at this time of day forgive Swift for having been a Tory. I feel little disturbance (whatever I might think of them) at his political sentiments, which died with him, considering how much else he has left behind him of a more solid and imperishable nature! If he had, indeed, (like some others) merely left behind him the lasting infamy of a destroyer of his country, or the shining example of an apostate from liberty, I might have thought the case altered.

The determination with which Swift persisted in a preconcerted theory, savoured of the morbid affection of which he died. There is nothing more likely to drive a man mad, than the being unable to get rid of the idea of the distinction between right and wrong, and an obstinate, constitutional preference of the true to the agreeable. Swift was not a Frenchman. In this respect he differed from Rabelais and Voltaire. They have been accounted the three greatest wits in modern times; but their wit was of a peculiar kind in each. They are little beholden to each other; there is some resemblance between Lord Peter in the Tale of a Tub, and Rabelais' Friar John; but in general they are all three authors of a substantive character in themselves. Swift's wit (particularly in his chief prose works) was serious, saturnine, and practical; Rabelais' was fantastical and joyous; Voltaire's was light, sportive, and verbal. Swift's wit was the wit of sense; Rabelais', the wit of nonsense; Voltaire's, of indifference to both. The ludicrous in Swift arises out of his keen sense of impropriety, his soreness and impatience of the least absurdity. He separates, with a severe and caustic air, truth from falsehood, folly from wisdom, 'shows vice her own image, scorn her own feature'; and it is the force, the precision, and the honest abruptness with which the separation is made, that excites our surprise, our admiration, and laughter. He sets a mark of reprobation on that which offends good sense and good manners, which cannot be mistaken, and which holds it up to our ridicule and contempt ever after. His occasional disposition to trifling (already noticed) was a relaxation from the excessive earnestness of his mind. *Indignatio facit versus.* His better genius was his spleen. It was the biting acrimony of his temper that sharpened his other faculties. The truth of his perceptions produced the pointed coruscations of his wit; his playful irony was the result of inward bitterness of thought; his imagination was the product of the literal, dry, incorrigible tenaciousness of his understanding. He endeavoured to escape from the persecution of realities into the regions of fancy, and invented his Lilliputians and Brobdingnagians, Yahoos, and Houynhyms, as a diversion to the more painful knowledge of the world around him: *they* only made him laugh, while men and women made him angry. His feverish impatience made him view the infirmities of that great baby the world, with the same scrutinizing glance and jealous irritability that a parent regards the failings of its offspring; but, as Rousseau has well observed, parents have not on this account been supposed to have more affection for other people's children than their own. In other respects, and except from the sparkling effervescence of his gall, Swift's brain was as 'dry as the remainder biscuit after a voyage.' He hated absurdity— Rabelais loved it, exaggerated it with supreme satisfaction, luxuriated in its endless varieties, rioted in nonsense, 'reigned there and revelled'. He dwelt on the absurd and ludicrous for the pleasure they gave him, not for the pain.

—WILLIAM HAZLITT, *Lectures on the English Poets: Delivered at the Surrey Institution*, 1818, pp. 217–224

SAMUEL TAYLOR COLERIDGE (1830)

Swift was *anima Rabelaisii habitans in sicco,*—the soul of Rabelais dwelling in a dry place.

—SAMUEL TAYLOR COLERIDGE, *Table Talk,* June 15, 1830

THOMAS CARLYLE (1838)

Between 1836 and 1840, Thomas Carlyle gave a number of well-attended if somewhat idiosyncratic lectures. Due to the short time he had to prepare, he mainly focused on German literature, a field he had spent a number of years researching. This extract is taken from his 1838 lectures on English literary history, in which Carlyle traces the influence of Teutonic culture on the British. Swift, in this view, is the "greatest man" of his time.

By far the greatest man of that time, I think, was Jonathan Swift: Dean Swift, a man entirely deprived of his natural nourishment, but of great robustness; of genuine Saxon mind, not without a feeling of reverence, though, from circumstances, it did not awaken in him, for he got unhappily, at the outset, into the Church, not having any vocation for it. It is curious to see him arranging, as it were, a little religion to himself. Some man found him one day giving prayers to his servants in a kind of secret manner, which he did, it seems, every morning, for he was determined, at any rate, to get out of cant; but he was a kind of cultivated heathen, no Christianity in him. He saw himself in a world of confusion and falsehood. No eyes were clearer to see into it than his. He was great from being of acrid temperament: painfully sharp nerves in body as well as soul, for he was constantly ailing, and his mind, at the same time, was soured with indignation at what he saw around him. He took up therefore, what was fittest for him, namely, sarcasm, and he carried it quite to an epic pitch. There is something great and fearful in his irony, for it is not always used for effect, or designedly to depreciate. There seems often to be a sympathy in it with the thing he satirises; occasionally it was even impossible for him so to laugh at any object without a sympathy with it, a sort of love for it; the same love as Cervantes universally shows for his own objects of merit. In his conduct, there is much that is sad and tragic, highly blameable; but I cannot credit all that is said of his cruel unfeeling dissipation. There are many circumstances to show that by nature he was one of the truest of men, of great pity for his fellow-men. For example, we read that he set up banks for the poor Irish in his neighborhood, and required nothing of them but that they should keep their word with him, when they came to borrow. 'Take your own time,' he said, 'but don't come back if you fail to keep the time you tell me.' And if they had failed, he would tell them, 'Come no more to me, if you have not so much method as to keep your time; if you cannot keep your word, what are you fit for?' All this proves him to have been a man of much affection, but too impatient of others' infirmities. But none of us can have any idea of the bitter misery which lay in him; given up to ambition, confusion, and discontent. He fell into fatalism at last, and madness, that was the end of it. The death of Swift was one of the awfullest; he knew his madness to be coming. A little before his death he saw a tree withered at the top, and he said that, 'like that tree, he, too, was dying at the top.' He was well called by Johnson a driveller and a show, a stern lesson to ambitious people.

—Thomas Carlyle, *Lectures on the*
History of Literature, 1838

Thomas Babington Macaulay
"Sir William Temple" (1838)

In this extract, Thomas Babington Macaulay, a renowned historian and essayist, discusses the life and achievements of Sir William Temple, Swift's employer in the 1690s. In particular, Macaulay analyzes the formal influence of Temple on Swift. Macaulay does so by comparing Swift with his prestigious younger contemporary, Dr. Johnson, as fellow political writers. Johnson might be considered a better stylist, he concedes, but Swift is the more authentic writer.

We think . . . that the obligations which the mind of Swift owed to that of Temple were not inconsiderable. Every judicious reader must be struck by the peculiarities which distinguish Swift's political tracts from all similar works produced by mere men of letters. Let any person compare, for example, the *Conduct of the Allies,* or the *Letter to the October Club,* with Johnson's *False Alarm,* or *Taxation no Tyranny,* and he will be at once struck by the difference of which we speak. He may possibly think Johnson a greater man than Swift. He may possibly prefer Johnson's style to Swift's. But he will at once acknowledge that Johnson writes like a man who has never been out of his study. Swift writes like a man who has passed his whole life in the midst of public business, and to whom the most important affairs of state are as familiar as his weekly bills.

> Turn him to any cause of policy,
> The Gordian knot of it he will unloose,
> Familiar as his garter.

The difference, in short, between a political pamphlet by Johnson, and a political pamphlet by Swift, is as great as the difference between an account of a battle by Mr. Southey and the account of the same battle by Colonel Napier. It is impossible to doubt that the superiority of Swift is to be, in a great measure, attributed to his long and close connection with Temple.

—THOMAS BABINGTON MACAULAY,
"Sir William Temple" (1838), *Critical, Historical,
and Miscellaneous Essays,* 1860, vol. 4, pp. 102–103

THOMAS ROSCOE (1841)

If, in proportion as Swift's productions were extensively spread abroad, his fame and popularity stood on a wider and a firmer basis, it forms a strong argument of their superior merit, of their ability and usefulness, and of the genuine wit and entertainment as well as the instruction which they contained. Swift wrote with no object but that of honest ambition to serve the cause which he conscientiously approved, and without even the common motives to stand foremost in literary fame, of which it is evident, from the little care he bestowed upon the publication or re-editions of his works, he was far less studious than of the purpose for which he wrote.

It was with a view of replacing the eccentric dean of St. Patrick's, his character and his writings, in the fair and full light of the public eye under which they formerly appeared by the same means of multiplied cheap editions, and of appealing from the merely select and patrician order, for which he never wrote, to the general and unbiassed judgment of the millions and of their posterity, that the following edition of his entire works was undertaken, and that a new life of the author was prepared, with scrupulous love of truth and fidelity, from the mass of voluminous materials placed at the disposal of the editor.

—*The Works of Jonathan Swift, D.D., and Dean
of St. Patrick's, Dublin: Containing Interesting and
Valuable Papers Not Hitherto Published,*
ed. Thomas Roscoe, 1841, "Advertisement"

Thomas Babington Macaulay
"The Life and Writings of Addison" (1843)

He moves laughter, but never joins in it. He appears in his works such as he appeared in society. All the company are convulsed with merriment, while the Dean, the author of all the mirth, preserves an invincible gravity, and even sourness of aspect, and gives utterance to the most eccentric and ludicrous fancies, with the air of a man reading the commination service.

—Thomas Babington Macaulay, "The Life and
Writings of Addison," 1843, *Critical, Historical,
and Miscellaneous Essays*, 1860, vol. 5, pp. 376–377

Thomas De Quincey "Schlosser's Literary History of the Eighteenth Century" (1847)

This extract is taken from Thomas De Quincey's review of F.C. Schlosser's multivolume *History of the Eighteenth Century*, translated into English and introduced by David Davison. Here we can see De Quincey's unique style of expression at work and, in this regard, students may wish to dwell on terms such as "unpretendingness." More productively, perhaps, students might also wish to consider De Quincey's position on the vernacular qualities of Swift's works.

Now ... you, commonplace reader, that (as an old tradition) believe Swift's style to be a model of excellence, hereafter I shall say a word to you, drawn from deeper principles. At present I content myself with these three propositions; which overthrow if you can:—

1. That the merit which justly you ascribe to Swift is *vernacularity*, and nothing better or finer: he never forgets his mother-tongue in exotic forms, unless we may call Irish exotic; for some Hibernicisms he certainly has. This merit, however, is exhibited—not, as *you* fancy, in a graceful artlessness, but in a coarse inartificiality. To be artless, and to be inartificial, are very different things,—as different as being natural and being gross, as different as being simple and being homely.

2. That, whatever, meantime, be the particular sort of excellence, or the value of the excellence, in the style of Swift, he had it in common with multitudes besides of that age. Defoe wrote a style for all the world the same as to kind and degree of excellence, only pure from Hibernicisms. So did every honest skipper (Dampier was something more) who had occasion to

record his voyages in this world of storms. So did many a hundred of religious writers. And what wonder should there be in this, when the main qualification for such a style was plain good sense, natural feeling, unpretendingness, some little scholarly practice in putting together the clockwork of sentences so as to avoid mechanical awkwardness of construction, but above all the advantage of a *subject* such in its nature as instinctively to reject ornament, lest it should draw off attention from itself? Such subjects are common; but grand impassioned subjects insist upon a different treatment; and *there* it is that the true difficulties of style commence, and thereit is that your worshipful Master Jonathan would have broke down irrecoverably.

3. (Which partly is suggested by the last remark.) That nearly all the blockheads with whom I have at any time had the pleasure of conversing upon the subject of style (and pardon me for saying that men of the most sense are apt, upon two subjects—viz. poetry and style—to talk *most* like blockheads) have invariably regarded Swift's style not as if *relatively* good (*i.e. given* a proper subject), but as if *absolutely* good—good unconditionally, no matter what the subject. Now, my friend, suppose the case that the Dean had been required to write a pendant for Sir Walter Raleigh's immortal apostrophe to Death, or to many passages that I could select in Sir Thomas Browne's *Religio Medici* and his *Um-Burial,* or to Jeremy Taylor's inaugural sections of his *Holy Living and Dying,* do you know what would have happened? Are you aware what sort of ridiculous figure your poor bald Jonathan would have cut? About the same that would be cut by a forlorn scullion from a greasy eating-house at Rotterdam, if suddenly called away in vision to act as seneschal to the festival of Belshazzar the king before a thousand of his lords.

—THOMAS DE QUINCEY, "Schlosser's Literary History
of the Eighteenth Century," 1847, *Collected Writings,*
ed. David Masson, 1889–90, vol. 11, pp. 17–18

WILLIAM MAKEPEACE THACKERAY (1852)

William Makepeace Thackeray was a popular novelist of the Victorian period, and *The History of Henry Esmond, Esq.* (1852) is widely ranked among his finest works. Written in the memoir style, the narrator and main character, Henry Esmond, in his twilight years on his estate in Virginia, recounts the worthy events of his life. The extract that follows is a typical digression on literary themes. Here we witness Swift at a distance, as a social climber with eyes only for the great men. He is, at the same time, an outdated man, one whose intellect has deteriorated and who has forgotten his venomous hatred of humanity. Now he stands in the background, a weakened bully from a bygone age.

—————

As for the famous Dr. Swift, I can say of him, "Vidi tantum." He was in London all these years up to the death of the Queen; and in a hundred public places where I saw him, but no more; he never missed Court of a Sunday, where once or twice he was pointed out to your grandfather. He would have sought me out eagerly enough had I been a great man with a title to my name, or a star on my coat. At Court the Doctor had no eyes but for the very greatest. Lord Treasurer and St. John used to call him Jonathan, and they paid him with this cheap coin for the service they took of him. He writ their lampoons, fought their enemies, flogged and bullied in their service, and it must be owned with a consummate skill and fierceness. 'Tis said he hath lost his intellect now, and forgotten his wrongs and his rage against mankind. I have always thought of him and of Marlborough as the two greatest men of that age. I have read his books (who doth not know them?) here in our calm woods, and imagine a giant to myself as I think of him, a lonely fallen Prometheus, groaning as the vulture tears him. Prometheus I saw, but when first I ever had any words with him, the giant stepped out of a sedan chair in the Poultry, whither he had come with a tipsy Irish servant parading before him, who announced him, bawling out his Reverence's name, whilst his master below was as yet haggling with the chairman. I disliked this Mr. Swift, and heard many a story about him, of his conduct to men, and his words to women. He could flatter the great as much as he could bully the weak; and Mr. Esmond, being younger and hotter in that day than now, was determined, should he ever meet this dragon, not to run away from his teeth and his fire.

—WILLIAM MAKEPEACE THACKERAY, *The History of Henry Esmond, Esq.*, 1852, book 3, chapter 5, p. 158

RALPH WALDO EMERSON "LITERATURE" (1856)

How realistic or materialistic in treatment of his subject is Swift! He describes his fictitious persons as if for the police.

—RALPH WALDO EMERSON, "Literature," *English Traits*, 1856, p. 131

DAVID MASSON "DEAN SWIFT" (1856)

An influential biographer, critic, and educator, David Masson frequently commented on the position of Swift in the national canon. In this essay

from his *Essays Biographical and Critical* (1856), Masson explores the general view of Swift's genius in comparison with the likes of Milton and
Shakespeare and looks closely at what he calls the "demoniac" element.

Have we said too much in declaring that of all the men who illustrated that
period of our literary history which lies between the Revolution of 1688 and
the beginning or middle of the reign of George II., Swift alone (excepting
Pope, and excepting him only on certain definite and peculiar grounds)
fulfils to any tolerable extent those conditions which would entitle him to
the epithet of "great," already refused by us to his age as a whole? We do not
think so. Swift *was* a great genius; nay, if by *greatness* we understand general
mass and energy rather than any preconceived peculiarity of quality, he was
the greatest genius of his age. Neither Addison, nor Steele, nor Pope, nor
Defoe, possessed, in anything like the same degree, that which Goethe and
Niebuhr, seeking a name for a certain attribute found always present, as they
thought, in the higher and more forcible order of historic characters, agreed
to call the *demoniac* element. Indeed very few men in our literature, from first
to last, have had so much of this element in them—the sign and source of all
real greatness—as Swift. In him it was so obvious as to attract notice at once.
"There is something in your looks," wrote Vanessa to him, "so awful that it
strikes me dumb"; and again, "Sometimes you strike me with that prodigious
awe, I tremble with fear"; and again, "What marks are there of a deity that
you are not known by?" True, these are the words of a woman infatuated with
love; but there is evidence that wherever Swift went, and in whatever society
he was, there was this magnetic power in his presence. Pope felt it; Addison
felt it; they all felt it. We question if, among all our literary celebrities, from
first to last, there has been one more distinguished for being personally
formidable to all who came near him.

   And yet in calling Swift a great genius we clearly do not mean to rank
him in the same order of greatness with such men among his predecessors
as Spenser, or Shakespeare, or Milton, or such men among his successors, as
Scott, Coleridge and Wordsworth. We even retain instinctively the right of
not according to him a certain kind of admiration which we bestow on such
men of his own generation as Pope, Steele, and Addison. How is this? What
is the drawback about Swift's genius which prevents us from referring him to
that highest order of literary greatness to which we do refer others, who in
respect of hard general capacity were apparently not superior to him, and on
the borders of which we also place some who in that respect were certainly
his inferiors? To make the question more special, why do we call Milton great

in quite a different sense from that in which we consent to confer the same epithet on Swift?

Altogether, it will be said, Milton was a greater man than Swift; his intellect was higher, richer, deeper, grander; his views of things are more profound, grave, stately, and exalted. This is a true enough statement of the case; and we like that comprehensive use of the word intellect which it implies, wrapping up, as it were, all that is in and about a man in this one word, so as to dispense with the distinctions between imaginative and non-imaginative, spiritual and unspiritual natures, and make every possible question about a man a mere question in the end as to the size or degree of his intellect. But such a mode of speaking is too violent and recondite for common purposes. According to the common use of the word intellect, it might be maintained (we do not say it would) that Swift's intellect, meaning his strength of mental grasp, was equal to Milton's; and yet that, by reason of the fact that his intellectual style was deficient, that he did not grasp things precisely in the Miltonic way, a distinction might be drawn unfavourable, on the whole, to his genius as compared with that of Milton. According to such a view, we must seek for that in Swift's genius, upon which it depends that while we accord to it all the admiration we bestow on strength, our sympathies with height or sublimity are left unmoved. Nor have we far to seek. When Goethe and Niebuhr generalized in the phrase, "the demoniac element," that mystic something which they seemed to detect in all men of unusual potency among their fellows, they used the word "demoniac," not in its English sense, as signifying what appertains specially to the demons or powers of darkness, but in its Greek sense, as equally implying the unseen agencies of light and good. The demoniac element in a man, therefore, may in one case be the demoniac of the etherial and celestial, in another the demoniac of the Tartarean and infernal. There is a demoniac of the supernatural—angels, and seraphs, and white-winged airy messengers swaying men's phantasies from above; and there is a demoniac of the infra-natural—fiends and shapes of horror tugging at men's thoughts from beneath. The demoniac in Swift was of the latter kind. It is false, it would be an entire mistake as to his genius, to say that he regarded, or was inspired by, only the worldly and the secular; that men, women, and their relations in the little world of visible life, were all that his intellect cared to recognise. He also, like our Miltons and our Shakespeares, and all our men who have been anything more than prudential and pleasant writers, had his being anchored in things and imaginations beyond the visible verge. But while it was given to them to hold rather by things and imaginations belonging to the region of the celestial, to hear angelic music and the rustling of seraphic wings; it was his unhappier lot to be related rather to the darker and subterranean mysteries. One might say of Swift that he had far less of belief in a God than of belief in a devil. He is like a man walking on the earth and among the busy haunts of his fellow-mortals, observing them and their ways, and taking his part in the bustle; all the while, however, conscious of the tuggings downward of secret chains reaching into the world of the demons. Hence his ferocity, his misanthropy, his *sæva indignatio,* all of them true forms of energy, imparting unusual potency to a life; but forms of energy bred of communion with what outlies nature on the lower or infernal side.

Swift, doubtless, had this melancholic tendency in him constitutionally from the beginning. From the first we see him an unruly, rebellious, gloomy, revengeful, unforgiving spirit, loyal to no authority, and gnashing under every restraint. With nothing small or weak in his nature, too proud to be dishonest, bold and fearless in his opinions, capable of strong attachments and of hatred as strong, it was to be predicted that if the swarthy Irish youth, whom Sir William Temple received into his house, when his college had all but expelled him for contumacy, should ever be eminent in the world, it would be for fierce and controversial, and not for beautiful or harmonious, activity. It is clear, however, on a survey of Swift's career, that the gloom and melancholy which characterised it, was not altogether congenital, but in part, at least grew out of some special circumstance or set of circumstances, having a precise date and locality among the facts of his life. In other words, there was some secret in Swift's life, some root of bitterness or remorse, diffusing a black poison throughout his whole existence. That communion with the invisible almost exclusively on the infernal side—that consciousness of chains wound round his own moving frame at the one end, and at the other tugged at by demons in the depths of their populous pit, while no cords of love were felt sustaining him from the countervailing heaven—had its origin, in part at least, in some one recollection or cause of dread. It was some one demon down in that pit that tugged the chains; the others but assisted him. Thackeray's perception seems to us exact when he says of Swift that "he goes through life, tearing, like a man possessed with a devil"; or again, changing the form of the figure, that, "like Abudah, in the Arabian story, he is always looking out for the Fury, and knows that the night will come, and the inevitable hag with it." What was this Fury, this hag that duly came in the night, making the mornings horrible by the terrors of recollection, the evenings horrible by those of anticipation, and leaving but a calm hour at full mid-day? There was a secret in Swift's life; what was it? His biographers as yet have failed to agree on this dark topic. Thackeray's hypothesis, that the cause of Swift's despair was chiefly his consciousness of disbelief in the creed to which he had sworn his professional faith, does not seem to us sufficient. In Swift's days, and even with his frank nature, we think that difficulty could have been got over. There was nothing, at least, so unique in the case as to justify the supposition that this was what Archbishop King referred to in that memorable saying to Dr. Delany, "You have just met the most miserable man on earth; but on the subject of his wretchedness you must never ask a question." Had Swift made a confession of scepticism to the Archbishop, we do not think the prelate would have been taken so very much by surprise. Nor can we think, with some, that Swift's vertigo (now pronounced to have been increasing congestion of the brain) and his life-long certainty that it would end in idiotcy or madness, are the true explanation of this interview and of the mystery which it shrouds. There was cause enough for melancholy here, but not exactly the cause that meets the case. Another hypothesis there is of a physical kind, which Scott and others hint at, and which finds great acceptance with the medical philosophers. Swift, it is said, was of "a cold temperament," &c. &c. But why a confession on the part of Swift that he was not a marrying man, even had he added that he desired, above all things in the world, to be a person of this sort, should have so moved the heart of an Archbishop, we cannot conceive. Besides, although this hypothesis might explain much of the Stella and Vanessa imbroglio, it would not explain all; nor do we see on what foundation it could rest. Scott's assertion that all through Swift's writings there is no evidence of his having felt the tender passion, is simply untrue. On the whole, the hypothesis which has been started of a too near consanguinity between Swift and Stella, either known from the first to one or both, or discovered too late, would most nearly suit the conditions of the case. And yet, so far as we have seen, this hypothesis also rests on air, with no one fact to support it. Could we suppose that Swift, like another Eugene Aram, went through the world with a murder on his mind, it might be taken as a solution of the mystery; but as we cannot do this, we must be content with supposing that either some one of the foregoing hypotheses, or some combination of them, is to be accepted, or that the matter is altogether inscrutable.

Such by constitution as we have described him—with an intellect strong as iron, much acquired knowledge, an ambition all but insatiable, and a decided desire to be wealthy—Swift, almost as a matter of course, flung himself impetuously into the Whig and Tory controversy, which was the question paramount in his time. In that he laboured as only a man of his powers could, bringing to the side of the controversy on which he chanced to be—and we believe when he was on a side it was honestly because he found a certain preponderance of right in it—a hard and ruthless vigour which served it immensely. But from the first, and, at all events, after the disappointments of a political career had been experienced by him, his nature would not work alone in the narrow warfare of Whiggism and Toryism, but overflowed in general bitterness of reflection on all the customs and ways of humanity. The following passage in *Gulliver's Voyage to Brobdingnag,* describing how the politics of Europe appeared to the King of Brobdingnag, shows us Swift himself in his larger mood of thought.

"This prince took a pleasure in conversing with me, inquiring into the manners, religion, laws, government, and learning of Europe; wherein I gave him the best account I was able. His apprehension was so clear, and his judgment so exact, that he made very wise reflections and observations upon all I said. But I confess that after I had been a little too copious in talking of my own beloved country, of our trade, and wars by sea and land, of our schisms in religion, and parties in the state, the prejudices of his education prevailed so far that he could not forbear taking me up in his right hand, and stroking me gently with the other, after an hearty fit of laughing, asking me, whether *I* was a Whig or Tory. Then turning to his first minister, who waited behind him with a white staff nearly as tall as the mainmast of the 'Royal Sovereign,' he observed how contemptible a thing was human grandeur, which could be mimicked by such diminutive insects as I; 'And yet,' says he, 'I dare engage these creatures have their titles and distinctions of honour; they contrive little nests and burrows, that they call houses and cities; they make a figure in dress and equipage; they love, they fight, they dispute, they cheat, they betray.' And thus he continued on, while my colour came and went several times with indignation to hear our noble country, the mistress of arts and arms, the scourge of France, the arbitress of Europe, the seat of virtue, piety, honour, truth, the pride and envy of the world, so contemptuously treated."

Swift's writings, accordingly, divide themselves, in the main, into two classes,—pamphlets, tracts, lampoons, and the like, bearing directly on persons and topics of the day, and written with the ordinary purpose of a partisan; and satires of a more general aim, directed, in the spirit of a cynic philosopher, against humanity on the whole, or against particular human classes, arrangements, and modes of thinking. In some of his writings the politician and the general satirist are seen together. The *Drapier's Letters* and most of the poetical lampoons, exhibit Swift in his direct mood as a party-writer; in the *Tale of a Tub* we have the ostensible purpose of a partisan masking a reserve of general scepticism; in the *Battle of the Books* we have a satire partly personal to individuals, partly with a reference to a prevailing tone of opinion; in the *Voyage to Laputa* we have a satire on a great class of men; and in the *Voyages to Lilliput* and *Brobdingnag,* and still more in the story of the *Houynhnms* and *Yahoos,* we have human nature itself analysed and laid bare.

Swift took no care of his writings, never acknowledged some of them, never collected them, and suffered them to find their way about the world as chance, demand, and the piracy of publishers directed. As all know, it is in his character as a humorist, an inventor of the preposterous as a medium for the reflective, and above all as a master of irony, that he takes his place as one of the chiefs of English literature. There can be no doubt that, as regards the literary form which he affected most, he took hints from Rabelais, as the greatest original in the realm of the absurd. Sometimes, as in his description of the Strulbrugs in the *Voyage to Laputa,* he approaches the ghastly power of that writer; on the whole, however, there is more of stern English realism in him, and less of sheer riot and wildness. Sometimes, however, Swift throws off the guise of the humorist, and speaks seriously and in his own name. On such occasions we find ourselves simply in the presence of a man of strong, sagacious, and thoroughly English mind, content, as is the habit of Englishmen, with vigorous proximate sense, expressed in plain and rather coarse idiom. For the speculative he shows in these cases neither liking nor aptitude; he takes obvious reasons and arguments as they come to hand, and uses them in a robust, downright Saxon manner. In one respect he stands out conspicuously even among plain Saxon writers—his total freedom from cant. Johnson's advice to Boswell, "above all things to clear his mind of cant," was perhaps never better illustrated than in the case of Dean Swift. Indeed, it might be given as a summary definition of Swift's character that he had cleared his mind of cant, without having succeeded in filling the void with song. It was Swift's intense hatred of cant—cant in religion, cant in morality, cant in literature—that occasioned many of those peculiarities which shock people in his writings. His principle being to view things as they are, irrespective of all the accumulated cant of orators and poets, he naturally prosecuted his investigations into those classes of circumstances which orators and poets have omitted as unsuitable for their purposes. If they had viewed men as angels, he would view them as Yahoos. If they had placed the springs of action among the fine phrases and the sublimities, he would trace them down into their secret connexions with the bestial and the obscene. Hence—as much as for any of those physiological reasons which some of his biographers assign for it—his undisguised delight in filth. And hence, also, probably—seeing that among the forms of cant he included the traditional manner of speaking of women in their relations to men—his studious contempt, whether in writing for men or women, of all the accustomed decencies. It was not only the more obvious forms of cant, however, that Swift had in aversion. Even to that minor form of cant which consists in the "trite" he gave no quarter. Whatever was habitually said by the majority of people, seemed to him, for that very reason, not worthy of being said at all, much less put into print. A considerable portion of his writings, as, for example, his *Tritical Essay on the Faculties of the Mind*, and his *Art of Polite Conversation*—in the one of which he strings together a series of the most threadbare maxims and quotations to be found in books, offering the compilation as an original disquisition of his own; and, in the other, imitates the insipidity of ordinary table-talk in society—may be regarded as showing a systematic determination on his part to turn the trite into ridicule. Hence, in his own writings, though he abstains from the profound, he never falls into the commonplace. Apart from all Swift's other merits, there are to be found scattered through his writings not a few distinct propositions of an innovative and original character respecting our social arrangements. We have seen his doctrine as to the education of women; and we may mention, as an instance of the same kind, his denunciation of the institution of standing armies as incompatible with freedom. Curiously enough, also, it was Swift's belief that, Yahoos as we are, the world is always in the right.

—David Masson, "Dean Swift,"
Essays Biographical and Critical:
Chiefly on English Poets, 1856, pp. 169–177

David Masson (1859)

In this extended extract from a section on Swift and Defoe in his *British Novelists and Their Styles* (1859), Masson talks at length about Swift's political and personal tempers, insisting, as many others have, that what categorizes Swift above all is his great variety.

Indubitably one of the most robust minds of his age, Swift, in the first place, went wholly along with his age, nay, tore it along with him faster than it could decorously go, in its renunciation of romance and all "the sublimities." He, a surpliced priest (as Rabelais had also been), a commissioned expositor of things not seen, *was* an expositor of things not seen; but it was of those that are unseen because they have to be dug for down in the concealing earth, and not of those that fill the upward azure, and tremble by their very nature beyond the sphere of vision. The age for him was still too full of the cant of older beliefs, preserved in the guise of "respectabilities"; and, to help to clear it of this, he would fix its gaze on its own roots, and on the physical roots of human nature in general, down in the disgusting and the reputedly bestial. I say this not in the way of judgment, but of fact. It is what we all know of Swift—they who see good in his merciless method, as well as they who abhor it. But, with all this excess of his age in its own spirit, even to what was considered profanity and blasphemy, Swift, in many respects, adjusted himself to it. He flung himself, none more energetically, into its leading controversy of Whiggism and Toryism. He was at first, somewhat anomalously, a Whig in civil politics and ecclesiastically a High Churchman, consenting to changes in the secular system of the State, but zealous for the preservation and extension of that apparatus of bishoprics, churches, and endowments, which the past had consolidated—though for what end, save that Swifts, as well as Cranmers and Lauds, could work it, he hardly permits us to infer. Later, he was a Tory in state-politics as well. In both stages of his political career, he took an active interest in current social questions. He was as laborious as a prime minister in his partisanship, as vehement and minute in his animosities. He had some peculiar tenets which he perseveringly inculcated—among which was that now called "The Emancipation of Women."

And yet, though he concerned himself in this manner with the controversies and social facts of his time, how, underneath such concern, we see a raging tumult of thought about humanity as a whole, over which all these facts and controversies of his time must have really floated as things ludicrous and contemptible! It is one of the peculiarities of Swift that, though belonging to an age in which Whiggism and Toryism had come in lieu of older distinctions and beliefs, and though himself sharing in the renunciation of these as effete fanaticism, yet in him, more than in any other man of his time, we see a mind bursting the bounds of Whiggism and Toryism, not dwelling in them, seeing round and round them, and familiar in its own recesses with more general and more awful contemplations. True, Swift's philosophy of human nature, in which his partisanship was engulphed, was not the same as that of the elder men—the Shakespeares and the Miltons, whose souls had also tended to the boundless and the general. It was a philosophy of misanthropy rather than of benevolence, of universal despair rather than of hope, of the blackness under the earth, and the demons tugging there at their connexions with man, rather than of the light and evangelism of the countervailing Heaven. But herein at least was a source of strength which made him terrible among his contemporaries. He came among them by day as one whose nights were passed in horror; and hence in all that he said and did there was a vein of ferocious irony.

While all Swift's fictions reveal his characteristic satirical humour, they reveal it in different degrees and on different themes and occasions. In some of his smaller squibs of a fictitious kind we see him as the direct satirist of a political faction. In the *Battle of the Books* we have a satire directed partly against individuals, partly against a prevailing tone of opinion and criticism. In the *Tale of a Tub* he appears as the satirist of the existing Christian Churches, the Papal, the Anglican, and the Presbyterian—treating each with the irreverence of an absolute sceptic in all that Churches rest upon, but arguing in behalf of the second. In the four parts of *Gulliver* he widens the ground. In the Voyage to Laputa, &c, we have a satire on various classes of men and their occupations; and in the Voyages to Lilliput and Brobdingnag, and still more in the story of the Houynhmns and Yahoos, we have satires on human nature and human society, down to their very foundations. With what power, what genius in ludicrous invention, these stories are written, no one needs to be reminded. Schoolboys, who read for the story only, and know nothing of the satire, read *Gulliver* with delight; and our literary critics, even while watching the allegory and commenting on the philosophy, break down in laughter from the sheer grotesqueness of some of the fancies, or are awed into pain and discomfort by the ghastly significance of others. Of Swift we may surely say, that, let our literature last for ages, he will be remembered in it, and chiefly for his fictions, as one of the greatest and most original of our writers—the likest author we have to Rabelais, and yet with British differences. In what cases one would recommend Swift is a question of large connexions. To all strong men he is and will be congenial, for they can bear to look round and round reality on all sides, even on that which connects us with the Yahoos. Universality is best. In our literature, however, there are varieties of spirits—

Black spirits and white,
  Green spirits and grey;

And so,

Mingle, mingle, mingle,
  Ye that mingle may.

—DAVID MASSON, *British Novelists and Their Styles*, 1859, pp. 90–94

W.E.H. Lecky "Jonathan Swift" (1861)

While still in his early twenties, the Irish historian William Edward Hartpole Lecky produced the anonymous *Leaders of Public Opinion in Ireland* (1861), which features sketches of the life and works of Swift, as well as Irish freedom fighters such as Henry Flood, Henry Grattan, and Daniel O'Connell. This book was republished a decade later, and the essay on Swift appeared again in 1897 as an introduction to a new edition of Swift's works. In this extract Lecky offers unconventional praise of his countryman.

In truth, the nature of Swift was one of those which neither seek nor obtain the sympathy of ordinary men. Through his whole life his mind was positively diseased, and circumstances singularly galling to a great genius and a sensitive nature combined to aggravate his malady. Educated in poverty and neglect, passing then under the yoke of an uncongenial patron and of an unsuitable profession, condemned during his best years to offices that were little more than menial, consigned after a brief period of triumph to life-long exile in a torpid country, separated from all his friends and baffled in all his projects, he learned to realise the bitterness of great powers with no adequate sphere for their display—of a great genius passed in every walk of worldly ambition by inferior men. His character was softened and improved by prosperity, but it became acrid and virulent in adversity. Hating hypocrisy, he often threw himself into the opposite extreme, and concealed his virtues as other men their vices. Possessing powers of satire perhaps as terrible as have ever been granted to a human being, he employed them sometimes in lashing impostors like Partridge, or arrogant lawyers like Bettesworth, but very often in unworthy personal or political quarrels. He flung himself unreservedly into party warfare, and was often exceedingly unscrupulous about the means he employed; and there is at least one deep stain on his private character; but he was capable of a very genuine patriotism, of an intense hatred of injustice, of splendid acts of generosity, of a most ardent and constant friendship, and it may be truly said that it was those who knew him best who admired him most. He was also absolutely free from those literary jealousies which were so common among his contemporaries, and from the levity and shallowness of thought and character that were so characteristic of his time. Of the intellectual grandeur of his career it is needless to speak. The chief sustainer of an English Ministry, the most powerful advocate of the Peace of Utrecht, the creator of public opinion in Ireland, he has graven his name indelibly in English history, and his writings, of their own kind, are unique in English literature. It has been the misfortune of Pope to produce a number of imitators, who made his versification so hackneyed that they produced a reaction against his poetry in which it is often most unduly underrated. Addison, though always read with pleasure, has lost much of his old supremacy. A deeper criticism, a more nervous and stimulating school of political writers have made much that he wrote appear feeble and superficial, and even in his own style it would be possible to produce passages in the writings of Goldsmith and Lamb that might be compared without disadvantage with the best papers of the *Spectator*. But the position of Swift is unaltered. *Gulliver* and the *Tale of a Tub* remain isolated productions, unrivalled, unimitated, and inimitable.

—W.E.H. Lecky, "Jonathan Swift," *The Leaders of Public Opinion in Ireland*, 1861

John Forster "The Life of Jonathan Swift" (1875)

The rule of measuring what is knowable of a famous man by the inverse ratio of what has been said about him, is applicable to Swift in a marked degree. Few men who have been talked about so much are known so little. His writings and his life are connected so closely, that to judge of either fairly with an imperfect knowledge of the other is not possible; and only thus can be excused what Jeffrey hardily said, and many have too readily believed—that he was an apostate in politics, infidel or indifferent in religion, a defamer of humanity, the slanderer of statesmen who had served him, and destroyer of the women who loved him. Belief in this, or any part of it, may be pardonable where the life is known insufficiently and the writings not at all; but to a competent acquaintance with either or both, it is monstrous as well as incredible.

Swift's later time, when he was governing Ireland as well as his deanery, and the world was filled with the fame of *Gulliver*, is broadly and intelligibly written. But as to all the rest, his life is a work unfinished; to which no one has brought the minute examination indispensably required, where the whole of a career has to be considered to get at the proper comprehension of single parts of it. The writers accepted as authorities for the obscurer portion are found to be practically worthless, and the defect is not supplied by the later and greater biographies. Johnson did him no kind of justice because of too little liking for him; and Scott, with much hearty liking as well as a generous admiration, has too much other work to do. Thus, notwithstanding noble passages in both memoirs, and Scott's pervading tone of healthy manly wisdom, it is left to an inferior hand to attempt to complete the tribute begun by those distinguished men.

—JOHN FORSTER, *The Life of Jonathan Swift,*
Volume the First: 1667–1711, 1875, pp. v–vi

JAMES RUSSELL LOWELL
"FORSTER'S LIFE OF SWIFT" (1876)

A Harvard graduate, James Russell Lowell was an American poet and critic associated with the Fireside Poets, a popular group of New England writers, sometimes referred to as the Schoolroom or Household Poets. This review of the first projected volume of John Forster's recent biography of Swift appeared in *The Nation* in 1876. Here Lowell discusses the "nobler temper" of Swift in contrast to his contemporary wits.

We cannot properly understand Swift's cynicism and bring it into any relation of consistency with our belief in his natural amiability without taking his whole life into account. Few give themselves the trouble to study his beginnings, and few, therefore, give weight enough to the fact that he made a false start. He, the ground of whose nature was an acrid common-sense, whose eye magnified the canker till it effaced the rose, began as what would now be called a romantic poet. With no mastery of verse, for even the English heroic (a balancing-pole which has enabled so many feebler men to walk the ticklish rope of momentary success) was uneasy to him, he essayed the Cowleian Pindarique, as the adjective was then rightly spelled with a hint of Parisian rather than Theban origin. If the master was but a fresh example of the disasters that wait upon every new trial of the flying-machine, what could be expected of the disciple who had not even the secret of the mechanic wings, and who stuck solidly to the earth while with perfect good faith he went through all the motions of soaring? Swift was soon aware of the ludicrousness of his experiment, though he never forgave Cousin Dryden for being aware of it also, and the recoil in a nature so intense as his was sudden and violent. He who could not be a poet if he would, angrily resolved that he would not if he could. Full-sail verse was beyond his skill, but he could manage the simpler fore-and-aft rig of Butler's octosyllabics. As Cowleyism was a trick of seeing everything as it was not, and calling everything something else than it was, he would see things as they were—or as, in his sullen disgust, they seemed to be—and call them all by their right names with a resentful emphasis. He achieved the naked sincerity of a Hottentot—nay, he even went beyond it in rejecting the feeble compromise of the breech-clout. Not only would he be naked and not ashamed, but everybody else should be so with a blush of conscious exposure, and human nature should be stripped of the hypocritical fig-leaves that betrayed by attempting to hide its identity with the brutes that perish. His sincerity was not unconscious, but self-willed and aggressive. But it would be unjust to overlook that he began with himself. He despised mankind because he found something despicable in Jonathan Swift, as he makes Gulliver hate the Yahoos in proportion to their likeness with himself. He had more or less consciously sacrificed self-respect for that false consideration which is paid to a man's accidents; he had preferred the vain pomp of being served on plate, as no other "man of his level" in Ireland was, to being happy with the woman who had sacrificed herself to his selfishness, and the independence he had won turned out to be only a morose solitude after all. "Money," he was fond of saying, "is freedom," but he never learned that self-denial is freedom with the addition of self-respect. With a hearty contempt for the ordinary objects of human ambition, he could yet bring himself for the sake of them to be the obsequious courtier of three royal strumpets. How should he be happy who had defined happiness to be "the perpetual possession of being well deceived," and who could never be deceived himself? It may well be doubted whether what he himself calls "that pretended philosophy which enters into the depth of things and then comes gravely back with informations and discoveries that in the inside they are good for nothing," be of so penetrative an insight as it is apt to suppose, and whether the truth be not rather that to the empty all things are empty. Swift's diseased eye had the miscroscopic quality of Gulliver's in Brobdingnag, and it was the loathsome obscenity which this revealed in the skin of things that tainted his imagination when it ventured on what was beneath. But with all Swift's scornful humor, he never made the pitiful mistake of his shallow friend Gay that life was a jest. To his nobler temper it was always profoundly tragic, and the salt of his sarcasm was more often, we suspect, than with most humorists distilled out of tears. The lesson is worth remembering that *his* apples of Sodom, like those of lesser men, were plucked from boughs of his own grafting.

—JAMES RUSSELL LOWELL, "Forster's Life of Swift,"
The Nation, April 20, 1876, p. 265

JAMES THOMSON "A NOTE ON FORSTER'S LIFE OF SWIFT" (1876)

Too strong and terrible for Thackeray and Macaulay, Swift is much more so for the average middle-class John Bull, who, while among the bravest of the brave in many respects, is one of the most timorous of mortals face to face with disagreeable truths, truths that perturb his eupeptic comfort, truths hostile to his easy old-fashioned way of thinking without thought, especially if these truths affront his fat inertia in religious, moral, or social questions. This middle-class John Bull, well-fed, well-clothed, well-housed, with a snug balance at his banker's, is the most self-satisfied of optimists, and is simply disgusted and alarmed by a fellow, who as a Dean ought surely to have been contented and sleekly jolly, who never omitted when his birthday came round to read the words of Job: "Let the day perish wherein I was born, and the night in which it was said, There is a man child conceived"; who asked a friend, "Do not the corruptions and villanies of men eat your flesh and exhaust your spirits?" and who wrote of himself in his epitaph: *"Ubi sæva indignatio ulterius cor lacerare nequit."*

—JAMES THOMSON, "A Note on Forster's Life of Swift,"
1876, *Essays and Phantasies,* 1881, pp. 287–288

LESLIE STEPHEN (1882)

The first editor of the compendious *Dictionary of National Biography,* Sir Leslie Stephen was a literary critic and educator who was highly esteemed among his peers. This extract is taken from his 1882 book titled *Swift,* which followed his 1880 *Pope* and his 1878 *Johnson.* In this extract, Stephen dwells on "the most unpleasant part of Swift's character," his "morbid interest" in the repulsive. In doing so, he draws on the testimonies of Swift's friends Patrick Delany and Laetitia Pilkington.

A word must here be said of the most unpleasant part of Swift's character. A morbid interest in the physically disgusting is shown in several of his writings. Some minor pieces, which ought to have been burnt, simply make the gorge rise. Mrs. Pilkington tells us, and we can for once believe her, that one "poem" actually made her mother sick. It is idle to excuse this on the ground of contemporary freedom of speech. His contemporaries were heartily disgusted. Indeed, though it is true that they revealed certain propensities more openly, I see no reason to think that such propensities were really stronger in them than in their descendants. The objection to Swift is not that he spoke plainly, but that he brooded over filth unnecessarily. No parallel can be found for his tendency even in writers, for example, like Smollett and Fielding, who can be coarse enough when they please, but whose freedom of speech reveals none of Swift's morbid tendency. His indulgence in revolting images is to some extent an indication of a diseased condition of his mind, perhaps of actual mental decay. Delany says that it grew upon him in his later years, and, very gratuitously, attributes it to Pope's influence. The peculiarity is the more remarkable, because Swift was a man of the most scrupulous personal cleanliness. He was always enforcing this virtue with special emphasis. He was rigorously observant of decency in ordinary conversation. Delany once saw him "fall into a furious resentment" with Stella for "a very small failure of delicacy." So far from being habitually coarse, he pushed fastidiousness to the verge of prudery. It is one of the superficial paradoxes of Swift's character that this very shrinking from filth became perverted into an apparently opposite tendency. In truth, his intense repugnance to certain images led him to use them as the only adequate expression of his savage contempt. Instances might be given in some early satires, and in the attack upon dissenters in the *Tale of a Tub*. His intensity of loathing leads him to besmear his antagonists with filth. He becomes disgusting in the effort to express his disgust. As his misanthropy deepened, he applied the same method to mankind at large. He tears aside the veil of decency to show the bestial elements of human nature; and his characteristic irony makes him preserve an apparent calmness during the revolting exhibition. His state of mind is strictly analogous to that of some religious ascetics, who stimulate their contempt for the flesh by fixing their gaze upon decaying bodies. They seek to check the love of beauty by showing us beauty in the grave. The cynic in Mr. Tennyson's poem tells us that every face, however full—

Padded round with flesh and blood,
Is but moulded on a skull.

Swift—a practised self-tormentor, though not in the ordinary ascetic sense—mortifies any disposition to admire his fellows by dwelling upon the physical necessities which seem to lower and degrade human pride. Beauty is but skin deep; beneath it is a vile carcase. He always sees the "flayed woman" of the *Tale of a Tub*. The thought is hideous, hateful, horrible, and therefore it fascinates him. He loves to dwell upon the hateful, because it justifies his hate. He nurses his misanthropy, as he might tear his flesh to keep his mortality before his eyes.

—Leslie Stephen, *Swift*, 1882, pp. 179–181

F.C. Montague "Political Pamphlets by Men of Genius" (1891)

Judged with reference to their object, [the] pamphlets of Swift are among the best things in our literature. They have lost much of their interest now that the occasions which prompted them are forgotten. Their constant bitterness, and now and then their nastiness, make them distasteful to sensitive readers. Their simplicity of style seems poverty-stricken to those who think that good writing means fine writing. But those who know what style means will own these pamphlets models of literary art. To be perfectly familiar yet by no means vulgar, to be precise without being pedantic, to argue without becoming tedious, to tell impossible things in a way which makes them seem quite natural, to prejudice your reader whilst yourself seemingly unprejudiced, to stir him to madness whilst yourself seemingly unmoved, to employ every artifice of the most dexterous advocate whilst never dropping the disguise of the modest parish priest or homely tradesman; all this Swift has done so often and with so much address, that after reading him it seems quite easy to do, and one forgets for a moment that in our literature it has been done by Swift alone. He has done the feat best in the *Drapier's Letters*. I know of nothing else like them, and I know of nothing else which may wait longer for a rival. The reader feels that they could not have been written by a tradesman; yet he cannot well believe that they were written by the Dean. The language has all the literary qualities, yet is that of an illiterate man. The arguments are often unsound enough to find general acceptance, yet the author conceals admirably his knowledge of their unsoundness. The result of the blending of the real author and his imagined trader is as piquant to us as it was exciting to his countrymen.

About the efficacy of Swift's polemical writings there can be no question; but there has been much question as to the nature of Swift's personal opinions. Nor is this surprising when we consider Swift's peculiar position. He put forth all his powers on behalf of the Tories; but he had reached middle-life before he quitted the Whigs. He fought the battles of the Church; but he certainly had no clerical vocation. He pleaded the cause of Ireland, but the country he disliked and the bulk of the people he despised. It is therefore natural that many, especially those who disagreed with him, should have regarded this puissant champion as a mere soldier of fortune, careless for whom he fought, and chagrined only because he failed to secure his booty. What seems to confirm their suspicion is the impartial and unqualified scorn which Swift, in his freer moods, pours out upon all factions, civil or ecclesiastical. What he thought of our venerable Constitution he has betrayed in Gulliver's conversation with the King of Brobdingnag. What he thought of politicians he has told us in the last of the *Drapier's Letters.* "Few politicians, with all their schemes, are half so useful members of a commonwealth as an honest farmer; who, by skilfully draining, fencing, manuring and planting, hath increased the intrinsic value of a piece of land, and thereby done a perpetual service to his country, which it is a great controversy whether any of the former ever did since the creation of the world; but no controversy that ninety-nine in a hundred have done abundant mischief." What Swift thought of ecclesiastical disputes he has pretty plainly told in his *Tale of a Tub,* and still more plainly in those famous lines on the Last Judgment, which, although disputed, seem too pungent to have come from any other author. Such a man might have been expected to set less store by the contentions of Whig and Tory, and to tolerate Nonconformists in a petty allowance of power and preferment. Yet as a Tory and Churchman Swift may have been sincere. If little prone to glorify an established order, he was apt enough to cry down the capacity of mankind. Vicious and foolish as they are, he seems to say, it is odd that they should have been able to set up any civil or ecclesiastical polity. What they have set up may be a poor contrivance; but it is as good as could be expected from them. Why trouble yourself to alter mere mechanical arrangements of state when the men upon whom all depends and for whom all exists are naturally base and necessarily miserable? Why vex your soul with the interminable wrangle of theologians when the very little which we know, or need to know, about religion is plain to every man possessed of common sense, if not puffed up with vanity and presumption? Rather let everything be and possess your soul in patience; for wisdom and endurance lessen the evils which they cannot cure. Let knaves and enthusiasts bawl for reformation; they know not what they want, or if they do, they know that they want their own advantage, not the public good.

Such, we may conjecture, was the real unaffected temper of Swift's mind. Expecting little from change, he was naturally conservative. Knowing how trivial are many of the subjects of political and ecclesiastical debate, he thought the disputants fools, and their noise a nuisance to be suppressed as speedily as possible. Sensitive to everything grotesque or frantic, he preferred a decent routine to the vagaries of enthusiasm. Constitutionally imperious and despotic, he followed his bent on taking the side of authority. Having chosen the clerical profession, he was confirmed in all those innate propensities. He took orders at a time when the Church was making her last effort to retain exclusive domination. He felt as a personal wrong the dissidence of the crowd, the unbelief of the fine gentlemen, and the mean estimation in which his calling was held. Upon considering all these things, we shall be surprised rather at his so long remaining a Whig than at his finally becoming a Tory. Once engaged in a party conflict, he was carried by his fierce, overbearing disposition into every excess which his keen, sceptical intellect might have been expected to condemn. The inconsistency may point his own satire upon man, it should surprise only those who have been able to regulate their lives by strict syllogism.

—F.C. Montague, "Political Pamphlets by
Men of Genius," *Murray's Magazine*,
November 1891, pp. 751–754

Henry Craik "Jonathan Swift" (1894)

A Scottish civil servant and author, Henry Craik wrote at length on Swift, most extensively in his *Life of Swift* (1882), *Selections from Swift* (1892), and this extract from his edited collection on *English Prose* (1894). Craik's writings on the subject were often quoted by his contemporaries in a period of relative decline in Swift studies.

"Proper words, in proper places, make the true definition of a style." This is Swift's own maxim in his *Letter to a Young Clergyman*, dated 1719. It has the common defect of such apophthegms, that we are left to interpret it each in his own way. But Swift has developed his views upon style with some fulness in several passages; and from these we can gather what his ideal was, although it is only natural that a genius such as his refused in practice to be bound very strictly by his own theories. In the *Tatler* for 28th September 1710 he commented severely upon the defects of contemporary prose—the mutilation of words and syllables, the introduction of what we should now call slang, and the sacrifice of dignity, taste, and orderly arrangement to caprice, affectation, and ever-changing fashion. He elaborated this more fully in his *Letter to the Lord Treasurer* (Lord Oxford) of the following year, in which he urged the minister to use his influence to check the vulgarising of our language, by founding an academy which should be empowered to regulate and fix the language, and preserve it against the changing whims of fashion. The project was a strange one, and it may be doubted whether there is not something of irony in Swift's advocacy of it; but his hatred of the absurd straining after originality, which succeeded only in attaining to an affected oddity and eccentricity, was not only serious and earnest, but was of a piece with the whole body of Swift's thought and taste. In both these pieces he points to the prose of the Elizabethan age as the most perfect type. Its distinctive mark he asserts to have been its simplicity—"The best and truest ornament of most things in human life," or, as he repeats in the *Letter to a Young Clergyman,* "That simplicity without which no human performance can arrive to any great perfection." As instances of this perfection he adduces Parsons the Jesuit and Hooker, and he contrasts them with the over-elaboration which was distinctive of the following age. Repeatedly he urges this as the first and most essential quality in good prose, and he found the excellence of the prose writers of the reign of Charles I. to be due to their having recovered for a few years some of the simplicity which marked the Elizabethan age. Clarendon was warmly admired by Swift, and was in great measure his model in his chief historical work, the *Memoirs of the Last Four Years of the Queen,* and he tells with approval of Lord Falkland's practice of testing the intelligibility of a word by consulting a servant, and being guided "by her judgment whether to receive or reject it." There is another passage—this time from Mrs. Pilkington's *Memoirs*—which helps us to understand Swift's conception of good prose. "I would have every man write his own English," said the Dean to Mrs. Pilkington; and when she assented, he followed up his dictum by asking her to explain it. "Not to confine one's self to a set of phrases, as some of our ancient English historians, Camden in particular, seems to have done, but to make use of such words as naturally occur on the subject." It was thus that Mrs. Pilkington represents herself to have replied. Swift seems to have approved the interpretation, and we may reasonably guess that he had given Mrs. Pilkington some help towards it.

These indications of the Dean's opinions are not without interest; but he was the last man to be bound by rules, even of his own making. He inveighs against grammatical errors and looseness of construction, but there is scarcely a page of his own writings in which some trifling infringement of grammatical accuracy is not to be found. Of all prose styles his is perhaps the least subject to parody or to imitation, because it is so admirably adapted to each variety in subject, in tone, in treatment. He wields it with the elastic power of the consummate master, so that, once expressed, each thought seems to be fitted with its natural dress, and no variation in the expression is conceivable without the obscuring and even the destruction of the thought. To the genuine lover of Swift the *Tale of a Tub* will probably always be the chief treasure in his works; and it is there that his style is seen at its perfection. The mere story in the book is of the flimsiest description, and the fact that the story is an allegory rather weakens than increases its interest. Its genius lies in the range of thought, in the light play of fancy, in the absolute ease with which he passes, in one undeviating mood of contemptuous sarcasm, through every varying phase of human interest—metaphysical and social, literary and historical, ecclesiastical and political, with no sign of effort, and yet without relaxing for one moment the restrained irony which dominates the reader with a sense of reserved power.

This is the quality of Swift's prose in which his genius shows its mastery. That genius had, of course, other elements; but merely as a writer of prose, Swift's highest excellence is his consummate ease, his absolute concealment of the art and the artist, and the perfect subordination of his instruments to his subject. It is a necessary consequence of this that his style should have variety; but although it is easy to trace the deliberate effort to assume a certain dialect with a view to dramatic effect, yet Swift never allows his reader to be impressed with the fact that the dialect is purposely assumed. Thus in the *Drapier Letters* there is a distinct homeliness of tone, but he is always careful to avoid any exaggeration; and he never openly imitates a jargon or reproduces peculiarities throughout a prose piece as he frequently does in his verse. Master of prose as he was, he yet denied himself any but what he deemed legitimate methods, and even in *Gulliver's Travels,* his imitations of nautical jargon are never carried on for more than a few lines, and even then they are introduced not so much for the purpose of caricature as to heighten the effect of reality in the narrative.

Of all English prose Swift's has the most of flexibility, the most of nervous and of sinewy force; it is the most perfect as an instrument, and the most deadly in its unerring accuracy of aim. It often disdains grammatical correctness, and violates not infrequently the rules of construction and arrangement. But it is significant that Swift attained the perfection of his art, not by deliberately setting aside the proprieties of diction, but by setting before himself consistently the first and highest ideal of simplicity, by disdaining eccentricity and paradox and the caprice of fashion, and that although he wrote "his own English," as no other did before or since, he was inspired from first to last by a deep reverence for the language, and an ardent desire to maintain its dignity and its purity unchanged and unimpaired.

—HENRY CRAIK, "Jonathan Swift,"
English Prose, 1894, vol. 3, pp. 387–390

EDMUND GOSSE (1898)

In this lengthy extract from Edmund Gosse's *Short History of Modern English Literature* (1898), we can identify a number of familiar ideas about Swift. Most pertinently, this Swift is a tainted genius, a man drawn, as Leslie Stephen and others argued, to the dirty and grotesque. Swift was, at the same time, a supreme master of surprise and "thunderbolts."

We have hitherto said nothing of JONATHAN SWIFT, yet he flows right across the present field of our vision, from William III. to George II. His course is that of a fiery comet that dashes through the constellation of the wits of Anne, and falls in melancholy ashes long after the occupation of the last of them. The friend and companion of them for a season, he pursues his flaming course with little real relation to their milder orbits, and is one of the most singular and most original figures that our history has produced. Swift was a bundle of paradoxes—a great churchman who has left not a trace on our ecclesiastical system, an ardent politician who was never more than a fly on the wheel. He is immortal on the one side on which he believed his genius ephemeral; he survives solely, but splendidly, as a man of letters. His career was a failure: he began life as a gentleman's dependent, he quitted it "like a poisoned rat in a hole"; with matchless energy and ambition, he won neither place nor power; and in the brief heyday of his influence with the Ministry, he who helped others was impotent to endow himself. Swift is the typical instance of the powerlessness of pure intellect to secure any but intellectual triumphs. But even the victories of his brain were tainted; his genius left a taste of brass on his own palate. That Swift was ever happy, that his self-torturing nature was capable of contentment, is not certain; that for a long period of years he was wretched beyond the lot of man is evident, and those have not sounded the depths of human misery who have not followed in their mysterious obscurity the movements of the character of Swift.

His will was too despotic to yield to his misfortunes; his pride sustained him, and in middle life a fund of restless animal spirits. We know but little of his early years, yet enough to see that the *splendida bilis,* the *sæva indignatio,* which ill-health exacerbated, were his companions from the first. We cannot begin to comprehend his literary work without recognising this. His weapon was ink, and he loved to remember that gall and copperas went to the making of it. It was in that deadest period, at the very close of the seventeenth century, that his prodigious talent first made itself apparent. With no apprenticeship in style, no relation of discipleship to any previous French or English writer, but steeped in the Latin classics, he produced, at the age of thirty, two of the most extraordinary masterpieces of humour and satire which were ever written, the *Tale of a Tub* and the *Battle of the Books.* It was not until five or six years later (1704) that he gave them together, anonymously, to the press. In the *Tale of a Tub* every characteristic of Swift's style is revealed—the mordant wit, the vehement graceful ease, the stringent simplicity. To the end of his days he never wrote better things than the description of the goddess

of Criticism drawn by geese in a chariot, the dedication to Prince Posterity
with its splendid hilarity and irony, the doubly distilled allegorical apologue
of the Spider and the Bee. In his poisonous attacks on the deists, in his gleams
of sulky misanthropy, in the strange filthiness of his fancy, in the stranger
exhilaration which seizes him whenever the idea of madness is introduced—
in all these things Swift reveals his essential character in this his first and
perhaps greatest book. Although every one admired it, the *Tale of a Tub* was
doubtless fatal to his ambition, thus wrecked at the outset on the reef of his
ungovernable satire. The book, to be plain, is a long gibe at theology, and it
is not surprising that no bishopric could ever be given to the inventor of the
Brown Loaf and the Universal Pickle. He might explain away his mockery,
declare it to have been employed in the Anglican cause, emphasise the denial
that his aim was irreligious; the damning evidence remained that when he
had had the sacred garments in his hands he had torn away, like an infuriated
ape, as much of the gold fringe as he could. The fact was that, without any
design of impiety, he knew not how to be devout. He always, by instinct, saw
the hollowness and the seamy side. His enthusiasms were negative, and his
burning imagination, even when he applied it to religion, revealed not heaven
but hell to him.

The power and vitality of such a nature could not be concealed; they drew
every sincere intellect towards him. Already, in 1705, Addison was hailing
Swift as "the most agreeable companion, the truest friend, and the greatest
genius of the age." We take him up again in 1711, when the slender volume
of *Miscellanies* reminds us of what he had been as a writer from the age of
thirty-five to forty-five. The contents of this strange book name for us the
three caustic religious treatises, the first of Swift's powerful political tracts
(the *Sacramental Test),* various other waifs and rags from his culminating
year, 1708, gibes and flouts of many kinds revealing the spirit of "a very
positive young man," trifles in verse and prose to amuse his friends the Whig
Ministers or the ladies of Lord Berkeley's family. Nothing could be more
occasional than all this; nothing, at first sight, less imbued with intensity
or serious feeling. Swift's very compliments are impertinent, his arguments
in favour of Christianity subversive. But under all this there is the passion
of an isolated intellect, and he was giving it play in the frivolities of a
compromising humour.

The published writings of Swift during the first forty-four years of his
life were comprised in two volumes of very moderate dimensions. But if the
purely literary outcome of all this period had been exiguous, it was now to
grow scantier still. At the very moment when the group of Anne wits, led
by Pope and Addison, were entering with animation upon their best work,

Swift, almost ostentatiously, withdrew to the sphere of affairs, and for ten years refrained entirely from all but political authorship. His unexampled *Journal to Stella,* it is true, belongs to this time of obscuration, but it is hardly literature, though of the most intense and pathetic interest. Swift now stood "ten times better" with the new Tories than ever he did with the old Whigs, and his pungent pen poured forth lampoons and satirical projects. The influence of Swift's work of this period upon the style of successive English publicists is extremely curious; he began a new order of political warfare, demanding lighter arms and swifter manoeuvres than the seventeenth century had dreamed of. Even Halifax seems cold and slow beside the lightning changes of mood, the inexorable high spirits of Swift. That such a tract as the *Sentiments of a Church of England Man,* with its gusts of irony, its white heat of preposterous moderation, led on towards Junius is obvious; but Swift is really the creator of the whole school of eighteenth-century rhetorical diatribe on its better side, wherever it is not leaden and conventional. It may be said that he invented a vital polemical system, which was used through the remainder of the century by every one who dealt in that kind of literature, and who was at the same time strong enough to wield such thunderbolts.

—EDMUND GOSSE, *A Short History of Modern
English Literature,* 1898, pp. 220–224

WORKS

The following extracts represent various critics' views of particular works by Swift, from his widely read novel *Gulliver's Travels* to his poetry and prose satires, including *A Tale of a Tub*. In each, once more, the art of Swift is inseparable from the critic's view of his character. Many of the extracts explore Swift's "sincerity" as being either aesthetically necessary to his art or its major flaw.

Although a number of later commentators would place *A Tale of a Tub* among the greatest of Swift's works, it is fair to say that many contemporaries did not know what to make of this scandalous prose satire when it first appeared anonymously in 1704. An extended allegory of corruptions and abuses within institutional religion, many viewed it as irreligious, while others commended its bravery. An early admirer was Francis Atterbury, who, in the year of its publication, described the work as "original in it's [sic] kind, full of wit, humour, good sense and learning." William Congreve was more ambivalent. He delights in several passages but, ultimately, "should not care to read it again." Later admirers include George-Monck Berkeley, who defends it as the "work of a very young man," and, half a century later, Henry Hallam, who feels it is "so full of real meaning, of biting satire, of felicitous analogy." Edmund Gosse, nearly another half century after that, suggests that it displays Swift's "finest qualities of imagination and irony when they were in their freshest and most ebullient condition." But of course, *A Tale of a Tub* has long had its critics too. An early detractor of note, Sir Richard Blackmore, damns it as yet another "pernicious Abuse of Wit." For William Wotton, it is a work that made fun not only of God and religion but also of learning, hard work, and morality. Later in the century, William Godwin, more prosaically, concedes that it is a work of great banter but not a fit model. By contrast, for Herbert Eveleth Greene nearly an additional century later, it is perhaps "the best sustained allegory that ever was written."

The Drapier's Letters, by contrast, received a great deal more praise at the outset. Thomas Sheridan, Swift's friend and biographer, was of the opinion that "the great talents of Swift never appeared in a more conspicuous light than on this occasion." *The Drapier's Letters* is the collective name of seven pamphlets produced between 1724 and 1725, which were first collected in George Faulkner's 1735 Dublin edition, replete with an allegorical frontispiece offering praise from the Irish people. Collectively these works had, by this time, acquired notice for their advocating the cause of Irish freedom. Under the pseudonym of the lowly M.B. Drapier, Swift sought to rouse public opinion in Ireland against an inferior coinage that was being circulated in the country and, by extension, against English corruption. Looking back on this episode, in 1808, John Wilson Croker argued for the importance of Swift to subsequent constructions of Irish patriotism. At the end of the century, Richard Ashe King concurred with his view and described the letters as "epoch-making." But the praise was not unanimous. In the midcentury, Adams Sherman Hill felt that, even if *The Drapier's Letters* "are the best known of Swift's efforts for Ireland," they were "no more useful than the tracts published subsequently."

While the debates over the value of *A Tale of a Tub* and *The Drapier's Letters* can be drawn to varying degrees of satisfaction, the immense cultural impact of Swift's most famous work can never be sufficiently defined. Streams of translations and adaptations appeared in increasing numbers, the English language was buttressed with a number of new words, such as *Lilliputian,* and reports of parliamentary debates in the periodical press mimicked Swift's universe. These references of course, are to *Gulliver's Travels* or, more properly as it is known, *Travels into Several Remote Nations of the World. In Four Parts by Lemuel Gulliver, First a Surgeon and then a Captain of several Ships.* "Here is a book come out," Lady Mary Wortley Montagu wrote in 1726, "that all our people of taste run mad about." That same year John Gay and Alexander Pope regaled Swift with their observations on the reception of *Gulliver's Travels.* In particular they gleefully inform him of the disapproval it had generated among their enemies. Such detractors were numerous, and some of them retaliated. Some, including Jonathan Smedley, demurred for the sake of railing against Swift's quickened fame: "The pious Dean has done what in him lies to render *Religion, Reason,* and *common Sense* ridiculous." Some readers delighted in the outlandish imagination on display. Horace Walpole, for instance, wrote a whimsical if caricatured "sequel" in a letter to a friend. But where Smedley and Walpole consider it to be a ridiculous work, others, including the pious Edward Young, are more damning of

Swift's skeptical outlook. Others, such as Lord Monboddo, praise *Gulliver's Travels* as a great exemplum of Swift's "simple . . . style." For Sir Walter Scott, in a lengthy extract included here, it is a work of great attraction to the whole strata of the reading public. Even conceding that it owed much to its classic influences, as well as to the current fashion for travelogues, Walter Scott praises the great originality of the work. Others made flattering comparisons with Daniel Defoe's *Robinson Crusoe*. John Churton Collins, in his 1893 study of Swift, asserts that Defoe "himself is not a greater master of the art of realistic effect." But, overwhelmingly, critics were concerned with the nature of realism in *Gulliver's Travels*. That is, did the book display a naked hatred of humanity in place of its artlessness? In the opinion of Gerald P. Moriarty, also first published in 1893, it would be churlish to assign a meaning to Swift's story. Rather it stands "for all time supreme and unapproachable," an uninterpretable primal scream. Alfred Ainger, a year later, feels the work demonstrated a lack of judgment on Swift's behalf, even if it captured his "matured powers." These accounts largely conformed to a much longer tradition that announced a concern for Swift's so-called disdain for humanity. In particular, commentators have focused on the final sections of the book, in which Gulliver exhibits a nauseated disdain for the humanlike Yahoos and humans alike, preferring instead the company of his horses in lieu of the idealized Houyhnhnms he had encountered on his travels. Nathan Drake, Leslie Stephen, Edward Young, James Beattie, Edmund Gosse, and many others have grappled with these problematic parts of the book. Thomas Tyler weighs these concerns, including the suggestion that the final sections are expendable—indeed, excised for children—and concludes that the book is consistent in its wallowing pessimism.

In general, Swift the poet has garnered less attention than Swift the prose writer. An often-repeated anecdote is of the formidable man of letters John Dryden telling a young Swift that he "will never be a poet." That is to say, Swift lacked the technical accomplishments a poet needed, abilities that were abundantly present in his friend Alexander Pope. More broadly, many commentators treated Swift's poetry as essentially prose in verse. For instance, in the 1880s, John Nichol observed that some of the "merits of our author's verse are those of his prose—condensation, pith, always the effect, generally the reality, of sincere purpose, and, with few exceptions, simplicity and directness." Crudely speaking, two schools of thought exist: Either Swift's verse is regarded as an extension of the satiric universe of the prose, or it is ignored completely. Such was the view held by Francis, Lord Jeffrey in 1816: "we cannot persuade ourselves that Swift was in any respect a poet." In 1871, Hippolyte Taine put it in a different, though equally damning way: "what is wanting most in his verses is poetry." Aside from technical considerations, many commentators, especially those speaking on behalf of their female audiences, grouped the poetry in with the prose and then forbade anyone from reading it on the grounds of decency. Many of the poems were, after all, too salacious for the minds of young readers, in the view of John Aikin and others. Some critics agreed with this in principle, though they sought to controvert the moral foundations. W.H. Dilworth, for example, suggests that, far from corrupting young minds, "Those verses upon women, which are deemed the most satirical," were actually written "with a view to correct their foibles." But Swift's achievements in verse must not be underestimated, especially in a number of established classical modes, from the Pindaric to the Juvenalian, as well as modern ones. One of his most accomplished pieces is included here, the morbidly self-reflexive "Verses on the Death of Dr. Swift," which, it is said, elicited a tear from Laetitia Pilkington upon reading it. Master of poetic technique or not, Jonathan Swift was, to be sure, a literary master capable of eliciting strong emotional responses to his works. His imaginative élan and intellectual vigor abounded in his writings, both verse and prose alike, as these testimonies, whether denunciatory or appreciatory, cannot help but reveal. Perhaps we should abandon the unhelpful distinctions between poetry and prose altogether in the case of Swift and instead follow Herbert Paul who, in the final extract, dubs him "The Prince of Journalists."

A TALE OF A TUB

FRANCIS ATTERBURY (1704)

Now widely ranked among Swift's best works, indeed among the best works in such a style in the English language, *A Tale of a Tub* baffled many of his contemporaries when it appeared in 1704. Here we have an early reader, Francis Atterbury, keen to insist that the book has great value even if it is profane and seemingly irreligious in parts. William Wotton (included later in this section), by contrast, attacks it precisely on the grounds of irreligiousness.

(June 15, 1704) I beg your Lordship (if the book is come down to Exon) to read the *Tale of a Tub*. For, bating the profaneness of it in some places, it is a book to be valued, being an original in it's kind, full of wit, humour, good sense and learning. It comes from Christ Church; and a good part of it is written in defence of Mr. Boyle against Wotton and Bentley. The town is wonderfully pleased with it.

(July 1, 1704) The author of *A Tale of a Tub* will not as yet be known; and if it be the man I guess, he hath reason to conceal himself, because of the prophane strokes in that piece, which would do his reputation and interest in the world more harm than the wit can do him good. I think your Lordship hath found out a very proper employment for his pen, which he would execute very happily. Nothing can please more than that book doth here at London.

—FRANCIS ATTERBURY, letters to
Bishop Trelawney, 1704

WILLIAM CONGREVE (1704)

I am of your mind as to the *Tale of a Tub*. I am not alone in the opinion, as you are there; but I am pretty near it, having but very few on my side; but those few are worth a million. However, I have never spoke my sentiments, not caring to contradict a multitude. Bottom admires it, and cannot bear my saying, I confess I was diverted with several passages when I read it, but I should not care to read it again. That he thinks not commendation enough.

—WILLIAM CONGREVE, letter to
Joseph Keally, October 28, 1704

WILLIAM WOTTON (1705)

Key combatants in the British version of the *Querelle des Anciens et des Modernes*, the "Battle of the Books," William Wotton and Richard Bentley were attacked by Sir William Temple for advocating the supremacy of the moderns over the ancients. Swift, Temple's secretary, entered the debate with "A Full and True Account of the Battel Fought last Friday, &c," a prose satire attached to *A Tale of a Tub* and arguing in favor of the ancients.

This way of printing Bits of Books in their Nature are intended for Continued Discourses, and are not loose Apophthegems, Occasional Thoughts, or incoherent Sentences, is what I have seen few Instances of; none more remarkable than this, and more which may be supposed to imitate this, *The Tale of a Tub*. . . . In which though Dr. *Bentley* and my self are coursely treated, yet I believe I may safely answer for us both, that we should not have taken any manner of notice of it, if upon this Occasion I had not been obliged to say something in answer to what has been seriously said against us.

For, believe me, Sir, what concerns us, is much the innocentest part of the Book, tending chiefly to make Men laugh for half an Hour, after which it leaves no farther Effects behind it. When Men are jested upon for what is in it self praiseworthy, the World will do them Justice: And on the other hand, if they deserve it, they ought to sit down quietly under it. Our Cause therefore we shall leave to the Public very willingly, there being no occasion to be concerned at any Man's Railery about it. But the rest of the Book which does not relate to us, is of so irreligious a nature, is so crude a Banter upon all that is esteemed as Sacred among all Sects and Religions among Men, that, having so fair an Opportunity, I thought it might be useful to many People who pretend they see no harm in it, to lay open the Mischief of the Ludicrous Allegory, and to shew what that drives at which has been so greedily brought up and read. In one Word, God and Religion, Truth and Moral Honesty, Learning and Industry are made a May-Game, and the most serious Things in the World are described as so many several scenes in a *Tale of a Tub.*

—WILLIAM WOTTON, *A Defense of the
"Reflections upon Ancient and Modern Learning,"
In Answer to the Objections of Sir W. Temple,
and Others. With Observations upon
"The Tale of the Tub,"* 1705, pp. 47–48

RICHARD BLACKMORE
"AN ESSAY UPON WIT" (1716)

A staunchly religious man, the dunce-poet Sir Richard Blackmore regularly spoke out against what he perceived to be the irreligiousness of modern literature. In particular, he held a running feud with Swift's co-satirist Alexander Pope for his supposed blasphemy. Swift himself, perhaps inevitably, incurred the wrath of Blackmore, as this passionate critique of *A Tale of a Tub* demonstrates.

Another pernicious Abuse of Wit is that which appears in the Writings of some ingenious Men, who are so hardy as to expose from the Press the most venerable Subjects, and treat Vertue and Sobriety of Manners with Raillery and Ridicule. Several, in their Books, have many sarcastical and spiteful Strokes at Religion in general, while others make themselves pleasant with the Principles of the Christian. Of the last kind this Age has seen a most audacious Example in the Book intitul'd, *A Tale of a Tub.* Had this Writing been publish'd in a Pagan or Popish Nation, who are justly impatient of all Indignity offer'd to the Establish'd Religion of their Country, no doubt but the Author would have receiv'd the Punishment he deserv'd. But the Fate of this impious Buffoon is very different;

for in a Protestant Kingdom, zealous of their Civil and Religious Immunities, he has not only escap'd Affronts and the Effects of publick Resentment, but has been caress'd and patroniz'd by Persons of great Figure and of all Denominations. Violent Party Men, who differ'd in all Things besides, agreed, in their Turn, to shew particular Respect and Friendship to this insolent Derider of the Worship of his Country, till at last the reputed Writer is not only gone off with Impunity, but triumphs in his Dignity and Preferment. I do not know, that any Inquiry or Search was ever made after this Writing, or that any Reward was ever offer'd for the Discovery of the Author, or that the infamous Book was ever condemn'd to be burnt in Publick: Whether this proceeds from the excessive Esteem and Love that Men in Power, during the late Reign, had for Wit, or their defect of Zeal and Concern for the Christian Religion, will be determin'd best by those, who are best acquainted with their Character.

—RICHARD BLACKMORE, "An Essay upon Wit,"
Essays upon Several Subjects, 1716, pp. 217–218

GEORGE-MONCK BERKELEY (1789)

A grandson of Swift's friend Bishop Berkeley, George-Monck Berkeley was a keen defender of Swift. Berkeley's *Literary Relics* contains a large store of letters to and from his grandfather, including a number involving Swift. In this extract, as elsewhere, Berkeley responds to specific accusations leveled at his subject by biographers. *A Tale of a Tub*, he argues here, was the work of a young man and must be appreciated as such.

'Of this work', says Johnson, 'charity may be persuaded to think, that it might be written by a man of peculiar character without bad intention; but it is certainly a dangerous example'. I confess myself unable to discern the danger. The *Tale of a Tub* holds up to ridicule superstitious and fanatical absurdities, which, having no weak side of common sense, defy argument and are unassailable by learning: but the essentials of religion are never attacked; and that church, for which Johnson entertained the highest veneration, is every where treated with the respect which is due to the glory of the reformation. If, in the book, a flight of fancy now and then occurs which a serious mind would wish away, before Swift be convicted of impiety, the following circumstances ought to be impartially weighed.

In the *first* place, *the Tale of a Tub* was the work of a very young man; and although the rule of Horace, *Nonum prematur in annum*, was observed, it still made its appearance at an early period of the author's life. To say, that he whose youth is not totally exempt from levity will be disgraced by an old age of blasphemy, is perhaps not perfectly consistent with that first of human virtues, *charity*. But of that virtue the persecutors of Swift seem to have had little or no idea. *Secondly*, I maintain, that in the work before us there is not a single passage which implies a disbelief of revelation: At the same time I must confess, there are many passages that, with the assistance of *well-meaning* and *able commentators*, might be so construed as to prove, that the author was an admirer of the *Gentoo* tenets, and not wholly averse to the *God* of *Thibet*. For although my reading cannot as yet have been very extensive, I have read enough to know, that there is not the least necessity for *any sort of connection* between the *text* and the *commentary*.

—George-Monck Berkeley, *Literary Relics: Containing Original Letters from King Charles II, King James II, The Queen of Bohemia, Swift, Berkeley, Addison, Steele, Congreve, The Duke of Ormond, and Bishop Rundle. To Which Is Prefixed, an Inquiry into the Life of Dean Swift*, 1789, pp. xxv–xxvi

William Godwin "Of English Style" (1797)

The *Tale of a Tub* is a work, of perhaps greater felicity of wit, and more ludicrous combinations of ideas, than any other book in the world. It is however, written in so strange a style of "banter," to make use of one of the author's words, or rather in so low and anomalous a slang, which perhaps Swift considered as the necessary concomitant of wit; that it is by no means proper to be cited as an example of just composition.

—William Godwin, "Of English Style," *The Enquirer*, 1797, p. 444

John Barrett (1808)

Identifying a lack of credible sources on the early part of Swift's life, John Barrett sought to provide a dedicated study in this area. He collected a number of obscure pamphlets and letters that might otherwise have vanished. In this extract, he quotes from a 1704 pamphlet on *A Tale of a Tub*.

But nothing is more observable in the true and undisputed productions of Swift, than the pains which he seems to take in raking together the most nauseous ideas, and dwelling upon the most indelicate images. It is unnecessary for me to bring examples of this strange propensity of his nature; which is the more serviceable to us, because he is almost singular in this respect, and it forms the strong outline that distinguishes him from almost every other writer. In a pamphlet which came out in 1704 at London, called "Some Remarks on the Tale of a Tub", he is thus described: "The Author's first aim is to be profane; but that part I shall leave to my betters, since matters of such a nature are not to be jested with, but punished. The second is, to show how great a proficient he is at hectoring and bullying, at ranting and roaring, and especially at cursing and swearing. His third is, to exceed all bounds of modesty. His next is, a great affectation for every thing nasty. He takes the air upon dunghills, in ditches, and in common sewers, and at my Lord Mayor's dog-kennel. By the first of these, he shews his religion, by the second his conversation, by the third his manners, and by the fourth his education. Now were the crow who at present struts so much in the gutter, stripped of these four sorts of feathers, he would be left quite naked".

—JOHN BARRETT, *An Essay on the Earlier Part of the Life of Swift*, 1808, pp. 28–29

HENRY HALLAM (1839)

It would not, perhaps, be unfair to bring within the pale of the seventeenth century an effusion of genius, sufficient to redeem our name in its annals of fiction. The Tale of a Tub, though not published till 1704, was chiefly written, as the author declares, eight years before; and the Battle of the Books subjoined to it has every appearance of recent animosity against the opponents of Temple and Boyle, in the question of Phalaris. The Tale of a Tub is, in my apprehension, the masterpiece of Swift; certainly Rabelais has nothing superior, even in invention, nor any thing so condensed, so pointed, so full of real meaning, of biting satire, of felicitous analogy.

—HENRY HALLAM, *Introduction to the Literature of Europe, in the Fifteenth, Sixteenth and Seventeenth Centuries*, 1839, vol. 4, p. 559

EDMUND GOSSE (1889)

After widespread befuddlement among readers in the early years of the eighteenth century, critics slowly began to appreciate the artistic merits of *A Tale of a Tub*. By 1889, the literary critic Edmund Gosse could happily insist that this work ought properly to rank among Swift's finest. He talks in detail about the intellectual rigor of the work, about the purity of style, and of the "prodigality of wit" on display.

The very extraordinary treatise called *A Tale of a Tub* is allowed to rank among the first of its author's productions. It displays his finest qualities of imagination and irony when they were in their freshest and most ebullient condition. Swift himself is said to have remarked, at the close of his life, "Good God, what a genius I had when I wrote that book." It is not long, and it is divided into so many varied sections that it seems shorter than it is. The reader is carried along so gaily on this buoyant tide of wit, that he puts the book down with regret to find it ended, when it seemed but just begun. In this, *A Tale of a Tub* forms a surprising contrast to almost all the prose which had preceded it for half a century, the writers of the Restoration, even where they are most correct and graceful, being devoid of this particular sparkle and crispness of phrase. The book is an allegorical romance, but surrounded by so many digressions, one outside the other, like the parts of an ivory puzzle-ball, that scarcely half of it is even nominally narrative. The name is given from the supposed custom of sailors to throw a tub to a whale to prevent him from rolling against their ship; the treatise being a tub for the leviathans of scepticism to sport with, instead of disturbing the orthodox commonwealth. . . . In *A Tale of a Tub* the intellectual interest never halts for a moment. There is infinite variety, and the reader is tantalised by the prodigality of wit, never fatigued for a moment by its expression. In pure style Swift never excelled this his first important essay. The polemical and humorous parts are direct and terse beyond anything that had preceded them in English, and when the author permits himself for a moment to be serious, he speaks with the tongue of angels. In the midst of the profane section on the Aeolists, there is a page which reaches as far as our language can reach in the direction of dignity and music; and at all times it may be noted that Swift in this work and in *The Battle of the Books* is more picturesque than anywhere else.

—EDMUND GOSSE, *A History of Eighteenth
Century Literature*, 1889, pp. 144–147

HERBERT EVELETH GREENE
"THE ALLEGORY AS EMPLOYED BY
SPENSER, BUNYAN, AND SWIFT" (1889)

In his larger essay on "The Allegory as Employed by Spenser, Bunyan, and Swift," appearing in the *Publications of the Modern Language Association of America* for 1889, Herbert Eveleth Greene discusses at length the technical

mastery of *A Tale of a Tub*. Taking into account certain inevitable restrictions
and obstacles, Greene asserts that the allegory is "well nigh perfect."

That SWIFT was able, when he chose, to fulfil the conditions of the allegory
is abundantly proved by 'The Tale of a Tub'. This work, written before he had
reached his thirtieth year, is full of spirit, wit, and power. The reader of such
vigorous and effective English, employed with so much directness and point,
cannot but sympathize with the feeling which prompted him to say in his old
age, when his mind was gradually failing, "Good God, what a genius I had
when I wrote that book!" Not only is the book his masterpiece, but it is also
his best allegory; indeed one would hazard little in making the assertion that
it is the best sustained allegory that ever was written.

Three brothers, born at a birth, named Peter, Martin, and Jack, represent
the Roman Catholics, the Church of England, and the Dissenters. To these
brothers their fathers had bequeathed a coat with strict injunctions never to
make any alteration in it; this coat is evidently the Christian religion. In his
will, that is, the Bible, were careful instructions as to how the coat should be
worn. After seven years, that is, centuries, of faithful obedience, the brothers
fell in with three ladies in great reputation at that time, the Duchess d'Argent,
Madame de Grand Titres, and the Countess d'Orgueil. A short digression
gives us the germ of the "clothes-philosophy," afterwards developed by
CARLYLE, whereby fine feathers make fine birds. This philosophy being in
vogue at that time, as since, the three brothers found their coats decidedly out
of fashion and themselves out of favor. Though the will said not a word about
shoulder-knots, which were then "the only wear," yet one of the brothers,
"more book-learned than the other two," found that the various letters of the
word could be picked out separately, with the exception of K; and it was soon
discovered that C was the equivalent of K. The interpretation is obvious. In
the same skillful manner are allegorized tampering with manuscripts, oral
tradition, the use of images, withholding the Bible from the common people,
the temporal sovereignty of the Pope, the doctrine of purgatory, penance,
confession, absolution, indulgences, holy water, the celibacy of the clergy,
transubstantiation, withholding the cup from the laity. Starting with the
three brothers, the coat, and the will, as the basis of his allegory, he follows
with amazing ingenuity the history of the Church through the centuries of
corruption to the Reformation, and thence onward far enough to show the
divisions that arose after the Reformation and the growth of sects. Such close
and logical correspondence between the sign and the thing signified, it would
be difficult to parallel elsewhere in an allegory that possesses a vital interest.

MACAULAY'S statement that 'The Tale of a Tub' swarms with errors in the conduct of its allegory, is not borne out by examination. Some parts, indeed, are expressed more directly than others; such are the celibacy of the clergy and the temporal power of the Pope, which it is scarcely possible to express otherwise than directly. In the entire narrative there are no personifications save those named above of wealth, ambition and pride. The allegory is necessarily historical, and that this is not the highest kind of allegory I shall have occasion later to show. In such an allegory and with the kind of figures that Swift habitually employed, there was little opportunity for true and ennobling symbolism. Setting aside all that should be deducted for the absence of two so important aids to the highest degree of success, and bearing in mind what SWIFT undertook to do, his allegory is well nigh perfect. The main lines of his narrative were already marked out for him; troublesome details he could omit, if he chose, but in the more important points he had no power of choice. His task was to contrive a close correspondence to the actual history of the church; and this he did in a masterly manner.

—HERBERT EVELETH GREENE,
"The Allegory as Employed by Spenser,
Bunyan, and Swift," *PMLA*, 1889, pp. 168–170

THE DRAPIER'S LETTERS

ALEXANDER POPE (1737)

Let Ireland tell, how Wit upheld her cause,
Her Trade supported, and supply'd her Laws;
And leave on SWIFT this grateful verse ingrav'd,
The Rights a Court attack'd, a Poet sav'd.
Behold the hand that wrought a Nation's cure,
Stretch'd to relieve the Idiot and the Poor,
Proud Vice to brand, or injur'd Worth adorn,
And stretch the Ray to Ages yet unborn.

—ALEXANDER POPE, *Imitations of Horace*,
1737, epistle II.i. 221–228

THOMAS SHERIDAN (1784)

In his biography of his friend Swift, Thomas Sheridan dedicates much space to the writings. In this extract, he discusses the literary merits of *The*

Drapier's Letters. He argues that, on the surface, the letters seem to have been written by a man of trade, in keeping with the expressed authorship, but, on closer inspection, we can find a great deal of consummate skill involved in this production.

Whoever examines the Drapier's Letters with attention will find, that the great talents of Swift never appeared in a more conspicuous light than on this occasion. He saw that a plan was formed by the British Minister to bring his country into the utmost distress. Notwithstanding the apparent opposition given to it by the Irish Parliament and Privy Council, he knew too well the servile disposition of all men in office at that time, and their abject dependence on the Minister, to suppose they would continue firm in their opposition, at the certain loss of their places, if he was determined to carry the point. He saw therefore no possible means of preventing the evil, but raising such a spirit in the whole body of the people, as would make them resolve on no account whatsoever to receive this coin. His writings in the character of a Drapier were in such plain language, as rendered them perfectly intelligible to the meanest capacities. His arguments were so naturally deduced, and in such an easy series, from simple and evident principles, as carried the fullest conviction to every mind. But as it was necessary to his purpose to rouse the feelings, as well as convince the understandings of mankind; without ever appearing to apply at all to the passions, he raises them to the highest pitch, by seemingly casual strokes here and there interspersed. So that the whole, on a transient view, appeared what it professed to be, the work of an honest shopkeeper, of plain common sense, who started out of his sphere to commence writer, upon a view of the imminent danger with which his country was threatened; and who could not, now and then, in the course of his argument, suppress the honest indignation which rose in his breast, at the unparalleled insolence of power, in treating a great and loyal kingdom with such indignity as would have been thought intolerable, even by the inhabitants of the Isle of Man. Yet plain and simple as these writings seem to be at first view, and such as every common Reader would imagine he could produce himself, upon a closer inspection they would be found to be works of the most consummate skill and art; and whoever should attempt to perform the like, would be obliged to say with Horace:

Sudet multum, frustraque laboret
Quivis speret idem.

—Thomas Sheridan, *The Life of the Rev.*
Dr. Jonathan Swift, Dean of St. Patrick's,
Dublin, 1784, pp. 239–240

John Wilson Croker (1808)

On this gloom, one luminary rose; and Ireland worshipped it with almost Persian idolatry: personal resentment was, perhaps, the first motive of the patriotism of SWIFT, but it assumed in its progress a higher port, and directed itself by nobler considerations. The jealousy of the partisan soon expanded into the generous devotion of a patriot, and the power of his mind and the firmness of his character raised him to an ascendancy which no other individual ever attained or deserved; above suspicion, he was trusted; above envy, he was beloved; above rivalry, he was obeyed. His wisdom was at once practical and prophetic; remedial for the present, warning for the future: he first taught Ireland that she might become a nation, and England that she might cease to be a despot. But he was a churchman. His gown impeded his course, and entangled his efforts; guiding a senate, or heading an army, he had perhaps been equal to Cromwell, and Ireland not less than England: as it was, he saved her by his courage, improved her by his authority, adorned her by his talents, and exalted her by his fame. His mission was but of ten years; and for ten years only did his personal power mitigate the government: but when no longer feared by the great, he was yet not forgotten by the wise; his influence, like his writings, has survived a century; and the foundations of whatever prosperity we have since erected, are laid in the disinterested and magnanimous patriotism of Swift.

—JOHN WILSON CROKER, *A Sketch of the State of Ireland, Past and Present*, 1808

Adams Sherman Hill "The Character of Jonathan Swift" (1868)

The Drapier's Letters are the best known of Swift's efforts for Ireland, but were perhaps no more useful than the tracts published subsequently, which are, says Scott, "a bright record of the unceasing zeal with which he continued, through successive years and until the total decay of his mental faculties, to watch over the interests of Ireland,—to warn his countrymen of their errors, to laugh them out of their follies, to vindicate their rights against the oppressions of their powerful neighbors, and to be, in the expressive language of Scripture, the man set for their watchman to blow the trumpet and warn the people." He inveighed, not always in the politest terms, against the luxury and extravagance of women, the folly of improvident marriages, the absenteeism of landlords, the extortions of their agents, the expenditure in England of money wrung from Irish tenants. He described the condition of the unhappy kingdom;—spacious harbors without shipping; fertile soil, capable of producing needed corn and potatoes, but grazed on by sheep whose wool was useless, since its exportation was forbidden; undrained morasses; unrepaired fences; wretched hovels; wretched roads; able-bodied laborers without work; beggars swarming everywhere: and, over all, the English governors, civil, military, clerical, whose sole anxiety was to squeeze as much as possible out of their subjects. Swift's was the single voice crying in that wilderness loudly enough to be heard across the Channel. With bursts of indignation against the oppressor who would not hear, and against the oppressed who, hearing, did not understand, he pleaded for his country, appealing to every motive that could influence the master or the slave. In one pamphlet he suggested, as the only remaining means of relief, that the people should sell their children to the rich, as a new delicacy for the table, and with the proceeds keep the wolf from their doors a little longer. The wonderful irony with which the advantages of the scheme are set forth, the scientific coolness with which the problem is worked out like a sum in arithmetic, so shocked the sensibilities of Thackeray, that he calls Swift an "ogre" in the nursery. But the meaning of the writer is apparent in every line. In numerous passages in previous tracts he had shown how inapplicable to Ireland was the generally received maxim that "People are the riches of a nation." If Swift played the ogre, it was not for the purpose of frightening children, but to warn parents, their landlords and rulers. England was the ogre whose part he assumed, in order the more forcibly to impress the fearful consequences of persistency in the policy which was ruining Ireland. Having assumed the part, he played it to the life, thinking less perhaps of the feelings of Thackeray and the ladies than of the serious work in hand. Bully Bottom had not been his instructor.

—ADAMS SHERMAN HILL, "The Character of
Jonathan Swift," *North American Review*,
January 1868, pp. 85–86

RICHARD ASHE KING (1895)

The Drapier's Letters are epoch-making in that they first taught Ireland the policy and the power of union, of dogged inert resistance, and of strategically organized and directed agitation. Their effect was, in fact, commensurate with their power, and their power of its kind was supreme. It is the power of a deft, vigorous, intent and unerring-eyed wielder of a hammer, who hits each nail on the head and home without one single feint, or flourish, or one single short, or wide, or weak, or wasted stroke. Swift's consummate mastery of the art which conceals art was never shown to such perfection as in these Letters, whose naked simplicity is so like naked truth as to be confounded with it. Yet there was about as much naked truth in them as in *Gullivers Travels!*

—RICHARD ASHE KING, *Swift in Ireland*,
1895, pp. 108–109

GULLIVER'S TRAVELS

MARY WORTLEY MONTAGU (1726)

Here is a book come out, that all our people of taste run mad about. Tis no less than the united Work of a dignify'd clergyman, an Eminent Physician, and the first poet of the Age, and very wonderfull it is, God knows. Great Eloquence have they employ'd to prove themselves Beasts, and show such a veneration for Horses that since the Essex Quaker no body has appear'd so passionately devoted to that species; and to say truth, they talk of a stable with so much warmth and Affection I can't help suspecting some very powerfull Motive at the bottom of it.

—MARY WORTLEY MONTAGU, letter
to the Countess of Mar, November 1726

JOHN ARBUTHNOT (1726)

Although many contemporaries, especially those of Swift's circle, were quick to appreciate the outlandish literary mastery on display in *Gulliver's Travels*, some took the mock travelogue seriously. Anecdotes abound of old sea dogs taking up their maps in search of Swift's mythical lands, as Swift's friend John Arbuthnot points out here.

Your books shall be sent as directed: they have been printed above a month, but I cannot get my subscribers' names. I will make over all my profits to you for the property of *Gulliver's Travels,* which, I believe, will have as great a run as John Bunyan. Gulliver is a happy man that at his age can write such a merry work. . . .

Lord Scarborough, who is no inventor of stories, told me, that he fell in company with a master of a ship, who told him, that he was very well acquainted with Gulliver, but that the printer had mistaken, that he lived in Wapping, and not in Rotherhithe. I lent the book to an old gentleman, who went immediately to his map to search for Lilliput.

—John Arbuthnot, letter to
Jonathan Swift, November 8, 1726

John Gay and Alexander Pope (1726)

Carrying on with the inside joke that Swift's authorship was unknown, in this witty letter John Gay and Alexander Pope comment wryly on the reception of *Gulliver's Travels,* which, as Lady Montagu had suggested in the extract included here, had caused quite a stir. Lord Bolingbroke, we learn, did not approve of the book, whereas Lord Harcourt, while enjoying the book overall, felt it went too far in places.

About ten days ago a Book was publish'd here of the Travels of one Gulliver, which hath been the conversation of the whole town ever since: The whole impression sold in a week; and nothing is more diverting than to hear the different opinions people give of it, though all agree in liking it extreamly. 'Tis generally said that you are the Author, but I am told, the Bookseller declares he knows not from what hand it came. From the highest to the lowest it is universally read, from the Cabinet-council to the Nursery. The Politicians to a man agree, that it is free from particular reflections, but that the Satire on general societies of men is too severe. Not but we now and then meet with people of greater perspicuity, who are in search for particular applications in every leaf; and it is highly probable we shall have keys published to give light into Gulliver's design. Your Lord [Bolingbroke] is the person who least approves it, blaming it as a design of evil consequence to depreciate human nature, at which it cannot be wondered that he takes most offence, being himself the most accomplish'd of his species, and so losing more than any other of that praise which is due both to the dignity and virtue of a man. Your friend, my Lord Harcourt, commends it very much, though he thinks in some places the matter too far carried. The Duchess Dowager of Marlborough is in raptures at it; she says she can dream of nothing else since she read it; she declares, that she hath now found out, that her whole life has been lost in caressing the worst part of mankind, and treating the best as her foes; and that if she knew Gulliver, tho' he had been the worst enemy she ever had, she should give up her present acquaintance for his friendship.

You may see by this, that you are not much injur'd by being suppos'd the Author of this piece. If you are, you have disoblig'd us, and two or three of your best friends, in not giving us the least hint of it while you were with us; and in particular Dr. Arbuthnot, who says it is ten thousand pitys he had not known it, he could have added such abundance of things upon every subject. Among Lady-critics, some have found out that Mr. Gulliver had a particular malice to maids of honour. Those of them who frequent the Church, say, his design is impious, and that it is an insult on Providence, by depreciating the works of the Creator. Notwithstanding I am told the Princess hath read it with great pleasure. As to other Critics, they think the flying island is the least entertaining; and so great an opinion the town have of the impossibility of Gulliver's writing at all below himself, 'tis agreed that Part was not writ by the same Hand, tho' this hath its defenders too. It hath pass'd Lords and Commons, *nemine contradicente;* and the whole town, men, women, and children are quite full of it.

Perhaps I may all this time be talking to you of a Book you have never seen, and which hath not yet reach'd Ireland; if it hath not, I believe what we have said will be sufficient to recommend it to your reading, and that you order me to send it to you.

But it will be much better to come over your self, and read it here, where you will have the pleasure of variety of commentators, to explain the difficult passages to you.

—JOHN GAY AND ALEXANDER POPE, letter to
Jonathan Swift, November 17, 1726

JONATHAN SMEDLEY (1728)

An outspoken defamer of Swift, Jonathan Smedley, the dean of Clogher, produced his anonymous *Gulliveriana* (1728) as a simulated further volume to Pope and Swift's *Miscellanies*. In this extract, Smedley attacks *Gulliver's Travels* for its vindictive jesting and empty-ended joshing.

The Divine who wrote the Travels of *Gulliver*, is not, it seems, content with turning the Heads of Men, Women and Children, in the present Age; he has prepar'd for Posterity Lessons for the *Art of Trifling*, and employing their Time and Thoughts upon *Nothing*. The pious Dean has done what in him lies to render *Religion*, *Reason*, and *common Sense* ridiculous, and to set up in their stead, *Buffoonry*, *Grimace*, and *Impertinence*, and, *like Harlequin*, carries if off all with a *Grin*. The Fellows that appear'd on a Stage at *Old Brentford*, to make Mouths for a *Pudding*, were of the same kind of Wits. They made the People laugh, and *Gulliver* does no more. The merry Author began with a *Tale of a Tub*, in which he made a Jest of every Religion in Christendom. He afterwards endeavour'd to joke us out of our Constitution in the Reign of his good Friend *Harley*, and now he is endeavouring to turn Reason into Ridicule, and put a *Fool's* Coat upon *Wit*. He has us'd his Readers so to Grinning, that they can't bring their Faces into Shape again, and are asham'd of *sober Thinking*, as it is with this Parson, a Mark of Ignorance, Stupidity, and *Sinking*. However, his best Quality is no better than that of the *Tarantula*: It causes Laughter, but it also causes Death to the Understanding. These Things, as little as they appear to be, are likely to have no less ill Effect, than to render the Minds of his Admirers as full of Trumpery as the Inside of a *Raree-Show* Man's Box; at which I shou'd not have been provok'd to trouble my self so much about him, if this same Dean *Gulliver* had not pick'd up in his Travels, a decrepid, diminutive *Lilliputian* Poet, whom he has plac'd by his Side on the Throne of Wit; an Empire to which they have just as much Right as their dear King at *Bologna* has to his Majesty's; which will be further made out in a very little while, and that these two Tyrants in Wit, are really just two such Monarchs as King *Phyz* and King *Ush* in the *Rehearsal*.

—JONATHAN SMEDLEY, *Gulliveriana:*
or, a Fourth Volume of Miscellanies. Being a
Sequel of the Three Volumes, Published by
Pope and Swift, 1728, pp. 267–268

DAVID HUME (1752)

'Tis dangerous to rely upon writers, who deal in ridicule and satire. What will posterity, for instance, infer from this passage of Dr. *Swift*? 'I told him, that in the kingdom of *Tribnia* (*Britain*) by the Natives call'd *Langdon*, (*London*) where I has sojourned some time in my travels, the bulk of the people consist, in a manner, wholly of discoverers, witnesses, informers, accusers, prosecutors, evidences, swearers, together with their several subservient and subaltern instruments, all under the colours, the conduct, and pay of ministers of state and their deputies. The plots in that kingdom are usually the workmanship of those persons, &c.', *Gulliver's travels*. Such a representation might suit the government of *Athens*; but not that of *England*, which is a prodigy, even in modern times, for humanity, justice and liberty. Yet the doctor's satire, tho' carry'd to extremes, as is usual with him, even beyond other satirical writers, did not altogether want an object. The bishop of *Rochester*, who was his friend and of the same party, had been banish'd a little before by a bill of attainder, with great justice, but without such a proof as was legal, or according to the strict forms of common law.

—David Hume, "Of the Populousness of
Antient Nations," *Political Discourses*,
1752, pp. 201–202

Edward Young (1759)

An important poet in his own right, Edward Young was also an influential aesthetician in the mid-eighteenth century. In his most famous work in this field, *Conjectures on Original Composition* (1759), he puts forward a case in favor of original genius. In this extract, he focuses on *Gulliver's Travels*, recounting in vividly poetic detail the incidents of the novel-cum-travel-narrative. Elsewhere referring to Swift's "tyranny in wit," Young was of the opinion that Swift's style was largely skeptical and damning.

O Gulliver! dost thou not shudder at thy brother *Lucian's* Vulturs hovering o'er thee? Shudder on! they cannot shock thee more, than Decency has been shocked by thee. How have thy *Houynhunms* thrown thy judgment from its seat, and laid thy imagination in the mire? In what ordure hast thou dipt thy pencil? What a monster hast thou made of the Human face Divine? Milt.

This writer has so satirised human nature, as to give a demonstration in himself, that it deserves to be satirised. But, say his wholesale admirers, Few could *so* have written; true, and Fewer *would*. If it required great abilities to commit the fault, greater still would have saved him from it. But whence arise such warm advocates for such a performance? From hence, (*viz.*) before a character is established, Merit makes Fame; afterwards fame makes merit. *Swift* is not commended for this piece, but this piece for *Swift*. He has given us some beauties which deserve all our praise; and our comfort is, that his faults will not become common; for none can be guilty of them, but who have Wit as well as Reputation to spare. His wit had been less wild, if his Temper had not jostled his Judgment. If his favourite *Houynhunms* could write, and *Swift* had been one of them, every Horse with him would have been an Ass, and he would have written a panegyric on mankind, saddling with much reproach the present heroes of his pen: On the contrary, being born amongst men, and, of consequence, piqued by many, and peevish at more, he has blasphemed a nature little lower than that of Angels, and assumed by far higher than they: But surely the contempt of the world is not a greater virtue, than the contempt of mankind is a vice. Therefore I wonder that, though forborn by others, the laughter-loving *Swift*, was not reproved by the venerable Dean, who could sometimes be very grave.

—EDWARD YOUNG, *Conjectures on
Original Composition*, 1759, pp. 62–64

HORACE WALPOLE "THE SEQUEL TO *GULLIVER'S TRAVELS*" (1771)

By no means the first, nor the last, person to adapt and extend Swift's novel, Horace Walpole offers here a witty if overelaborated "sequel" to *Gulliver's Travels*. He carries logic to extreme levels, mimics the comical names used, and describes local customs in Swiftian terms.

The two nations of the giants and the fairies had long been mortal enemies, and most cruel wars had happened between them. At last in the year 2000096 Oberon the 413th had an only daughter who was called Illipip, which signified the corking-pin, from her prodigious stature, she being full eighteen inches high, which the fairies said was an inch taller than Eve the first fairy. Gob, the Emperor of the giants, had an only son, who was as great a miracle for his diminutiveness, for at fifteen he was but seven and thirty feet high, and though he was fed with the milk of sixteen elephants every day, and took three hogsheads of jelly of lions between every meal, he was the most puny child that ever was seen, and nobody expected that he would ever be reared to man's estate. However as it was indispensably necessary to marry him, that the imperial family might not be extinct, and as an opportunity offered of terminating the long wars between the two nations by an union of the hostile houses, ambassadors were sent to demand the Princess of the Fairies, for the Prince of the Giants, who I forgot to say was called the Delicate Mountain. The Queen of the Fairies, who was a woman of violent passions, was extremely offended at the proposal, and vowed that so hopeful a girl as Corking-Pin should not be thrown away upon a dwarf—however as Oberon was a very sage monarch and loved his people, he overruled his wife's impetuosity and granted his daughter. Still the Queen had been so indiscreet as to drop hints of her dissatisfaction before the Princess, and Corking-Pin set out with a sovereign contempt for her husband, whom she said she supposed she should be forced to keep in her toothpick-case for fear of losing him. This witticism was so applauded by all the Court of Fairy that it reached the ears of Emperor Gob and had like to have broken off the match.

On the frontiers of the two kingdoms the Princess was met by the Emperor's carriages. A litter of crimson velvet, embroidered with seed pearls as big as ostriches' eggs, and a little larger than a cathedral was destined for the Princess, and was drawn by twelve dromedaries. At the first stage she found the bridegroom, who for fear of catching cold, had come in a close sedan, which was but six and forty feet high. He had six under-waistcoats of bearskin, and a white handkerchief about his neck twenty yards long. He had the misfortune of having weak eyes, and when the Princess descended from her litter to meet him he could not distinguish her. She was wonderfully shocked at his not saluting her, but when his governor whispered to him which was she, he spit upon his finger, and stretched out his hand to bring her nearer to his eye, but unluckily fixed upon the great Mistress of the Queen's Household and lifted her up in the air in a very unseemly attitude, to the great diversion of the young fairy lords. The lady squalled dreadfully, thinking the Prince was going to devour her. As misfortune would have it, notwithstanding all the Empress's precautions, the Prince had taken cold, and happening at that very instant to sneeze, he blew the old lady ten leagues off, into a millpond, where it was forty to one but she had been drowned. The whole cavalcade of the fairies was put into great disorder likewise by this untoward accident, and the cabinet councillors deliberated whether they should not carry back the Princess immediately to her father—but Corking-Pin it seems had not found the Prince quite so disagreeable as she had expected, and declared that she would not submit to the disgrace of returning without a husband. Nay, she said, that to prevent any more mistakes, she would have the marriage solemnized that night. The nuptial ceremony was accordingly performed by the Archbishop of Saint Promontory, but the governor declaring that he had the Empress's express injunctions not to let them live together for two years in consideration of the Prince's youth and tender constitution, the Princess was in such a rage, that she swore and stamped like a madwoman, and spit in the Archbishop's face. Nothing could equal the confusion occasioned by this outrage. By the laws of Giantland it was death to spit in a priest's face. The Princess was immediately made close prisoner, and couriers were dispatched to the two courts to inform them of what had happened. By good fortune the chief of the law, who did not love the Archbishop, recollected an old law which said that no woman could be put to death for any crime committed on her wedding day. This discovery split the whole nation of giants into two parties, and occasioned a civil war which lasted till the whole nation of giants was exterminated; and as the fairies from a factious spirit took part with the one side or other, they were all trampled to death, and not a giant or fairy remained to carry on either race.

—Horace Walpole, "The Sequel to *Gulliver's Travels*,"
letter to the Countess of Upper Ossery,
December 14, 1771

Lord Monboddo (1776)

A significant figure in the Scottish Enlightenment, James Burnett, Lord Monboddo, was a distinguished lawyer and judge who frequented the literary circles of London. This extract is taken from the third volume of his own six-volume work *Of the Origin and Progress of Language* (1773–1792). Here he praises *Gulliver's Travels* as a modern example of the "simple . . . style" of antiquity.

The author, in English, that has excelled the most in this style is Dr Swift, in his *Gulliver's Travels*; of which the narrative is wonderfully plain and simple, minute likewise, and circumstantial, so much, as to be disgusting to a reader without taste or judgment, and the character of an English sailor is finely kept up in it. In short, it has every virtue belonging to this style; and I will venture to say, that those monstrous lies so narrated, have more the air of probability than many a true story unskilfully told. And, accordingly, I have been informed, that they imposed upon many when they were first published. The voyage to Lilliput, in my judgment, is the finest of them all, especially in what relates to the politics of that kingdom, and the state of parties there. The debate in the King's council, concerning Gulliver, is a master-piece; and the original papers it contains, of which he says he was so lucky as to get copies, give it an air of probability that is really wonderful. When we add to all this, the hidden satire which it contains, and the grave ridicule that runs through the whole of it, the most exquisite of all ridicule, I think I do not go too far when I pronounce it the most perfect work of the kind, antient or modern, that is to be found. For, as to Lucian's true history, which is the only antient work of the kind that has come down to us, it has nothing to recommend it, except the imitation of the grave style of the antient historians, such as Herodotus; but it wants the satire and exquisite ridicule that is to be found in the Dean's work.

—James Burnett, Lord Monboddo,
Of the Origin and Progress of Language,
1776, vol. 3, pp. 196–197

James Beattie (1783)

The comments offered by James Beattie, a popular poet and aesthetician in the eighteenth century, are notable for two compelling reasons. On one hand, Beattie offers some insights into the technical achievements of *Gulliver's Travels* as a "sort of allegory." On the other, he questions whether a distasteful work can be properly considered in aesthetic terms. This extract is taken from his essay "On Fable and Romance" in his *Dissertations Moral and Critical* (1783).

———————

Gulliver's Travels are a sort of allegory; but rather Satirical and Political, than Moral. The work is in every body's hands; and has been criticised by many eminent writers. As far as the satire is levelled at human pride and folly; at the abuses of human learning; at the absurdity of speculative projectors; at those criminal or blundering expedients in policy, which we are apt to overlook, or even to applaud, because custom has made them familiar; so far the author deserves our warmest approbation, and his satire will be allowed to be perfectly just, as well as exquisitely severe. His fable is well conducted, and, for the most part consistent with itself, and connected with probable circumstances. He personates a sea-faring man; and with wonderful propriety supports the plainness and simplicity of the character. And this gives to the whole narrative an air of truth; which forms an entertaining contraste, when we compare it with the wildness of the fiction. The style too deserves particular notice. It is not free from inaccuracy; but, as a model of easy and graceful simplicity, it has not been exceeded by any thing in our language; and well deserves to be studied by every person, who wishes to write pure English.—These, I think, are the chief merits of this celebrated work; which has been more read, than any other publication of the present century. Gulliver has something in him to hit every taste. The statesman, the philosopher, and the critick, will admire his keenness of satire, energy of description, and vivacity of language: the vulgar, and even children, who cannot enter into these refinements, will find their account in the story, and be highly amused with it.

But I must not be understood to praise the whole indiscriminately. The last of the four voyages, though the author has exerted himself in it to the utmost, is an absurd, and an abominable fiction. It is absurd: because, in presenting us with rational beasts, and irrational men, it proceeds upon a direct contradiction to the most obvious laws of nature, without deriving any support from either the dreams of the credulous, or the prejudices of the ignorant. And it is abominable: because it abounds in filthy and indecent images; because the general tenor of the satire is exaggerated into absolute falsehood; and because there must be something of an irreligious tendency in a work, which, like this, ascribes the perfection of reason, and of happiness, to a race of beings, who are said to be destitute of every religious idea.—But, what, is yet worse, if any thing can be worse, this tale represents human nature itself as the object of contempt and abhorrence. Let the ridicule of wit be pointed at the follies, and let the scourge of satire be brandished at the crimes of mankind: all this is both pardonable, and praiseworthy; because it may be done with a good intention, and produce good effects. But when a writer endeavours to make us dislike and despise, every one his neighbour, and be dissatisfied with that Providence, who has made us what we are, and whose dispensations toward the human race are so peculiarly, and so divinely beneficent; such a writer, in so doing, provides himself the enemy, not of man only, but of goodness itself; and his work can never be allowed to be innocent, till impiety, malevolence, and misery, cease to be evils.

—James Beattie, *Dissertations Moral and Critical*, 1783, pp. 514–516

NATHAN DRAKE (1805)

This singular work displays a most fertile imagination, a deep insight into the follies, vices, and infirmities of mankind, and a fund of acute observation on ethics, politics, and literature. Its principal aim appears to have been to mortify the pride of human nature, whether arising from personal or mental accomplishments: the satire, however, has been carried too far, and degenerates into a libel on the species. The fourth part, especially, notwithstanding all that has been said in its defence by Sheridan and Berkeley, apparently exhibits such a malignant wish to degrade and brutalize the human race, that with every reader of feeling and benevolence it can occasion nothing but a mingled sensation of abhorrence and disgust. Let us hope, though the tendency be such as we have described, that it was not in the contemplation of Swift; but that he was betrayed into this degrading and exaggerated picture, by that habitual and gloomy discontent which long preyed upon his spirits, which at length terminated in insanity, and which for ever veiled from his eyes the fairest portion of humanity.

—Nathan Drake, *Essays, Biographical, Critical, and Historical, Illustrative of the Tatler, Spectator, and Guardian*, 1805, vol. 3, pp. 148–149

WALTER SCOTT (1814)

The leading novelist of his generation, Sir Walter Scott was also a prolific, and often adept, editor and reviewer. In 1814, he edited an annotated edition of Swift's works, which was reissued with some minor changes a decade later. His comments are interesting for two contradictory reasons.

First, he provides a useful and often detailed overview of Swift's reception
in the eighteenth century, not just in England but throughout Europe.
Second, his comments tend to be somewhat unusual.

Perhaps no work ever exhibited such general attractions to all classes. It
offered personal and political satire to the readers in high life, low and coarse
incident to the vulgar, marvels to the romantic, wit to the young and lively,
lessons or morality and policy to the grave, and maxims of deep and bitter
misanthropy to neglected age, and disappointed ambition. The plan of the
satire varies in the different parts. The voyage to Liliput refers chiefly to the
court and politics of England, and Sir Robert Walpole is plainly intimated
under the character of the Premier Flimnap, which he afterwards probably
remembered to the prejudice of the Dean's view of leaving Ireland. The
factions of High-Heels and Low-Heels express the factions of Tories and
Whigs, the Small-Endians and Big-Endians the religious divisions of Papist
and Protestant; and when the Heir-Apparent was described as wearing one
heel high and one low, the Prince of Wales, who at that time divided his favour
between the two leading political parties of England, laughed very heartily at
the comparison. Blefescu is France, and the ingratitude of the Liliputian court,
which forces Gulliver to take shelter there rather than have his eyes put out,
is an indirect reproach upon that of England, and a vindication of the flight
of Ormond and Bolingbroke to Paris. Many other allusions may be traced
by those well acquainted with the secret history of the reign of George I. The
scandal which Gulliver gave to the Empress, by his mode of extinguishing the
flames in the royal palace, seems to intimate the author's own disgrace with
Queen Anne, founded upon the indecorum of *A Tale of a Tub*, which was
remembered against him as a crime, while the service which it had rendered
the cause of the high church was forgotten. It must also be remarked, that the
original institutions of the empire of Liliput are highly commended, as also
their system of public education, while it is intimated, that all the corruptions
of the court had been introduced during the last three reigns. This was Swift's
opinion concerning the English Constitution.

In the 'Voyage to Brobdingnag' the satire is of a more general character;
nor is it easy to trace any particular reference to the political events or
statesmen of the period. It merely exhibits human actions and sentiments as
they might appear in the apprehension of beings of immense strength, and, at
the same time, of a cold, reflecting, and philosophical character. The monarch
of these sons of Anak is designed to embody Swift's ideas of a patriot king,
indifferent to what was curious, and cold to what was beautiful, feeling only

interest in that which connected with general utility and the public weal. To such a prince, the intrigues, scandals, and stratagems, of a European court, are represented as equally odious in their origin, and contemptible in their progress. A very happy effect was also produced by turning the telescope, and painting Gulliver, who had formerly been a giant among the Liliputians, as a pigmy amidst this tremendous race. The same ideas are often to be traced, but, as they are reversed in the part which is performed by the narrator, they are rather illustrated than repeated. Some passages of the court of Brobdingnag were supposed to be intended as an affront upon the maids of honour, for whom, Delany informs us, that Swift had very little respect.

The 'Voyage to Laputa' was disliked by Arbuthnot, who was a man of science, and probably considered it as a ridicule upon the Royal Society; nor can it be denied that there are some allusions to the most respectable philosophers of the period. An occasional shaft is even said to have been levelled at Sir Isaac Newton. The ardent patriot had not forgot the philosopher's opinion in favour of Wood's halfpence. Under the parable of the tailor, who computed Gulliver's altitude by a quadrant, and took his measure by a mathematical diagram, yet brought him his clothes very ill made and out of shape, by the mistake of a figure in the calculation, Swift is supposed to have alluded to an error of Sir Isaac's printer, who, by carelessly adding a cypher to the astronomer's computation of the distance between the sun and the earth, had increased it to an incalculable amount. Newton published, in the *Amsterdam Gazette*, a correction of this typographical error, but the circumstance did not escape the malicious acumen of the Dean of St Patrick's. It was also believed by the Dean's friends, that the office of flapper was suggested by the habitual absence of mind of the great philosopher. The Dean told Mr D. Swift that Sir Isaac was the worst companion in the world, and that, if you asked him a question, 'he would revolve it in a circle in his brain, round, and round, and round, (here Swift described a circle on his own forehead,) before he could produce an answer.'

But, although Swift may have treated with irreverence the first philosopher of the age, and although it must be owned that he evinces, in many parts of his writings, an undue disrespect for mathematics, yet the satire in *Gulliver* is rather aimed against the abuse of philosophical science than at its reality. The projectors in the academy of Laputa are described as pretenders, who had acquired a very slight tincture of real mathematical knowledge, and eked out their plans of mechanical improvement by dint of whim and fancy. The age in which Swift lived had exhibited numerous instances of persons of this description, by whom many of the numerous *bubbles*, as they were emphatically termed, had been set on foot, to the impoverishment of credulous individuals, and the general detriment of the community. In ridiculing this class of projectors, whose character was divided between self-confidence in their chimaeras, and a wish to impose upon others Swift, who peculiarly hated them, has borrowed several illustrations, and perhaps the general idea, from Rabelais, Book v, cap. xxiii, where Pantagruel inspects the occupations of the courtiers of Quinte-Essence, Queen of Entelechie.

The professors of speculative learning are represented as engaged in prosecution of what was then termed Natural and Mathematical Magic, studies not grounded upon sound principles, or traced out and ascertained by experiment, but hovering between science and mysticism. Such are the renowned pursuits of alchemy—the composition of brazen images that could speak; or wooden birds that could fly; of powders of sympathy, and salves, which were applied, not to the wound, but to the weapon by which it was inflicted; of vials of essence, which could manure acres of land, and all similar marvels, of which imposters propagated the virtue, and which dupes believed to their cost. The machine of the worthy professor of Lagado, for improving speculative knowledge, and composing books on all subjects, without the least assistance from genius or knowledge, seems to be designed in ridicule of the art invented by Raimond Lully, and advanced by his sage commentators; the mechanical process, namely, by which, according to Cornelius Agrippa, (himself no mean follower of Lully) 'everye man might plentifullye dispute of what matter he wolde, and with a certain artificial and huge heap of nownes and verbes invente and dispute with ostentation, full of trifling deceites upon both sides'. A reader might supposed himself transported to the grand academy of Lagado when they read of this 'Brief and great art of invention and demonstration', which consisted in adjusting the subject to be treated of, according to a machine composed of divers circles, fixed and moveable. The principle circle was fixed, and inscribed with the substances of all things that may be treated of, arranged under general heads, as GOD, ANGEL, EARTH, HEAVEN, MAN, ANIMAL, &c. Another circle was placed within it, which is moveable, bearing inscribed thereon what logicians call the accidents, as QUANTITY, QUALITY, RELATION, &c. Other circles again contained the predicates absolute and relative, &c. and the forms of the questions; and by turning the circles, so as to bring the various attributes to bear upon the question proposed, there was effected a species of mechanical logic, which it cannot be doubted was in Swift's mind when he described the celebrated machine for making books. Various refinements upon this mechanical mode of composition and ratiocination were contrived for the purpose of improving this Art of arts, as it was termed. Kircher, the teacher of an hundred arts, modernized and refitted the machine of Lully. Knittel, the

Jesuit, composed, on the same system, his Royal Road to all sciences and arts; Brunus invented the art of logic on the same mechanical plan; and Kuhlman makes our very hair bristel, by announcing such a machine as should contain, not only an art of knowledge, comprehending a general system of all sciences, but the various acts of acquiring languages, of commentary, of criticism, of history, sacred and profane, of biography of every kind, not to mention a library of libraries, comprehending the essence of all the books that ever were written. When it was gravely announced by a learned author, in tolerable latinity, that all this knowledge was to be acquired by the art of a mechanical instrument, much resembling a child's whirligig, it was time for the satirist to assume the pen. It was not real science, therefore, which Swift attacked, but those chimerical and spurious studies with which the name has been sometimes disgraced. In the department of the political projectors we have some glances of his Tory feelings; and when we read the melancholy account of the Struldbrugs, we are affectingly reminded of the author's contempt of life, and the miserable state in which his own was at length prolonged.

The voyage to the land of the Houynhms is what an editor of Swift must ever consider with pain. The source of such a diatribe against human nature could only be, that fierce indignation which he has described in his epitaph as so long gnawing his heart. Dwelling in a land where he considered the human race as divided between petty tyrants and oppressed slaves, and being himself a worshipper of that freedom and independence which he beheld daily trampled upon, the unrestrained violence of his feelings drove him to loath the very species by whom such iniquity was done and suffered. To this must be added, his personal health, broken and worn down by the recurring attacks of a frightful disorder; his social comfort destroyed by the death of one beloved object, and the daily decay and peril of another; his life decayed into autumn, and its remainder, after so many flattering and ambitious prospects, condemned to a country which he disliked, and banished from that in which he had formed his hopes, and left his affections—when all these considerations are combined, they form some excuse for that general misanthropy which never prevented a single deed of individual benevolence. Such apologies are personal to the author, but there are also excuses for the work itself. The picture of the Yahoos, utterly odious and hateful as it is, presents to the reader a moral use. It was never designed as a representation of mankind in the state to which religion, and even the lights of nature, encourage men to aspire, but of that to which our species is degraded by the wilful subservience of mental qualities to animal instincts, of man, such as he may be found in the degraded ranks of every society, when brutalized by ignorance and gross vice. In this view, the more coarse and disgusting the picture, the more impressive is the moral to be derived from it, since, in proportion as an individual indulges in sensuality, cruelty, or avarice, he approaches in resemblance to the detested Yahoo. It cannot, however, be denied, that even a moral purpose will not justify the nakedness with which Swift has sketched this horrible outline of mankind degraded to a bestial state; since a moralist ought to hold with the Romans, that crimes of atrocity should be exposed when punished, but those of flagitious impurity concealed. In point of probability, too, for there are degrees of probability proper even to the widest fiction, the fourth part of *Gulliver* is inferior to the three others. Giants and pigmies the reader can conceive; for, not to mention their being the ordinary machinery of romance, we are accustomed to see, in the inferior orders of creation, a disproportion of size between those of the same generic description, which may parallel (among some reptile tribes at least) even the fiction of *Gulliver*. But the mind rejects, as utterly impossible, the supposition of a nation of horses placed in houses which they could not build, fed with corn which they could neither sow, reap, nor save, possessing cows which they could not milk, depositing that milk in vessels which they could not make, and, in short, performing an hundred purposes of rational and social life, for which their external structure altogether unfits them.

But under every objection, whether founded in reason or prejudice, the *Travels of Gulliver* were received with the most universal interest, merited indeed by their novelty, as well as their internal merit. Lucian, Rabelais, More, Bergerac, Alletz, and many other authors, had indeed composed works, in which may be traced such general resemblance as arises from the imaginary voyage of a supposed traveller to ideal realms. But every Utopia which had hitherto been devised, was upon a plan either extravagant from its puerile fictions, or dull from the speculative legislation of which the story was made the vehicle. It was reserved for Swift to enliven the morality of his work with humour; to relieve its absurdity with satire; and to give the most improbable events an appearance of reality, derived from the character and stile of the narrator. Even Robinson Crusoe (though detailing events so much more probable,) hardly excels Gulliver in gravity and verisimilitude of narrative. The character of the imaginary traveller is exactly that of Dampier, or any other sturdy nautical wanderer of the period, endowed with courage and common sense, who sailed through distant seas, without losing a single English prejudice which he had brought from Portsmouth or Plymouth, and on his return gave a grave and simple narrative of what he had seen or heard in foreign countries. The character is perhaps strictly English, and can be hardly relished by a foreigner. The reflections and observations of Gulliver are never more refined or deeper than might be expected from a plain master of a merchant-man, or surgeon in the Old Jewry; and there was such a reality given to his whole person, that one seaman is said to have sworn he knew Captain Gulliver very well, but he lived at Wapping, not at Rotherhithe. It is the contrast between the natural ease and simplicity of such a stile, and the marvels which the volume contains, that forms one great charm of this memorable satire on the imperfections, follies, and vices of mankind. The exact calculations preserved in the first and second part, have also the effect of qualifying the extravagance of the fable. It is said that in natural objects, where proportion is exactly preserved, the marvellous, whether the object be gigantic or diminutive, is lessened in the eyes of the spectator, and it is certain, in general, that proportion forms an essential attribute of truth, and consequently of verisimilitude, or that which renders a narration probable. If the reader is disposed to grant the traveller his postulates as to the existence of the strange people whom he visits, it would be difficult to detect any inconsistence in his narrative. On the contrary, it would seem that he and they conduct themselves towards each other, precisely as must necessarily have happened in the respective circumstances which the author has supposed. In this point of view, perhaps the highest praise that could have been bestowed on *Gulliver's Travels* was the censure of a learned Irish prelate, who said the book contained *some* things which he could not prevail upon himself to believe. It is a remarkable point of the author's art, that, in Liliput and Brobdignag, Gulliver seems gradually, from the influence of the images by which he was surrounded, to lose his own ideas of comparative size, and to adopt those of the pigmies and giants by whom he was surrounded. And, without further prolonging these reflections, I would only request the reader to notice the infinite art with which human actions are divided between these two opposite races of ideal beings, so as to enhance the keenness of the satire. In Liliput political intrigue and *tracasserie*, the chief employment of the highest ranks in Europe, are ridiculed by being transferred to a court of creatures about six inches high. But in Brobdignag, female levities, and the lighter follies of a court, are rendered monstrous and disgusting, by being attributed to a race of such tremendous stature. By these, and a thousand masterly touches of which we feel the effect, though we cannot trace the cause without a long analysis, the genius of Swift converted the sketch of an extravagant fairy tale into a narrative, unequalled for the skill with which it is sustained, and the genuine spirit of satire of which it is made the vehicle.

The renown of Gulliver's travels soon extended into other kingdoms. Voltaire, who was at this time in England, spread their fame among his correspondents in France, and recommended a translation. The Abbé Desfontaines undertook the task, but with so many doubts, apprehensions, and apologies, as make his Introduction a curious picture of the mind and opinions of a French man of letters. He admits, that he was conscious of offending against rules; and, while he modestly craves some mercy for the prodigious fictions which he had undertaken to clothe in the French language, he confesses, that there were passages at which his pen escaped his hand, from actual horror and astonishment at the daring violations of all critical decorum: then he becomes alarmed, lest some of Swift's political satire might be applied to the Court of Versailles, and protests, with much circumlocution, that it only concerns the *Toriz and Wigts*, as he is pleased to term them, of the factious kingdom of Britain. Lastly, he assures his readers, that not only has he changed many of the incidents, to accommodate them to the French taste, but moreover, they will not be annoyed, in his translation, with the nautical details, and minute particulars, so offensive in the original. Notwithstanding all this affectation of superior taste and refinement, the French translation is very tolerable.

—WALTER SCOTT, *The Works of Jonathan Swift,*
D.D., Dean of St. Patrick's Dublin,
1814, vol. 1, pp. 328–343

SAMUEL TAYLOR COLERIDGE (1818)

In Swift's writings there is a false misanthropy grounded upon an exclusive contemplation of the vices and follies of mankind, and this misanthropic tone is also disfigured or brutalized by his obtrusion of physical dirt and coarseness. I think *Gulliver's Travels* the great work of Swift. In the voyages to Lilliput and Brobdingnag he displays the littleness and moral contemptibility of human nature; in that to the Houyhnhnms he represents the disgusting spectacle of man with the understanding only, without the reason or the moral feeling, and in his horse he gives the misanthropic ideal of man—that is, a being virtuous from rule and duty, but untouched by the principle of love.

—SAMUEL TAYLOR COLERIDGE, *A Course of Lectures,*
1818, *Literary Remains,* ed. Henry Nelson
Coleridge, 1836, vol. 1, p. 140

WILLIAM MONCK MASON (1819)

The Travels of Captain Lemuel Gulliver, by Swift, can only be compared to the *Life and Adventures of Robinson Crusoe,* by Defoe: between these two writers there are many points of resemblance; both are remarkable for the unaffected simplicity of their narratives, the variety of their incidents, but, most of all, for the air of truth with which they have enveloped the whole; a circumstance which was incomparably more difficult to Swift than to the other, because the matters whereof he treated were marvellous beyond credibility, whereas the events related by Defoe were mere ordinary occurrences. This appearance of truth is effected by the intermixture of minute circumstances, which state, particularly, dates, names of places, and persons, some of whom are referred to as actually living; the incidents too are described in so circumstantial a manner, and embellished with so many minute particulars, which we are apt to think would hardly be mentioned if they were not true, that we are induced to believe what we are perusing is a real story.

—WILLIAM MONCK MASON, *The History and Antiquities of the Collegiate and Cathedral Church of St. Patrick, near Dublin*, 1819, p. 355

THOMAS TYLER (1883)

In this short extract, taken from a larger commentary on *Gulliver's Travels* in *The Academy*, Thomas Tyler enters into the long-running debate over the final part of the novel. In particular, many readers questioned the moral and artistic validity of the voyages to Laputa and to the land of the Houyhnhnms, most especially the latter. In idolizing the talking horses he encounters at the expense of the filthy, humanlike Yahoos, this part is often interpreted as Swift's self-loathsome rejection of humanity late in his life. For Tyler, this argument is nonsensical, as the novel should be properly treated holistically, as a "building" erected on consistent foundations. For further thoughts on this debate, contrast this extract with the following entry from Edmund Gosse.

Gulliver has been sometimes bisected; and the voyages to Liliput and Brobdingnag have been published alone. No reasonable objection can be urged against this course when the object in view is merely the amusement of children. But assent can certainly not be given to Mr. Leslie Stephen's opinion (*Swift*, "English Men of Letters") that the voyages to Laputa and to the Houyhnhnms are to be regarded as "wrung from him in later years, after a life tormented by constant disappointment and disease", while the voyages to Liliput and Brobdingnag give occasion for "a harmless play of fancy". Accepting Swift's own statements, we must look upon the work as one "building", erected on a definite foundation, and in accordance with well-considered principles. If the intention of the book was to express "misanthropy", or pessimism, it was to be expected that there would be a growing intensity in the expression as the work advanced towards its conclusion. And, however offensive to some of us the glare may at last become, Swift has fully observed the Horatian maxim—

"Non fumum ex fulgore, sed ex fumo dare lucem." . . .

Mr. Leslie Stephen seems to think that, in the behaviour and in the polity of the Houyhnhnms (which is a socialistic, though aristocratic, republic), Swift may have intended to describe a Utopia, something after the fashion, I suppose, of Plato or of More. And Swift may, indeed, very well have delineated what he considered would be the conduct and polity perfectly accordant with reason, but certainly with no practical aim. On this point Mr. Craik need entertain no doubt. To have had in view the improvement of mankind would have been contrary to Swift's express statement. And that he had no such aim is clearly shown by various satirical touches; as, for example, what is said of conjugal and parental love, and of the Houyhnhnm widow's excuse for her want of punctuality. No; as the life according to original and essential human nature, the life of the Yahoos, is exhibited as revolting, so the life according to perfect reason—that of the Houyhnhnms—is set forth as impracticable and even absurd. There is hope for mankind neither on the one side nor the other. And thus the "Voyage to the Country of the Houyhnhnms" becomes the fullest expression of the fundamental pessimism. We may dislike the foundation; but on it "the whole building" firmly rests.

—Thomas Tyler, "Recent Criticism of
'Gulliver's Travels,'" *The Academy*,
August 18, 1883, pp. 113–114

Edmund Gosse (1889)

Critical ingenuity has laboured to discover the sources of the peculiar form taken by this celebrated romance. The author presented the world with one obvious suggestion by stating, in a mock prefatory epistle, that he was the cousin of William Dampier, the famous navigator of the preceding generation. But *Gulliver's Travels* owes most of its external shape to the *Vera Historia* of Lucian, itself a travesty of lost works on geography. The French poet Cyrano de Bergerac (1620–1655) had written a *Voyage a la lune* and a *Histoire comique des itats empires du Soleil,* from which Fontenelle had borrowed some hints. Several slight points which Swift used he is said to have taken from a tract by Francis Goodwin, Bishop of Llandaff. There can be no doubt, moreover, that the particular narrative manner of Defoe, whose *Robinson Crusoe* had appeared in 1719, produced an effect upon Swift. All these critical speculations, however, are rather curious than essential. Swift, always among the most original of writers, is nowhere more thoroughly himself than in his enchanting romance of Lemuel Gulliver. Whether we read it, as children do, for the story, or as historians, for the political allusions, or as men of the world, for the satire and philosophy, we have to acknowledge that it is one of the wonderful and unique books of the world's literature.

From internal evidence, it is highly probable that the composition of *Gulliver's Travels* was distributed over a good many years. In the voyages to Lilliput and Brobdingnag there is but little to justify the charges of brutality and cruel violence which are brought against Swift's later satires. They belong to the period of his mental health. The third section of *Gulliver's Travels* is really a miscellany: it has never interested the public so much as the rest of the book; it deals with speculations with which, it is supposed, Swift could not deal without help from Arbuthnot; and it holds no very distinct place among the leading works of the writer. The floating island, though described with unusual picturesqueness of phrase, baffles the most willing faith. When he comes to Lagado, Swift flies too modestly beneath the wing of Rabelais. In Glubbdubdrib the reader soon grows like the narrator, and finds that the domestic spectres "give him no emotion at all." Indeed, this portion of *Gulliver's Travels* would hardly live, were it not for the pathetic imagination of the Struldbrugs, a people whose peculiarities appeal to the most secret instincts of mankind. But in all these miscellaneous excursions there is little or nothing which displays to us the darker side of Swift's genius. That side is, however, exemplified to excess in the final part, the Voyage to the Country of the Houyhnhnms. It is difficult not to believe that this was written during the last illness of Stella, when Swift was aware that his best companion was certainly leaving him, and when that remorse which he could not but feel for his conduct to the woman who had so long loved him was turning what milk remained in his nature to gall. In the summer of 1726 the loss of Stella's conversation made him, he tells us, weary of life, and he fled from Ireland in a horror lest he should be a witness of her end. Delany tells us that from the time of her death, and probably from a few months earlier, Swift's character and temper underwent a change. His vertigo became chronic, and so did his misanthropy, and it seems probable that the first literary expression of his rage and despair was the awful satire of the Yahoos. It was with the horrible satisfaction of disease that Swift formed a story which would enable him to describe men as being, though "with some appearance of cunning, and the strongest disposition to mischief, yet the most unteachable of all brutes," and there is something which suggests a brain not wholly under control in the very machinery of this part of the romance. In Lilliput and in Brobdingnag we are struck by the ingenious harmony of the whole design, there being no detail which is not readily credible if we admit the possibility of the scheme; but among the Houyhnhnms probability is ruthlessly sacrificed to the wild pleasure the author takes in trampling human pride in the mire of his sarcasm. Of the horrible foulness of this satire on the Yahoos enough will have been said when it is admitted that it banishes from decent households a fourth part of one of the most brilliant and delightful of English books.

—EDMUND GOSSE, *A History of Eighteenth Century Literature*, 1889, pp. 160–162

JOHN CHURTON COLLINS (1893)

In his biographical and critical study of Swift, John Churton Collins seeks to uncover the secrets of the author's success. Other writers surpass him technically and in imagination, and yet *Gulliver's Travels* is a work of "exact and elaborate propriety." Once one recovers from the shock of Swift's writing style, Collins insists, his great merits as a realistic writer can be truly appreciated.

It would be easy to point to fictions which in wealth of imagination and fancy, in humour, in wit, in originality, would suffer nothing from comparison with Swift's masterpiece. Such in ancient times would be the *Birds* and the *True Art of Writing History*; such, in later times, would be the romances of Rabelais and Cervantes. But what distinguishes Swift's satire from all other works of the same class is not merely its comprehensiveness and intensity, but its exact and elaborate propriety. The skill with which every incident, nay, almost every allusion, in a narrative as rich in incident as the *Travels* of Pinto, and as minutely particular as the *Journal of the Plague*, is invested with satirical significance, is little short of marvellous. From the commencement to the end there is nothing superfluous, and there is nothing irrelevant. The merest trifle has its point. Where the satire is not general, it is personal and local; where the analogies are not to be found in the vices and follies common to all ages, they are to be found in the social and political history of Swift's own time. But the fiction has been framed with such nice ingenuity, that the allegory blends what is ephemeral with what is universal; and a satire which is on the one hand as wide as humanity, is on the other hand as local and particular as the *History of John Bull* or *The Satyre Menippée*. Regarded simply as a romance, the work is not less finished.

De Morgan has pointed out the scrupulous accuracy with which in the first two voyages the scale of proportions is adjusted and maintained. So artfully, he observes, has Swift guarded against the possibility of discrepancy, that he has taken care to baffle mathematical scrutiny by avoiding any statement which would furnish a standard for exact calculation. And this minute diligence, this subtle skill, is manifest in the delineation of the hero Gulliver, who is not merely the ironical embodiment of Swift himself, but a portrait as true to life as Bowling or Trunnion—in the style, which is at once a parody of the style of the old voyagers, and a style in itself of a high order of intrinsic excellence—in the fine and delicate touches, which give to incidents, in themselves monstrously extravagant, so much verisimilitude, that as we follow the story we are almost cheated into believing it. In all works of a similar kind every incident is, as Scott well observes, a new demand upon the patience and credulity of the reader. In Swift's romance, as soon as the first shock of incredulity is over, the process of illusion is uninterrupted. If the premises of the fiction be once granted, if the existence of Lilliput and Brobdingnag, of Laputa and Balnibarbi, be postulated, we have before us a narrative as logical as it is consistent and plausible. No writer, indeed, has excelled, or perhaps equalled, Swift in the art of what Aristotle describes as 'deception'—the art, that is to say, of inducing false inference. When, says that great critic, one thing is observed to be constantly accompanied or followed by another, men are apt to conclude that if the latter is or has happened, the former must also be or must have happened. For, knowing the latter to be true, the mind is betrayed into the false inference that the first is true also. Indeed, the skill with which Swift has by a thousand minute strokes contrived to invest the whole work with the semblance of authenticity is inimitable. De Foe himself is not a greater master of the art of realistic effect.

—John Churton Collins,
*Jonathan Swift: A Biographical and
Critical Study*, 1893, pp. 202–204

Gerald P. Moriarty (1893)

What does *Gulliver's Travels* mean? It is not an unfair question to ask, though it might be an unsatisfying one. Working on the assumption that literature must have a meaning, or even plural meanings, this question has perplexed readers for centuries. In his 1893 study of Swift and his works, Gerald P. Moriarty cannot help but argue against the numerous commentators who clamor for their own definitive interpretations. Quite simply, this novel has no meaning, no "theory," no moral insights into mankind and society, Moriarty asserts, but rather it is an animalistic howl against the world. And, as such, it is a highly successful one.

———⟋⟍⟋⟍⟍——— ———⟋⟍⟋⟍⟍——— ———⟋⟍⟋⟍⟍———

Attempts have been made to assign a definite aim to "Gulliver's Travels". According to some critics it was to mortify pride; according to others it sought to exalt the virtues of simplicity; others again have looked on it as a political allegory applicable solely to the time at which it was written. But on a careful reading of the work I feel unable to accept this view. It is not so much a satire at all as a universal denunciation. It is Timon howling out curses against the world; or Mephistopheles counting up the sins and follies of mankind with a sneer of triumph. According to Gulliver, man's instincts are vile, his civilisation is vile, and the two together produce the most execrable combination in nature. No sex, no class, no institution, no sentiment, no theory is mentioned save for sweeping condemnation. The simplicity of the style, the protestations of partiality for his fellows, the affected disregard for an inevitable conclusion, all serve to bring out with greater force the underlying contempt and hate. In the records of misanthropy "Gulliver's Travels" stands for all time supreme and unapproachable.

—GERALD P. MORIARTY, *Dean Swift and His Writings*, 1893, pp. 247–248

ALFRED AINGER "SWIFT—HIS LIFE AND GENIUS" (1894)

This extract is taken from Alfred Ainger's two-volume *Lectures and Essays*, which was put together after his death by H.C. Beeching, the dean of Norwich. *Gulliver's Travels*, Ainger insists, is the "key" to Swift's life and works. Written in a period of "matured powers" if not—crucially—"matured judgment," this novel indicates that Swift's scorn only developed further as he aged. Nonetheless, it is a work marked by the perfection of Swift's grand intellect and one that continues to charm the reading public, adults and children alike.

———⟋⟍⟋⟍⟍——— ———⟋⟍⟋⟍⟍——— ———⟋⟍⟋⟍⟍———

Gulliver's Travels is the one work of Swift's which is known to the universal reading public, I suppose, in all European countries. It is in every way his greatest and most characteristic work. Swift's purely intellectual gifts are there in perfection; his vigour, clearness, and ease of style; invention of the first order; wit and humour of the most exquisite. We read it in an abridged form as children; for its marvels, and for the verisimilitude which makes them seem possible, if not wholly credible, and for the Defoe-like handling of detail, which makes it so like what a man would have written had he had such adventures as Gulliver. We are not surprised at the Irish bishop who pronounced it most interesting, but added there were things in it which he could hardly believe. Then, as we grow older, our eyes are opened to the pungent satire scattered through the narrative, upon the trivial or foolish quarrels of men or nations, on the pomps and vanities which men will live and die for; the wars of the "Big-endians" and the "Little-endians," of which, with amazing gravity (and this gravity is a special feature of Swift's irony), the author relates that "it is computed that eleven thousand persons have at several times suffered death rather than submit to break their eggs at the smaller end." We become aware what is meant by the strips of blue and red ribbon for which prominent men at court would contend by jumping over sticks; and it is not till last of all, the sublime audacity of the whole purpose flashes upon the reader. For, besides the incidental satire upon particular blemishes and weaknesses in any one particular state of society, such as that among which Swift dwelt, Swift, by the machinery of his allegory, was able to inflict a deeper, wider wound upon the credit of human nature. He wielded a two-edged sword—a two-handed engine. For the Lilliputians and Brobdingnagians were *men,* though on vaster or more diminutive scale than ordinary; and Swift thereby contrives, without showing that he had any such intention, to show human nature as contemptible when exhibited in the manikins of Lilliput, and gross, horrible, and revolting when magnified into the size of the Brobdingnagian. [Lemuel] Gulliver, from this point of view, is the author himself, looking from a height of calm contemplation, alternately on the pettiness and on the grossness of human vanities or pursuits. And this is what, of course, makes *Gulliver* Swift's most characteristic, most representative work, and places it in a different category from that earlier satire, the *Tale of a Tub.* Taking up that book once in the years of his decay, he was heard to exclaim, "What a genius I had when I wrote that book!" But, brilliant as it is, it is not Swift's masterpiece. There was underlying it—for those who had eyes to see—the scorn for his kind, the grudge and the impeachment of human nature. It was then in the germ, as we have seen, but though the book was profane enough, Swift had not conceived the more profane, the more awful idea, of cursing the very image of his Maker, and hooting and yelling at the flesh and blood which he, the author, was himself compelled to wear. And *Gulliver* belongs, as we see, to Swift's matured powers, if not matured judgment, and the years which should have brought the philosophic mind, but which had brought him only a deadlier hate and scorn. *Gulliver* is the key to Swift's life and works. Swift, writing about human nature, is always either in Lilliput or in Brobdingnag—either pitying and scorning its littleness, or enlarging and dilating on its horror. Yet no one who has watched, in friend and neighbour, or in himself, the manifold inconsistencies which make up the individual life will be surprised that the man who thus looked upon his kind was at the same time capable of affection and admiration for individuals. Swift could love Arbuthnot and Gay and Addison, while he affected to loathe the clay out of which they were formed. Yes, and worse than this, he could be drawn to, and dearly love, the converse and the sympathy of women like Stella and Vanessa, and be aware at the same time that, in accordance with this creed, he was bound to loathe and despise them; yes, and to loathe and despise himself for not being superior to the vulgar affections and needs of mankind. And here may well have been a clue to some portion of his conduct, and to certain elements of his misery. His heart and his creed were in deadly conflict. His heart pleaded with him to be human; his creed said, "to be human is to be despicable or brutal." When he looked on Stella, his heart may have often said, "take her, and be happy"; his creed said, "no, wedded love is also a delusion and a snare." Samuel Taylor Coleridge, in familiar lines, has told us that "to be wrath with one we love, doth work like madness in the brain." But what is even that struggle between love and anger to compare with this conflict of love and scorn, this self-imposed obligation of disgust and revolt. "I have just beheld," said the Archbishop of Dublin to a friend, after an interview with Swift, "the most miserable man in the world"; and one thinks he must have deserved this description, as truly as any man that ever lived. Of *Gulliver* the world at large knows chiefly the portions referring to Lilliput and Brobdingnag. It is these only, and then only with careful editings, that one cares to leave about in the schoolroom. The other portions are most surely not "meat for babes"; not because of immorality, or even of coarseness, as ordinarily understood, but because of the horror of the continuous presentation of human nature in every light that can lower it and make it hateful. To compare it unfavourably with the lower animals—such as that indeed noble animal "the horse"—to exaggerate the *animal* aspect of the man, and minimise the spiritual, by ignoring, not only the soul, but *any* sense of dignity and self-respect in the creature—this is the ignoble work Swift set himself to do. And the disastrous character of his method lies in its very skill and adroitness. Here is no Thersites, scattering abuse and ribaldry right and left, but a man, standing a head and shoulders, in cleverness and plausibility, above his contemporaries; employing this ability to sow broadcast the seeds of misanthropy; for though the satire is ostensibly directed against Swift's own country, by making the criticisms of it proceed from a kind of "Utopia," the censure passed is not on this or that country at all, but on the human subject.

—Alfred Ainger, "Swift—His Life and Genius,"
1894, *Lectures and Essays*, 1905, vol. 1,
pp. 252–256

WALTER RALEIGH (1894)

In this extract from his 1894 book, *The English Novel*, the Cambridge scholar Sir Walter Raleigh provides a detailed account of the intellectual content of Swift's prose, specifically *Gulliver's Travels*. He also considers the generic status of the book, whether it is properly designated as a novel in the realist mode.

The close simulation of the truth employed by Defoe to gain credence for the story of *Robinson Crusoe* was imitated by Swift to lend plausibility to the *Travels into Several remote Nations of the World by Lemuel Gulliver* (1726–1727). Imaginary voyages and travels cannot, for the most part, be regarded as pure romances; they have generally some ulterior purpose in view, political or satirical. Thus Sir Thomas More's *Utopia* (1516) pictures an ideal polity; Francis Godwin's *The Man in the Moon*, written before 1603, borrows its inspiration from Lucian; Bacon's fragment called *The New Atlantis* (1635) sets forth a scheme for the advancement of science; the Duchess of Newcastle's *Description of New World, called the Blazing World* (1666), tells mechanical wonders of a fairy people living at the North Pole; the anonymous *Memoirs of Gaudentio di Lucca* (1737), by Simon Berington, describe an imaginary State conducted on philanthropic principles under a patriarchal government; and Swift's great work, after storming the outposts of human policy and human learning, breaks at last in a torrent of contempt and hatred on the last stronghold of humanity itself. The strength of Swift's work as a contribution to the art of fiction lies in the portentous gravity and absolute mathematical consistency wherewith he develops the consequences of his modest assumptions. In the quality of their realism the voyages to Lilliput and Brobdingnag are much superior to the two later and more violent satires: he was better fitted to ridicule the politics of his time than to attack the "men of Gresham," of whose true aims and methods he knew little or nothing; and the imagination stumbles at many of the details of the last book. But the wealth of illustration whereby he maintains the interest of his original conception of pigmies and giants is eternally surprising and delightful. Defoe could have made of Captain Lemuel Gulliver a living man; he, too, could have recorded with the minutest circumstance of date and place the misadventures and actions of his hero: it may well be doubted whether he could have carried into an unreal world that literalism, accuracy of proportion, and imaginative vividness of detail wherewith Swift endows it. The cat in Brobdingnag makes a noise in purring like "a dozen Stocking-weavers at work"; Gulliver is clad in clothes of the thinnest silk, "not much thicker than an English blanket, very cumbersome, till I was accustomed to them"; the sailing-boat wherein he shows his skill in navigation is taken, when he has done, and hung upon a nail to dry. These are the sources of the pleasure that children take in the book; the astonishing strokes of savage satire that are its chief attraction for their elders derive most of their force from the imperturbable innocence and quietude of manner that disarms suspicion. Like Iago, Gulliver is a fellow "of exceeding honesty," and he goes about his deadly work the better for his bluntness and scrupulous pretence of veracity. But the design of the book forbids its classification among works of pure fiction; it is enough to remark that in *Gulliver* realism achieved one of the greatest of its triumphs before its ultimate conquest of the novel.

—WALTER RALEIGH,
The English Novel, 1894, pp. 136–138

SELECTED POETRY

JONATHAN SWIFT "VERSES ON THE DEATH OF DR. SWIFT" (1731)

Fittingly, perhaps, Swift anatomized his own life and career in verse. In his iconic poem "Verses on the Death of Dr. Swift," he surveys his grieving friends, offering insights into their likely responses to his death. He does so wryly, of course, offering us his own uniquely humorous response to the world around him. This version of the text is taken from the "authoritative" George Faulkner collection of 1739.

The Time is not remote, when I
Must by the Course of Nature dye:
When I foresee my special Friends,
Will try to find their private Ends:
Tho' it is hardly understood,
Which way my Death can do them good;
Yet, thus methinks, I hear 'em speak;
See, how the Dean begins to break:
Poor Gentleman, he droops apace,
You plainly find it in his Face:
That old Vertigo in his Head,
Will never leave him, till he's dead:
Besides, his Memory decays,

He recollects not what he says;
He cannot call his Friends to Mind;
Forgets the Place where last he din'd:
Plyes you with Stories o'er and o'er,
He told them fifty Times before.
How does he fancy we can sit,
To hear his out-of-fashion'd Wit?
But he takes up with younger Fokes,
Who for his Wine will bear his Jokes:
Faith, he must make his Stories shorter,
Or change his Comrades once a Quarter:
In half the Time, he talks them round;
There must another Sett be found.

    For Poetry, he's past his Prime,
He takes an Hour to find a Rhime:
His Fire is out, his Wit decay'd,
His Fancy sunk, his Muse a Jade.
I'd have him throw away his Pen;
But there's no talking to some Men.

    And, then their Tenderness appears,
By adding largely to my Years:
"He's older than he would be reckon'd,
And well remembers *Charles* the Second.

    "He hardly drinks a Pint of Wine;
And that, I doubt, is no good Sign.
His Stomach too begins to fail:
Last Year we thought him strong and hale;
But now, he's quite another Thing;
I wish he may hold out till Spring.

    "Then hug themselves, and reason thus;
It is not yet so bad with us."

    In such a Case they talk in Tropes,
And, by their Fears express their Hopes:
Some great Misfortune to portend,
No Enemy can match a Friend;
With all the Kindness they profess,
The Merit of a lucky Guess,
(When daily Howd'y's come of Course,
And Servants answer; *Worse and Worse*)
Wou'd please 'em better than to tell,

That, GOD be prais'd, the Dean is well.
Then he who prophecy'd the best,
Approves his Foresight to the rest:
"You know, I always fear'd the worst,
And often told you so at first:"
He'd rather chuse that I should dye,
Than his Prediction prove a Lye.
Not one foretels I shall recover;
But, all agree, to give me over.

    YET shou'd some Neighbour feel a Pain,
Just in the Parts, where I complain;
How many a Message would he send?
What hearty Prayers that I should mend?
Enquire what Regimen I kept;
What gave me Ease, and how I slept?
And more lament, when I was dead,
Than all the Sniv'llers round my Bed.

    MY good Companions, never fear,
For though you may mistake a Year;
Though your Prognosticks run too fast,
They must be verify'd at last.

    "BEHOLD the fatal Day arrive!
How is the Dean? He's just alive.
Now the departing Prayer is read:
He hardly breathes. The Dean is dead.
Before the Passing-Bell begun,
The News thro' half the Town has run.
O, may we all for Death prepare!
What has he left? And who's his Heir?
I know no more than what the News is,
'Tis all bequeath'd to publick Uses.
To publick Use! A perfect Whim!
What had the Publick done for him!
Meer Envy, Avarice, and Pride!
He gave it all:—But first he dy'd.
And had the Dean, in all the Nation,
No worthy Friend, no poor Relation?
So ready to do Strangers good,
Forgetting his own Flesh and Blood?"

    Now Grub-Street Wits are all employ'd;

With Elegies, the Town is cloy'd:
Some Paragraph in ev'ry Paper,
To *curse* the *Dean,* or *bless* the *Drapier.*[1]
THE Doctors tender of their Fame,
Wisely on me lay all the Blame:
"We must confess his Case was nice;
But he would never take Advice:
Had he been rul'd, for ought appears,
He might have liv'd these Twenty Years:
For when we open'd him we found,
That all his vital Parts were sound.
FROM *Dublin* soon to *London* spread,
'Tis told at Court, the Dean is dead.[2]
KIND Lady *Suffolk* in the Spleen,[3]
Runs laughing up to tell the Queen.
The Queen, so Gracious, Mild, and Good,
Cries, "Is he gone? 'Tis time he shou'd.
He's dead you say; why let him rot;
I'm glad the Medals were forgot.[4]
I promis'd them, I own; but when?
I only was the Princess then;
But now as Consort of the King,
You know 'tis quite a different Thing."
Now, *Chartres*[5] at Sir *Robert's* Levee,
Tells, with a Sneer, the Tidings heavy:
"Why, is he dead without his Shoes?"
(Cries *Bob*)[6] "I'm Sorry for the News;
Oh, were the Wretch but living still,
And in his Place my good Friend *Will;*[7]
Or, had a Mitre on his Head
Provided *Bolingbroke*[8] were dead."
Now *Curl*[9] his Shop from Rubbish drains;
Three genuine Tomes of *Swift's* Remains.
And then to make them pass the glibber,
Revis'd by *Tibbalds, Moore, and Cibber.*[10]
He'll treat me as he does my Betters.
Publish my Will, my Life, my Letters.[11]
Revive the Libels born to dye;
Which POPE must bear, as well as I.
HERE shift the Scene, to represent

How those I love, my Death lament.
Poor POPE will grieve a Month; and GAY
A Week; and ARBUTHNOTT a Day.

    ST. JOHN himself will scarce forbear,
To bite his Pen, and drop a Tear.
The rest will give a Shrug and cry,
I'm sorry; but we all must dye.
Indifference clad in Wisdom's Guise,
All Fortitude of Mind supplies:
For how can stony Bowels melt,
In those who never Pity felt;
When *We* are lash'd, *They* kiss the Rod;
Resigning to the Will of God.

    THE Fools, my Juniors by a Year,
Are tortur'd with Suspence and Fear.
Who wisely thought my Age a Screen,
When Death approach'd, to stand between:
The Screen remov'd, their Hearts are trembling,
They mourn for me without dissembling.

    MY female Friends, whose tender Hearts
Have better learn'd to act their Parts.
Receive the News in *doleful Dumps,*
"The Dean is dead, (*and what is Trumps?*)
Then Lord have Mercy on his Soul.
(Ladies I'll venture for the *Vole.*)
Six Deans they say must bear the Pall.
(I wish I knew what *King* to call.)
Madam, your Husband will attend
The Funeral of so good a Friend.
No Madam, 'tis a shocking Sight,
And he's engag'd To-morrow Night!
My Lady *Club* wou'd take it ill,
If he shou'd fail her at *Quadrill.*
He lov'd the Dean. (*I lead a Heart.*)
But dearest Friends, they say, must part.
His Time was come, he ran his Race;
We hope he's in a better Place."

    WHY do we grieve that Friends should dye?
No Loss more easy to supply.
One Year is past; a different Scene;

No further mention of the Dean;
Who now, alas, no more is mist,
Than if he never did exist.
Where's now this Fav'rite of *Apollo*?
Departed; *and his Works must follow*:
Must undergo the common Fate;
His Kind of Wit is out of Date.
Some Country Squire to *Lintot*[12] goes,
Enquires for Swift in Verse and Prose:
Says *Lintot*, "I have heard the Name:
He dy'd a Year ago." The same.
He searcheth all his Shop in vain;
"Sir you may find them in *Duck-lane*:[13]
I sent them with a Load of Books,
Last *Monday* to the Pastry-cooks.
To fancy they cou'd live a Year!
I find you're but a Stranger here.
The Dean was famous in his Time;
And had a Kind of Knack at Rhyme:
His way of Writing now is past;
The Town hath got a better Taste:
I keep no antiquated Stuff;
But, spick and span I have enough.
Pray, do but give me leave to shew em;
Here's *Colley Cibber's* Birth-day Poem.
This Ode you never yet have seen,
By *Stephen Duck,* upon the Queen.
Then, here's a Letter finely penn'd
Against the *Craftsman* and his Friend;
It clearly shews that all Reflection
On Ministers, is disaffection.
Next, here's Sir *Robert's* Vindication,[14]
And Mr. *Henly's*[15] last Oration:
The Hawkers have not got 'em yet,
Your Honour please to buy a Set?
    "Here's *Wolston's*[16] Tracts, the twelfth Edition;
'Tis read by ev'ry Politician:
The Country Members, when in Town,
To all their Boroughs send them down:
You never met a Thing so smart;

The Courtiers have them all by Heart:
Those Maids of Honour (who can read)
Are taught to use them for their Creed.
The Rev'rend Author's good Intention,
Hath been rewarded with a Pension:
He doth an Honour to his Gown,
By bravely running *Priest-craft* down:
He shews, as sure as GOD's in *Gloc'ster,*
That *Jesus* was a Grand Impostor:
That all his Miracles were Cheats,
Perform'd as Juglers do their Feats:
The Church had never such a Writer:
A Shame, he hath not got a Mitre!"
   SUPPOSE me dead; and then suppose
A Club assembled at the *Rose;*
Where from Discourse of this and that,
I grow the Subject of their Chat:
And, while they toss my Name about,
With Favour some, and some without;
One quite indiff'rent in the Cause,
My Character impartial draws:
   "THE Dean, if we believe Report,
Was never ill receiv'd at Court:
As for his Works in Verse and Prose,
I own my self no Judge of those:
Nor, can I tell what Criticks thought 'em;
But, this I know, all People bought 'em;
As with a moral View design'd
To cure the Vices of Mankind:
His Vein, ironically grave,
Expos'd the Fool, and lash'd the Knave:
To steal a Hint was never known,
But what he writ was all his own.
   "HE never thought an Honour done him,
Because a Duke was proud to own him:
Would rather slip aside, and chuse
To talk with Wits in dirty Shoes:
Despis'd the Fools with Stars and Garters,
So often seen caressing *Chartres:*[17]
He never courted Men in Station,

Nor Persons had in Admiration;
Of no Man's Greatness was afraid,
Because he sought for no Man's Aid.
Though trusted long in great Affairs,
He gave himself no haughty Airs:
Without regarding private Ends,
Spent all his Credit for his Friends:
And only chose the Wise and Good;
No Flatt'rers; no Allies in Blood;
But succour'd Virtue in Distress,
And seldom fail'd of good Success;
As Numbers in their Hearts must own,
Who, but for him, had been unknown.
"WITH Princes kept a due Decorum,
But never stood in Awe before 'em:
He follow'd *David's* Lesson just,
In *Princes never put thy Trust.*
And, would you make him truly sower;
Provoke him with *a slave in Power:*
The *Irish* Senate, if you nam'd,
With what Impatience he declaim'd!
Fair LIBERTY was all his Cry;
For her he stood prepar'd to die;
For her he boldly stood alone;
For her he oft expos'd his own.
Two Kingdoms, just as Faction led,[18]
Had set a Price upon his Head;
But, not a Traytor cou'd be found,
To sell him for Six Hundred Pound.
   "HAD he but spar'd his Tongue and Pen,
He might have rose like other Men:
But, Power was never in his Thought;
And, Wealth he valu'd not a Groat:
Ingratitude he often found,
And pity'd those who meant the Wound:
But, kept the Tenor of his Mind,
To merit well of human Kind:
Nor made a Sacrifice of those
Who still were true, to please his Foes.
He labour'd many a fruitless Hour[19]

To reconcile his Friends in Power;
Saw Mischief by a Faction brewing,
While they pursu'd each others Ruin.
But, finding vain was all his Care,
He left the Court in meer Despair.

    "AND, oh! how short are human Schemes!
Here ended all our golden Dreams.
What ST. JOHN's Skill in State Affairs,
What ORMOND's *Valour*, OXFORD's Cares,
To save their sinking Country lent,
Was all destroy'd by one Event.
Too soon that precious Life was ended,[20]
On which alone, our Weal depended.
When up a dangerous Faction starts,[21]
With Wrath and Vengeance in their Hearts:
By *solemn League and Cov'nant bound,*
To ruin, slaughter, and confound;
To turn Religion to a Fable,
And make the Government a *Babel:*
Pervert the Law, disgrace the Gown,
Corrupt the Senate, rob the Crown;
To sacrifice old *England's* Glory,
And make her infamous in Story.
When such a Tempest shook the Land,
How could unguarded Virtue stand?

    "WITH Horror, Grief, Despair the Dean
Beheld the dire destructive Scene:
His Friends in Exile, or the Tower,
Himself within the Frown of Power;[22]
Pursu'd by base envenom'd Pens,
Far to the Land of Slaves and Fens;[23]
A servile Race in Folly nurs'd,
Who truckle most, when treated worst.

    "BY Innocence and Resolution,
He bore continual Persecution;
While Numbers to Preferment rose;
Whose Merits were, to be his Foes.
When, *ev'n his own familiar Friends*
Intent upon their private Ends;
Like Renegadoes now he feels,

Against him lifting up their Heels.
   "THE Dean did by his Pen defeat
An infamous destructive Cheat.[24]
Taught Fools their Int'rest how to know;
And gave them Arms to ward the Blow.
Envy hath own'd it was his doing,
To save that helpless Land from Ruin,
While they who at the Steerage stood,
And reapt the Profit, sought his Blood.
   "To save them from their evil Fate,
In him was held a Crime of State.
A wicked Monster on the Bench,[25]
Whose Fury Blood could never quench;
As vile and profligate a Villain,
As modern *Scroggs,* or old *Tressilian;*[26]
Who long all Justice had discarded,
Nor fear'd he GOD, nor Man regarded;
Vow'd on the Dean his Rage to vent,
And make him of his Zeal repent;
But Heav'n his Innocence defends,
The grateful People stand his Friends:
Not Strains of Law, nor Judges Frown,
Nor Topicks brought to please the Crown,
Nor Witness hir'd, nor Jury pick'd,
Prevail to bring him in convict.
   "IN Exile[27] with a steady Heart,
He spent his Life's declining Part;
Where, Folly, Pride, and Faction sway,
Remote from ST. JOHN,[28] POPE, and GAY.
   "HIS Friendship there to few confin'd,[29]
Were always of the midling Kind:
No Fools of Rank, a mungril Breed,
Who fain would pass for Lords indeed:
Where Titles give no Right or Power,[30]
And Peerage is a wither'd Flower,
He would have held it a Disgrace,
If such a Wretch had known his Face.
On Rural Squires, that Kingdom's Bane,
He vented oft his Wrath in vain:
Biennial Squires, to Market brought;[31]

Who sell their Souls and Votes for Naught;
The Nations stript go joyful back,
To rob the Church, their Tenants rack,
Go Snacks with Thieves and Rapparees,[32]
And, keep the Peace, to pick up Fees:
In every Jobb to have a Share,
A Jayl or Barrack" to repair;[33]
And turn the Tax for publick Roads
Commodious to their own Abodes.

    "PERHAPS I may allow, the Dean
Had too much Satyr in his Vein;
And seem'd determin'd not to starve it,
Because no Age could more deserve it.
Yet, Malice never was his Aim;
He lash'd the Vice but spar'd the Name.
No Individual could resent,
Where Thousands equally were meant.
His Satyr points at no Defect,
But what all Mortals may correct;
For he abhorr'd that senseless Tribe,
Who call it Humour when they jibe:
He spar'd a Hump or crooked Nose,
Whose Owners set not up for Beaux.
True genuine Dulness mov'd his Pity,
Unless it offer'd to be witty.
Those, who their Ignorance confess'd,
He ne'er offended with a Jest;
But laugh'd to hear an Idiot quote,
A Verse from *Horace,* learn'd by Rote.

    "HE knew an hundred pleasant Stories,
With all the Turns of Whigs and *Tories:*
Was chearful to his dying Day,
And Friends would let him have his Way.

    "HE gave the little Wealth he had,
To build a House for Fools and Mad:
And shew'd by one satyric Touch,
No Nation wanted it so much:
That Kingdom[34] he hath left his Debtor,
I wish it soon may have a Better.

Notes

1. The Author imagines, that the Scriblers of the prevailing Party, which he always opposed, will libel him after his Death; but that others will remember him with Gratitude, who consider the Service he had done to *Ireland,* under the Name of M. B. Drapier, by utterly defeating the destructive Project of Wood's Half-pence, in five Letters to the People of *Ireland,* at that Time read universally, and convincing every Reader.

2. The Dean supposeth himself to dye in *Ireland.*

3. Mrs. *Howard,* afterwards Countess of *Suffolk,* then of the Bed chamber to the Queen, professed much Friendship for the dean. The Queen then Princess, sent a dozen times to the Dean (then in *London*) with her Command to attend her; which at last he did, by advice of all his Friends. She often sent for him afterwards, and always treated him very Graciously. He taxed her with a Present worth Ten Pounds, which she promised before he should return to *Ireland,* but on his taking Leave, the Medals were not ready.

4. The Medals were to be sent to the Dean in four Months, but she forgot them, or thought them too dear. The Dean, being in *Ireland,* sent Mrs. *Howard* a Piece of *Indian* Plad made in that Kingdom: which the Queen seeing took from her, and wore it herself, and sent to the Dean for as much as would cloath herself and Children, desiring he would send the Charge of it. He did the former. It cost thirty-five Pounds, but he said he would have nothing except the Medals. He was the Summer following in *England,* was treated as usual, and she being then queen, the Dean was promised a Settlement in *England,* but returned as he went, and, instead of Favour or Medals, hath been ever since under her Majesty's Displeasure.

5. *Chartres* is a most infamous, vile Scoundrel, grown from a Foot-Boy, or worse, to a prodigious Fortune both in *England* and *Scotland:* He had a Way of insinuating himself into all Ministers under every Change, either as Pimp, Flatterer, or Informer. He was Tryed at Seventy for a Rape, and came off by sacrificing a great Part of his Fortune (he is since dead, but this Poem still preserves the Scene and Time as was writ in.)

6. Sir *Robert Walpole,* Chief Minister of State, treated the *Dean* in 1726, with great Distinction, invited him to Dinner at *Chelsea,* with the *Dean's* Friends chosen on Purpose; appointed an Hour to talk with him of *Ireland,* to which *Kingdom* and *People* the *Dean* found him no great Friend; for he defended *Wood's* Project of Half-pence, &c. The *Dean* would see him no more, and upon his next Year's return to *England,* Sir

Robert on an accidental Meeting, only made a civil Compliment, and never invited him again.

7. Mr. *William Pultney,* from being Mr. *Walpole's* intimate Friend, detesting his Administration, opposed his Measures, and joined with my *Lord Bolingbroke,* to represent his Conduct in an excellent Paper, called the *Craftsman,* which is still continued.

8. *Henry St. John,* Lord Viscount *Bolingbroke,* Secretary of State to *Queen Anne of blessed Memory.* He is reckoned the most Universal Genius in *Europe; Walpole* dreading his Abilities, treated him most injuriously, working with King *George,* who forgot his promise of restoring the said Lord, upon the restless Importunity of *Walpole.*

9. *Curl* hath been the most infamous Bookseller of any Age or Country: His Character in Part may be found in Mr. PoPE's *Dunciad.* He published three Volumes all charged on the Dean, who never writ three Pages of them: He hath used many of the Dean's Friends in almost as vile a Manner.

10. Three stupid Verse Writers in *London,* the last to the Shame of the Court, and the highest Disgrace to Wit and Learning, was made Laureat. Moore, commonly called *Jemmy Moore,* Son of *Arthur Moore,* and *Tibbalds, Theobald* in the *Dunciad.*

11. *Curl* is notoriously infamous for publishing the Lives, Letters, and last Wills and Testaments of the Nobility and Ministers of State, as well as of all the Rogues, who are hanged at *Tyburn.* He hath been in Custody of the House of Lords for publishing or forging the Letters of many Peers; which made the Lords enter a Resolution in their Journal Book, that no Life or Writings of any Lord should be published without the Consent of the next Heir at Law, or Licence from their House.

12. *Bernard Lintot,* a Bookseller in *London.* Vide Mr. Pope's *Dunciad.*

13. A Place in *London* where old Books are sold.

14. *Walpole* hires a Set of Party Scriblers, who do nothing else but write in his Defence.

15. *Henly* is a Clergyman who wanting both Merit and Luck to get Preferment, or even to keep his Curacy in the Established Church, formed a new Conventicle, which he calls an Oratory. There, at set Times, he delivereth strange Speeches compiled by himself and his Associates, who share the Profit with him. Every Hearer pays a Shilling each Day for Admittance. He is an absolute Dunce, but generally reputed crazy.

16. *Wolston* was a Clergyman, but for want of Bread, hath in several Treatises, in the most blasphemous Manner, attempted to turn *Our Saviour* and his Miracles into Ridicule. He is much caressed by many great Courtiers, and by all the Infidels, and his Books read generally by the Court Ladies.

17. See the Notes before on *Chartres*.

18. In the Year 1713, the late Queen was prevailed with by an Address of the House of Lords in *England*, to publish a Proclamation, promising Three Hundred Pounds to whatever Person would discover the Author of a Pamphlet called, *The Publick Spirit of the Whiggs*; and in *Ireland*, in the Year 1724, my Lord *Carteret* at his first coming into the Government, was prevailed on to issue a Proclamation for promising the like Reward of Three Hundred Pounds, to any Person who could discover the Author of a Pamphlet called, *The Drapier's Fourth Letter*, &c. writ against that destructive Project of coining Half-pence for *Ireland*; but in neither Kingdoms was the Dean discovered.

19. Queen ANNE's Ministry fell to Variance from the first Year after their Ministry began: *Harcourt* the Chancellor, and Lord *Bolingbroke* the Secretary, were discontented with the Treasurer *Oxford*, for his too much Mildness to the Whig Party; this Quarrel grew higher every Day till the Queen's death: The Dean, who was the only Person that endeavoured to reconcile them, found it impossible; and thereupon retired to the Country about ten Weeks before that fatal Event: Upon which he returned to his Deanry in *Dublin*, where for many Years he was worried by the new People in Power, and had Hundreds of Libels writ against him in *England*.

20. In the Height of the Quarrel between the Ministers, the Queen died.

21. Upon Queen ANNE's death the Whig Faction was restored to Power, which they exercised with the utmost Rage and Revenge; impeached and banished the Chief Leaders of the Church Party, and stripped all their Adherents of what Employments they had, after which *England* was never known to make so mean a Figure in *Europe*. The greatest Preferments in the Church in both Kingdoms were given to the most ignorant Men, Fanaticks were publickly caressed, *Ireland* utterly ruined and enslaved, only great Ministers heaping up Millions, and so Affairs continue until this present third Day of May, 1732, and are likely to go on in the same Manner.

22. Upon the Queen's Death, the Dean returned to live in *Dublin*, at his Deanry-House: Numberless Libels were writ against him in *England*, as a Jacobite; he was insulted in the Street, and at Nights was forced to be attended by his Servants armed.

23. The Land of Slaves and Fens, is *Ireland*.

24. One *Wood*, a Hardware-man from *England*, has a Patent for coining Copper Half-pence in *Ireland*, to the Sum of 108.000 *l*. which in the Consequence, must leave that Kingdom without Gold or Silver (see *Drapier's* Letters).

25. One *Whitshed* was then Chief Justice: He had some Years before prosecuted a Printer for a Pamphlet writ by the Dean, to persuade the People of *Ireland* to wear their own Manufactures. *Whitshed* sent the Jury down eleven Times, and kept them nine Hours, until they were forced to bring in a special Verdict. He sat as Judge afterwards on the Tryal of the Printer of the *Drapier's* Fourth Letter; but the Jury, against all he could say or swear, threw out the Bill: All the Kingdom took the *Drapier's* Part, except the Courtiers, or those who expected Places. The *Drapier* was celebrated in many Poems and Pamphlets: His Sign was set up in most Streets of *Dublin* (where many of them still continue) and in several Country Towns.

26. *Scroggs* was Chief Justice under King *Charles* the Second: His Judgment always varied in State Tryals, according to Directions from Court. *Tressilian* was a wicked Judge, hanged above three hundred Years ago.

27. In *Ireland,* which he had Reason to call a Place of Exile; to which Country nothing could have driven him, but the Queen's Death, who had determined to fix him in *England,* in Spight of the Dutchess of *Somerset,* &c.

28. *Henry St. John,* Lord Viscount *Bolingbroke,* mentioned before.

29. In *Ireland* the Dean was not acquainted with one single Lord Spiritual or Temporal. He only conversed with private Gentlemen of the Clergy or Laity, and but a small Number of either.

30. The Peers of *Ireland* lost a great Part of their Jurisdiction by one single Act, and tamely submitted to this infamous Mark of Slavery without the least Resentment, or Remonstrance.

31. The Parliament (as they call it) in *Ireland* meet but once in two Years; and, after giving five Times more than they can afford, return Home to reimburse themselves by all Country Jobs and Oppressions, of which some few only are here mentioned.

32. The Highway-Men in *Ireland* are, since the late Wars there, usually called Rapparees, which was a name given to those *Irish* soldiers who in small Parties used, at that time, to plunder the Protestants.

33. The Army in *Ireland* is lodged in Barracks, the building and repairing whereof, and other Charges, have cost a prodigious Sum to that unhappy Kingdom.

34. Meaning *Ireland,* where he now lives, and probably may dye.

—JONATHAN SWIFT, *Verses on the death of Dr. Swift,*
D.S.P.D. Occasioned by Reading a Maxim
in Rochefoulcault. Written by Himself,
November 1731, 1739, pp. 9ff

GEORGE FAULKNER (1735)

As the first significant editor of Swift's works, the Dublin printer George
Faulkner is of great importance to Swiftian studies. In many ways, he was
Swift's "authoritative" editor, but this must not be taken for granted as
he omitted a number of key works. This extract is taken from the second
volume of the *Works* printed in 1735. In it, Faulkner discusses the rationale
for his treatment of the poems included in the volume. He is fully aware
that some poems might cause offence, but he also wishes to remain faithful to the texts.

The following poems chiefly consist either of Humour or Satyr, and very often of
both together. What Merit they may have, we confess ourselves to be no Judges
of in the least; but out of due Regard to a Writer, from whose Works we hope
to receive some Benefit, we cannot conceal what we have heard from several
Persons of great Judgment; that the Author never was known either in Verse or
Prose to borrow any Thought, Simile, Epithet, or particular Manner of Style; but
whatever he writ, whether good, bad, or indifferent, is an Original in itself.

Although we are sensible, that in some of the following Poems, the Ladies
may resent certain satyrical Touches against the mistaken Conduct in some
of the fair Sex: And that, some warm Persons on the prevailing Side, may
censure this Author, whoever he be, for not thinking in publick Matters exactly
like themselves: Yet we have been assured by several judicious and learned
Gentlemen, that what the Author hath here writ, on either of those two Subjects,
had no other Aim than to reform the Errors of both Sexes. If the Publick be
right in its Conjectures of the Author, nothing is better known in London, than
that while he had Credit at the Court of Queen Anne, he employed so much
of it in favour of Whigs in both Kingdoms, that the Ministry used to railly him
as the Advocate of that Party, for several of whom he got Employments, and
preserved others from losing what they had: Of which some Instances remain
even in this Kingdom. Besides, he then writ and declared against the Pretender,
with equal Zeal, though not without equal Fury, as any of our modern Whigs;
of which Party he always professed himself to be as to Politicks, as the Reader
will find in many Parts of his Works.

Our Intentions were to print the Poems according to the Time they were
writ in; but we could not do it so exactly as we desired, because we could
never get the least Satisfaction in that or many other Circumstances from the
supposed Author.

—GEORGE FAULKNER, *The Works of J.S., D.D.,
D.S.P.D. in Four Volumes*, 1735, vol. 2, pp. i–ii

W.H. DILWORTH (1758)

If it cannot be denied on one hand, that there runs an unabating vein of satire throughout all the writings of Dean Swift, it must be owned on the other, as he himself declares, no age could have more deserved it than that in which he was destined to live.

He is, therefore, justly entitled to all the praise we can bestow upon him, for having exerted his abilities (which were uncommonly great) in the defence of honour, virtue, and his country.

An article worthy of special observation is, that in his general satire, wherein, perhaps, thousands were equally meant, he hath never once, through malice, inserted the name of any one person. The vice, nevertheless, he exposed to contempt and ridicule.

But, in his particular satire, when egregious monsters, traitors to the commonwealth, and slaves to party, are the objects of his resentment, he cuts without mercy; in order that those, who trespass in defiance of laws, might live in fear of him.

If our readers expect that, in this work, we should enter into a minute detail of Swift's poetry, in order to point out his most striking beauties; our humble answer is, That, as for the dull or ignorant, such a disquisition would be quite fruitless: so all persons of taste and learning are enabled to judge for themselves, as well as to admire the real beauties of an author, and accompany his flights into the most distant regions of poetry, without a guide or monitor.

From these considerations we shall be very sparing in references and quotations of that sort. It is proper, however, to observe, that, in general, Swift's poetical writings, which, in their present situation, are only a beautiful heap of confusion, rather distracting the eye, and flashing upon the imagination, that conducting our fancies into poetical scenes, and commanding our approbation, while they improve our faculties, might easily be reduced to a number of classes under proper heads; and those which are too miscellaneous for any particular scenes, might follow the rest to posterity, in a course by themselves.

In such an order as here hinted, for the sake of the inimitable Swift's reputation, we earnestly recommend their being published by all future editors.

Nay, we farther assert, that the arrangement of his works in prose and verse (for indeed they are both strangely confused, through his own carelessness) would not be a difficult task to a man of common abilities, with any degree of attention.

One of the most distinguishing characters of Dr. Swift was, a bright and clear genius; so extremely piercing, that every, the most striking, circumstance, arising from any subject whatever, quickly occurred to his happy imagination; and those he frequently so accumulated one upon another, that, perhaps beyond all other poets, of all ages and countries, he deserves in this particular to be the most universally admired.

And this choice of circumstances (if any stress can be laid on the opinions of Longinus, that great director of our taste and judgment) renders a composition truly noble and sublime. For his masterly sentiments theron, we refer our readers to his tenth section.

The most remarkable pieces of this are, *The furniture of a woman's mind*; BETTY, *the Grizette*; *The journal of a modern lady*; *His poem on reading Dr. Young's satires*; *Mordanto*; *The description of a city shower*; *The description of Quilca*; *The description of the morning*; and, *The place of the damned*.

His great powers of the mind gave him also that *desperate hand*, as Pope terms it, in taking off all sorts of characters. We shall omit, for the present, those of a political nature, and mention but *The progress of poetry*; the second part of *Traulus*; *The progress of love*; *The character of Corinna*; and, *The beautiful young nymph just going to bed*.

By the last of these poems it appears, that his imagination could even dream in the character if an old battered strumpet. From the same inexhaustible fund he acquired the historic arts, both of designing and colouring, either in groups or in single portraits.

For instance: how exact, how lively and spirited, is that group of figures in *The journal of a modern lady*! how admirable also in point of single portrait if we consider the design, the attitude, the drapery, or the colouring, is that excellent representation of Cassinus, in *The tragical elegy*!

Throughout all Dean Swift's poetical productions, although many of them be dedicated immediately to the fair sex, there cannot be found, to the best of our recollection, one single distich addressed in the character of a love to any person. If he wrote any poems of that sort in his younger days, they must have been destroyed; for, after the strictest research we have been able to make, we could never come to the knowledge of any.

Those verses upon women, which are deemed the most satirical, were written principally with a view to correct their foibles, to improve their taste, and to make them as agreeable companions at threescore, as at the age of five and twenty.

By all that ever we could hear, the most exceptionable of his poems in that way, have produced some very extraordinary effects in the public world; which was, in truth, the ultimate design of his writing *The lady's dressing-room*, and other pieces, which are acknowledged to be somewhat liable to censure on account of their indelicacy.

It is impossible to remark on the poetical works of Dean Swift, without being somewhat particular on the piece entitled, *Cadenus and Vanessa*; for that poem is built on the finest model, supported with infinite humour, wit and gaiety, embellished with ideas the most lovely and delicate, beautifully adorned with variety of the most attractive images, and conducted, throughout the whole, with such perfect regularity, that, beyond all other pieces, whether of Dean Swift, or of any other poet that has writ the English language, it appears the best calculated to abide the severest examination of the critics.

—W.H. DILWORTH, *The Life of Dr. Jonathan Swift,*
Dean of Saint Patrick's, Dublin, 1758, pp. 80–86

JOSEPH WARTON (1782)

Although Joseph Warton first produced his important study of Alexander Pope—and, tangentially, Pope's circle—in 1756, this footnoted comment was added to the expanded version of 1782. In this anecdotal aside, Warton posits a reason as to why Swift resented the celebrated poet and dramatist John Dryden: envy.

I remember to have heard my father say, that Mr. Elijah Fenton, who was his intimate friend, and had been his master, informed him that Dryden, upon seeing some of Swift's earliest verses, said to him "Young man, you will never be a poet".

—JOSEPH WARTON, *An Essay on the Genius and*
Writings of Pope, 1782, pp. 312–313

JOHN AIKIN (1804)

Like many other critical commentators of the period, the physician John Aikin sought to render the rougher elements of great works of literature more accessible to a wider audience. Aikin often goes into great detail when describing the poetry, more so than many of his contemporaries, who often discussed Swift's poetry and prose alike in abstractly moral terms. In particular, this extract, which is taken from Aikin's *Letters to a Young Lady on a Course of English Poetry* (1804), is, as the title indicates, addressed to impressionable female readers. Students might well consider the cultural politics of this. Although many commentators insisted that readers, male and female alike, ought to steer clear of Swift's crudest writings, does Aikin

go too far in his suggestion that his intended readership ought to completely ignore the majority of Swift's poems?

Dean SWIFT is in our language the master in *familiar poetry*. Without the
perusal of his works no adequate conception can be formed of wit and
humour moving under the shackles of measure and rhyme with as much
ease as if totally unfettered; and even borrowing grace and vigour from the
constraint. In your progress hitherto, although it has been through some of
our most eminent poets, you cannot but have observed, that the necessity of
finding a termination to a line of the same sound with that of the preceding,
has frequently occasioned the employment of an improper word, such as
without this necessity would never have suggested itself in that connexion.
Indeed, it is not uncommon in ordinary versifiers to find a whole line thrown
in for no other purpose than to introduce a rhyming word. How far rhyme
is a requisite decoration of English verse, you will judge from your own
perceptions, after perusing the best specimens of blank verse. It is manifest,
however, that when employed, its value must be in proportion to its exactness,
and to its coincidence with the sense. In these respects, Swift is without
exception the most perfect rhymer in the language; and you will admire how
the very word which by its meaning seems most fit for the occasion, slides in
without effort as the echo in sound to the terminating word of the preceding
line. Even double and triple rhymes are ready at his call, and, though
suggesting the most heterogeneous ideas, are happily coupled by some of
those whimsical combinations in which comic wit consists.

The diction of Swift is the most complete example of colloquial ease that
verse affords. In aiming at this manner, other writers are apt to run into
quaintness and oddity; but in Swift not a word or phrase occurs which does
not belong to the natural style of free conversation. It is true, this freedom is
often indecorous, and would at the present day be scarcely hazarded by any
one who kept good company, still less by a clergyman. Yet he has known how
to make distinctions; and while many of his satirical and humorous pieces are
grossly tainted with indelicacies, some of his best and longest compositions are
void of any thing that can justly offend. It is evident, indeed, that Swift, though
destitute of genius for the sublimer parts of poetry, was sufficiently capable
of elegance, had he not preferred indulging his vein for sarcastic wit. No one
could compliment more delicately when he chose it, as no one was a better
judge of proprieties of behaviour, and the graces of the female character.

From the preceding representation, you will conclude that I cannot set you
to read Swift's poetry straight forwards. In fact, your way through them must

be picked very nicely, and a large portion of them must be unvisited. It should be observed, however, to do him justice, that their impurities are not of the moral kind, but are chiefly such as it is the scavenger's office to remove.

—JOHN AIKIN, *Letters to a Young Lady on a*
Course of English Poetry, 1804, pp. 62–65

FRANCIS, LORD JEFFREY
"SCOTT'S EDITION OF SWIFT" (1816)

A leading critical voice for the *Edinburgh Review* in the nineteenth century, Francis, Lord Jeffrey offers here a scathing critique of Swift and, by extension, Swift's recent editor, Sir Walter Scott. More particularly, in this extract, Jeffrey elaborates a commonly rehearsed view that Swift was much less successful as a poet than as a prose satirist.

Of his Poetry, we do not think there is much to be said;—for we cannot persuade ourselves that Swift was in any respect a poet. It would be proof enough, we think, just to observe, that, though a popular and most miscellaneous writer, he does not mention the name of Shakespeare above two or three times in any part of his works, and has nowhere said a word in his praise. His partial editor admits that he has produced nothing which can be called either sublime or pathetic; and we are of the same opinion as to the beautiful. The merit of correct rhymes and easy diction, we shall not deny him; but the diction is almost invariably that of the most ordinary prose, and the matter of his pieces no otherwise poetical, than that the Muses and some other persons of the Heathen mythology are occasionally mentioned. He has written lampoons and epigrams, and satirical ballads and abusive songs in great abundance, and with infinite success. But these things are not poetry;—and are better in verse than in prose, for no other reason than that the sting is more easily remembered, and the ridicule occasionally enhanced, by the hint of a ludicrous parody, or the drollery of an extraordinary rhyme. His witty verses, where they are not made up of mere filth and venom, seem mostly framed on the model of *Hudibras;* and are chiefly remarkable, like those of his original, for the easy and apt application of homely and familiar phrases, to illustrate ingenious sophistry or unexpected allusions. One or two of his imitations of Horace, are executed with spirit and elegance, and are the best, we think, of his familiar pieces; unless we except the verses on his own death, in which, however, the great charm arises, as we have just stated, from the singular ease and exactness with which he has imitated the style of ordinary society, and the neatness with which he has brought together and reduced to metre such a number of natural, characteristic and commonplace expressions. The *Cadenus and Vanessa* is, of itself, complete proof that he had in him none of the elements of poetry. It was written when his faculties were in their perfection, and his heart animated with all the tenderness of which it was ever capable—and yet it is as cold and as flat as the ice of Thule. Though describing a real passion, and a real perplexity, there is not a spark of fire, nor a throb of emotion in it from one end to the other. All the return he makes to the warm-hearted creature who had put her destiny into his hands, consists in a frigid mythological fiction, in which he sets forth, that Venus and the Graces lavished their gifts on her in her infancy, and moreover got Minerva, by a trick, to inspire her with wit and wisdom. The style is mere prose—or rather a string of familiar and vulgar phrases tacked together in rhyme, like the general tissue of his poetry.

—Francis, Lord Jeffrey, "Scott's Edition of Swift,"
Edinburgh Review, September 1816, pp. 49–50

Hippolyte Taine (1871)

Will poetry calm such a mind? Here, as elsewhere, he is most unfortunate. He is excluded from great transports of imagination, as well as from the lively digressions of conversation. He can attain neither the sublime nor the agreeable; he has neither the artist's rapture, nor the entertainment of the man of the world. Two similar sounds at the end of two equal lines have always consoled the greatest troubles; the old muse, after three thousand years, is a young and divine nurse; and her song lulls the sickly natures whom she still visits, like the young, flourishing races amongst whom she has appeared. The involuntary music, in which thought wraps itself, hides ugliness and unveils nature. Feverish man, after the labors of the evening and the anguish of the night; sees at morning the beaming whiteness of the opening heaven; he gets rid of himself and the joy of nature from all sides enters with oblivion into his heart. If misery pursues him, the poetic afflatus, unable to wipe it out, transforms it; it becomes ennobled, he loves it, and thenceforth he bears it; for the only thing to which he cannot resign himself is littleness. Neither Faust nor Manfred have exhausted human grief; they drank from the cruel cup a generous wine, they did not reach the dregs. They enjoyed themselves and nature; they tasted the greatness which was in them, and the beauty of creation; they pressed with their bruised hands all the thorns with which necessity has made our way thorny, but they saw them blossom with roses, fostered by the purest of their noble blood. There is nothing of the sort in

Swift: what is wanting most in his verses is poetry. The positive mind can neither love nor understand it; it sees therein only a machine or a fashion, and employs it only for vanity and conventionality. When in his youth he attempted Pindaric odes, he failed lamentably. I cannot remember a line of his which indicates a genuine sentiment of nature: he saw in the forests only logs of wood, and in the fields only sacks of corn. He employed mythology, as we put on a wig, ill-timed, wearily and scornfully. . . .

But in prosaic subjects, what truth and force! How this masculine nakedness crushes the artificial poetry of Addison and Pope! There are no epithets; he leaves his thought as he conceived it, valuing it for and by itself, needing neither ornaments, nor preparation, nor extension; above the tricks of the profession, scholastic conventionalisms, the vanity of the rhymester, the difficulties of the art; master of his subject and of himself. This simplicity and naturalness astonish us in verse. Here, as elsewhere, his originality is entire, and his genius creative; he surpasses his classical and timid age; he tyrannizes over form, breaks it, dare utter anything, spares himself no strong word. Acknowledge the greatness of this invention and audacity; he alone is a superior, who finds everything and copies nothing. . . .

All poetry exalts the mind, but this depresses it; instead of concealing reality, it unveils it; instead of creating illusions, it removes them. When he wishes to give a *description of morning,* he shows us the street-sweepers, the "watchful bailiffs," and imitates the different street cries. When he wishes to paint the rain, he describes "filth of all hues and odors," the "swelling kennels," the "dead cats," "turnip-tops," "stinking sprats," which "come tumbling down the flood." His long verses whirl all this filth in their eddies. We smile to see poetry degraded to this use; we seem to be at a masquerade; it is a queen travestied into a rough country girl. We stop, we look on, with the sort of pleasure we feel in drinking a bitter draught. Truth is always good to know, and in the splendid piece which artists show us, we need a manager to tell us the number of the hired applauders and of the supernumeraries.

—Hippolyte Taine, *History of English Literature,*
translated by H. Van Laun, 1871, vol. 2,
book 3, chapter 5, p. 135–139

Charles Cowden Clarke "On the Comic Writers of England: VI. Swift" (1871)

This lengthy extract is taken from a series of essays "On the Comic Writers of England" by the elderly public lecturer and writer Charles Cowden

Clarke for *Gentleman's Magazine*. Here Clarke discusses at length the general merits of the works of Swift. In particular, he seeks to redress the balance between the much celebrated prose and the largely ignored poetry. "The poetry of Swift has been wholly—at all events, in a great degree—eclipsed by the predominant excellence of his prose inventions and dissertations." Clarke challenges this assumption on the grounds that the "same strong sense, ... the same natural, indigenous diction, and the same caustic humour characterise his poetical effusions." Swift is seen as a poet of "sterling, downright sense, and not of speculative fancy, or of excursive imagination." Johnson offered a similar assessment in the late 1770s, but Clarke regards this in much more positive terms. After all, for Clarke, his subject must be characterized without prejudice as a "British classic."

Had Swift written no other verses than those on his own death, he would have deserved honourable mention among our national poets; had he written no other history than the "Tale of a Tub" he must have ranked among our greatest wits; had he produced no other work of imagination than "Gulliver's Travels", he would have been great among the greatest satirists; had he put forth no other tracts than the "Drapier Letters", he would have deserved a votive offering from the nation whose interests he had undertaken to protect; and had he projected no other scheme than the plan of an Academy for the correcting and enlarging, polishing and fixing of his native language, he might have claimed the gratitude and reverence of the whole British people. Even one of these productions would furnish an ample capital to establish and support a good literary reputation; and a single one of them (the "Gulliver") has perhaps commanded a more extended share of popularity than any prose work in the language ("Robinson Crusoe" excepted); and it will continue to be a stable satire so long as court servility, national vanity and conceit, with the mania for scheme-projection, shall continue to form a feature in the human character, and to maintain an influence over human action. Swift's other great satire, the "Tale of a Tub", will retain every particle of its freshness and verdure so long as the three master-dogmas of the Christian religion (those of the Roman, the Lutheran, and the Calvinistic Churches) shall preserve their sway in the Christian world. The subjects of his two great satires being quite as familiar with our every-day habits, feelings, and associations, as they were with society at the period of their production; to all appearance they will continue so after very many generations shall have passed away; and this circumstance has given Swift an advantage over his brother satirists, who, in attacking the epidemic weaknesses, follies, or vices of their contemporaries, which were the mania of their age, and not of universal humanity, have passed into matter of curious investigation with the literary antiquary, and are not familiar with or cognisable by the million. Who, for example, would be bold enough to name the period when it shall become a question of legendary history, and not, as it now is, a matter of every day notoriety, that the leaders in the different sects of Christianity have interpreted the doctrinal portions of Scripture in conformity with their own articles of faith, warping the texts by the heat of argument; or, where they happen to be stubbornly plain, denying their authenticity altogether? and this, in the "Tale of a Tub", Swift has, with a caustic satire, represented under the form of the three brothers interpreting their father's will. When will the allegory of Brother Peter's loaf, which comprised the essence of beef, partridge, apple-pie, and custard, require a black-letter annotator to expound its interpretation? The "Tale of a Tub" was written when Swift was but nineteen years old. This circumstance renders the performance of the work the more surprising; not on account of the invention and learning displayed in it, neither of which was miraculous in a naturally strong mind, and in one educated for the clerical profession: but the staidness with which the history is conducted, and the consistency preserved throughout, have all the air of matured practice in authorship. The style, too, is so easy, and so purely idiomatical, that none of his later works exhibits material improvement upon it in this respect. There is a remarkable determination of purpose in the style of Swift, with perfect transparency; and these are but the reflexes of the natural man, for these were the prominent features of his character. It will be observed that in his writings we rarely meet with a superfluous word, and never with a superfluous epithet. Now this is one of the besetting sins of modern writing. Swift is the most English, the most thoroughly national in his diction of all our classic writers. On no occasion does he employ an exotic term, if one indigenous to the language be at hand. He is also sparing of connecting particles and introductory phrases and flourishes; using also the simplest forms of construction; and, moreover, he is master of the idiomatic peculiarities, and lurking, unapparent resources of the language to a degree of perfection that leaves him almost without a competitor. The cultivation of a plain, unornamented style demands considerably more care and research than that of the florid and redundant style; and for this obvious reason, that, in the one instance, it is a task of no ordinary severity to restrain, retrench, and condense, remaining all the while clear and perspicuous; whereas, in the inflated, verbose style, the very redundancy of words pressed into the service is commonly the result of indolence, indifference, and carelessness. The former, on account of its simplicity in appearance, is thought to be easily imitable, while the latter has the effect of laborious and scientific construction,—than which a greater mistake does not exist. For the one man who by bestowing thought and care shall be able to write with the nervous plainness and perspicuity of Swift, fifty could with little exertion imitate the artificial manner of Dr. Johnson; and hence the number of followers and admirers of the latter. "Fit words in fit places" is the best and indeed the only axiom to form the best style in writing: for in expressing our thoughts there may be several native words, which differ only in shades of meaning, that are all available for carrying out the idea; nevertheless, each word or term must express the thought with varied force and propriety; but out of all these there is only one we really want, and that is *the* one which punctually accords with the idea we design to convey. The usages of society have apportioned to each word employed in common conversation its conventional associations and graduated tints of meaning; and the stubbornness of custom has assigned to each its nicety of distinction. The having all these ready for use, with the judgment to decide upon the one best fitted for the occasion, constitutes the clearest conversational prose style; and that is the finest diction which most nearly approaches a familiar and refined discourse. In the florid and artificial style of writing the same tax of selection, and the same niceness of propriety, are not severely demanded. It is sufficient that, in construction, the members of sentences be involved, that qualifying terms and epithets be multiplied, and the employment of learned words from the classical and dead languages be not spared. One cannot be supposed familiar with the minute varieties and shades of signification in a language that has no longer a "local habitation." The attainment of this last finish in writing is sufficiently perplexing even in the living dialects; the broadly accepted meaning, therefore, of dead foreign words is sufficient for the cultivator of the artificial and florid style; and they offer this advantage to the writer, that they all impose upon the general reader, because they are out of the every-day familiar path of language; and the more unfamiliar and occult the words, the more learned and grand, of course, will be thought the style. The location of words, rather than the novelty of ideas, soonest attracts the reading million. A verbose commonplace will gain the day over simple originality—at least where the election goes by "universal suffrage." Swift's own designation of the three styles of writing cannot be too often repeated. "There is one style (he says) that cannot be understood; and there is another that can be understood: but there is a third style, that cannot be misunderstood, and that is the best"; and it is eminently characteristic of his own, for it may be safely affirmed that throughout the whole of his voluminous writings not a single sentence occurs the meaning of which any intellect above a baboon's need stumble at. The most remarkable style of our own day for simplicity, with clearness and brevity, was, perhaps, that of the late Duke of Wellington. I know of nothing in writing more suited to their subject-matter than those official despatches. They are to be studied for their economy and yet sufficiency of language. They are models for young men who may be employed in business correspondence. A principal clerk in one of our public offices told me that at one period, when they were not much engaged, he was in the habit of receiving official communications from the Duke, and that he used to amuse himself by endeavouring to express the same ideas in fewer words, but that he remembered in no instance to have succeeded. And now to return to our "Tale of a Tub".

One curious feature in the work is the several introductory papers that the author has appended before the reader is ushered into the "real presence"; like passing a suite of rooms in progress to a Prince at his levee. There is first an "Apology," or defence of the character and principles of the tale; wherein, defending the freedom with which he has assailed the superstition and folly of the religious sectaries, he concludes with the question, "Why any clergyman of our Church should be angry to see the follies of fanaticism and superstition exposed, though in the most ridiculous manner; since that is the most probable way to cure them, or at least to hinder them from farther proceeding?" and he frankly adds, that he "will forfeit his life if any one opinion can be fairly deduced from the book, which is contrary to religion or morality." The "Apology" comprises sixteen pages of small type, closely printed, and ably written with temper and judgment. This is followed by a "Postscript," which is succeeded by a noble and worthy "Dedication" to the great Lord Chancellor Somers, one of the most shining lights of his age. The language of this dedication is of itself calculated to exalt Swift in our esteem; for in addressing this nobleman, he has shown how (like all magnanimous spirits) he could sink the mere party-politician in the intellectual cosmopolite. Swift was a Tory, and Somers was the Whig Chancellor; nevertheless, the tribute to the public virtues of the first patron of the *Paradise Lost* is urged with as much neatness and elegance of wit as manliness of spirit. . . .

The weight and force of Swift's argumentative power, with perspicuity of thought and transparency of diction, are seen to great advantage in that admirable series of political essays known under the title of "The Drapier Letters", a collection of papers drawn up in so masterly a manner, and directed to their object of attack with such vehemence and effect, that his single energy and exertion withstood the unconstitutional attempt of the whole Ministerial phalanx to debase the Irish coin; and, finally, he succeeded in frustrating their iniquitous purpose. The event, which forms a prominent feature in Swift's career, was briefly this: In the year 1724 an obscure tradesman, and a bankrupt, of the name of Wood, alleging the great want of copper money in Ireland, obtained a patent for issuing one hundred and eight thousand pounds in that metal, to pass there as current money; the metal for which, however, was so debased that six parts out of seven were composed of brass. Swift at this period had almost wholly withdrawn from political writing; but, seeing at a glance the fatal consequences that would ensue to the whole kingdom if the measure were allowed to succeed, and believing it to be a vile job from the beginning to the end, and that the chief procurers of the patent were to be sharers in the profits which would arise from the ruin of a kingdom, he rushed from his retirement to the rescue, and in the first instance drew up a remonstrance to both Houses of Parliament, in which, after a number of masterly arguments, he makes the following nervous appeal:—"Is it, was it, can it, or will it ever be a question, not whether such a kingdom, or William Wood, should be a gainer; but whether such a kingdom should be wholly undone, destroyed, sunk, depopulated, made a scene of misery and desolation, for the sake of William Wood? God of His infinite mercy avert this dreadful judgment; and it is our universal wish that God would put it into your hearts to be His instrument for so good a work." And he concludes with the following determination in case the Parliament should persist in urging on the measure:—"For my own part, who am but one man, of obscure condition, I do solemnly declare, in the presence of Almighty God, that I will suffer the most ignominious and torturing death, rather than submit to receive this accursed coin, or any other that shall be liable to the same objections, until they shall be forced upon me by a *law of my own country*" (the Irish, it will be remembered, had then a Parliament of their own); "and if that shall ever happen, I will transport myself into some foreign land, and eat the bread of poverty among a free people." Well may it be said: "When shall the Irish have such another rector of Laracor?"

The Ministry, however, persisted in their injustice; and then Swift began his famous attack in the series of letters (there are seven of them) under the signature "M. B. Drapier" (a supposed tradesman), which are dictated in so plain a language that the most barren capacity could understand them. His arguments are so naturally adduced, and his principles are so clear and homely, that perusal and conviction are simultaneous. So perfectly did he sustain the character of the writer he had assumed, that the letters have all the appearance of being the common-sense outpourings of an honest, homespun shop-keeper, who had issued from his obscurity, and had perforce turned author, through indignation at the insolence of power exerted over himself and fellow-citizens. And yet, plain and simple as these compositions appear at first sight, and such as any ordinary writer might imagine he himself could produce, as he would a letter of ceremony; yet inspect them critically, and they will be found to have been constructed with consummate art and skill. Moreover, Swift has displayed a thoroughly comprehensive view of his subject, and shown himself to have been a political economist (especially as regards the monetary question) of no ordinary standard. Had this iniquitous job (for "job" it certainly was—there is no courtlier term for it) been forced upon the Irish people, their trading interest must have been swamped. His attacks, therefore, are terrific, from their force and certainty of aim. They are rifle-cannon shot. His fourth letter brought out a proclamation from the Lord Lieutenant (Carteret) offering £300 reward for the discovery of the author of it. The printer was imprisoned; a bill was sent to the grand jury. Swift addressed a letter to every member of the pannel—so convincing in its argument, that, to a man, they threw out the bill; and so furious was the then tide of party, that the time-serving Lord Chief Justice, Whitshed, in his rage, unconstitutionally discharged the whole of the grand jury; and when the Parliament refused to impeach the judge for his breach of the law of the land, Swift darted upon him like a bull-dog, tore, and worried him out of all his patience by squibs, epigrams, and bitter attacks in all directions, till he made him ridiculous, as well as odious, to the whole country—in short, he succeeded in making the universal trading community of Ireland determine to refuse the coin in payment for their goods. . . .

What service Demosthenes rendered to the Athenians by his renowned orations, the author of these remarkable, yet unostentatious, letters effected for his countrymen by his silent pen. This is the true and the most effective "agitation"; steam-force arguments, with a righteous cause to back them; and indeed Swift undertook a greater labour, and produced a greater effect, than any single man, before or since, has been able to accomplish. "Every person, of every rank, party, and denomination, was convinced," says Lord Orrery; "the Papist, the fanatic, the Tory, the Whig, all listed themselves volunteers under the banner of M. B. Drapier, and were all equally zealous to serve the common cause. Much heat, and many fiery speeches against the Administration, were the consequences of this union." All the threats and proclamations of the Government produced not the slightest effect till the coin was totally suppressed and Wood had withdrawn his patent. As a proof of the intrinsic merit of these letters, as compositions, they are so interesting that the reader must indeed be inert who can quit them; or who, as he reads on, does not so identify himself with the object they are intended to serve as to revive their local political interest after a lapse of more than a hundred and forty years. Swift was a thorough master of "political agitation." It is curious, and as amusing, to note the various measures in which he harps upon that odious coin, constantly using the word "brass." When he was not writing essays, addresses, petitions, and letters, he let off squibs and epigrams, and all addressed to the level of the common intellect. The circumstance of Lord Carteret succeeding the unprincipled Duke of Grafton in the government of Ireland, supplied him with an epigram:—

Cart'ret was welcom'd to the shore,
First with the *brazen* cannons' roar;
To meet him next the soldier comes,
With *brazen* trumps and *brazen* drums;
Approaching near the town, he hears
The *brazen* bells salute his ears;
But when Wood's *brass* began to sound,
Guns, trumpets, drums, and bells were drown'd.

It was not at all Swift's vein to cant about the "dignity and morality of virtue," or to pat his brethren on the back and to assure them that, after all, men are not so bad as they are represented; he left that course to the dealers in hypocrisy and mouth honour; but he has, by implication, constantly shown his reverence for *true* honour, social worth, and unpalavering integrity; and "he that runneth may read" this moral throughout his most popular prose satire, meaning the "Gulliver's Travels". We have the meanness, the littleness, the low cunning, the national conceit and chicanery, in the small people of Lilliput. Just so long as blue ribands and red ribands, and silver sticks and gold sticks, and other trumpery are retained and revered as the insignia of services performed, just so long will the leaps and the vaultings and the summersaults of my lord Flimnap and his noble competitors at the Court of Lilliput be appreciated by and amuse the reflecting reader. And as long as men will prostrate their souls in the mire of servility and dishonour, in order that they may bask in the sunshine of favour, so long will the service in the Court of Lilliput rebound from every worthy breast, that the chief merit of every courtier there is made to consist in the neatness with which he licks up the dust while crawling upon his hands and knees to the foot of the throne. All these acts are the characteristics of miniature-minded and low people. On the other hand, to the gigantic Brobdignagians he has dispensed a bland nature and a large benevolence, the baser properties being the result of diminutive intellectual conformation. Swift, therefore, as it appears, designs to portray that true grandeur of character and magnanimity consist in gentleness, sympathy, and an expansive benevolence. His prototype, Rabelais, has anticipated him in this moral of his allegory; for Gargantua and his father, Grangousier, are the most forbearing and beneficent of giants. How agreeable is the description of Gulliver's nurse, Glumdalclitch; and how fine and racy the satire put into the mouth of the good-tempered King. How triumphant his reception of the little traveller's account of the wars and disputes in his own country—religious and political—after a hearty laugh asking him whether he was a Whig or a Tory. What a capital rebuke to the fussiness of party! And how stinging the concluding remark of his Brobdignagian majesty:—

> "Then turning to his First Minister, who waited behind him with a white staff near as tall as the mainmast of the *Royal Sovereign,* he observed how contemptible a thing was human grandeur, which could be mimicked by such contemptible creatures as I; and yet, says he, I dare engage, these creatures have their titles and distinctions of honour; they contrive little nests and burrows, that they call houses and cities; they make a figure in dress and equipage; they love, they fight, they dispute, they cheat, they betray."

The only malicious creature among the whole race is the Dwarf.

Throughout this masterly work, Swift has taken such a view of human nature as might be supposed to emanate from a being of a higher sphere and in a superior state of existence. Who more contemptuously than he has exposed the worthlessness, if not the wickedness, of party feud? two races in a nation tearing each other to pieces in order that the question may be decided whether they shall break their eggs at the big or the little end: as Voltaire, in his biting way, records of the Spaniards in America, "They roasted thirty thousand people at slow fires, in order to *convert* them."

Dr. Johnson, who seems to have had a personal antipathy to Swift, has endeavoured to depreciate his literary reputation by denying—or, at all events, questioning—that, in the one case, he was the author of the "Tale of a Tub"; and, in the other, by asserting that there was no merit in "Gulliver" beyond the mechanical execution of the story; because the first idea of it was taken from the "Gargantua" of Rabelais.

That Swift was answerable for all the merits and demerits in the allegory of the Brothers Peter, Martin, and Jack, its internal evidence of style and manner were alone all but sufficient. Johnson should have said who was the author, if Swift was not. His biographer and friend, Dr. Sheridan, however, speaks of the work as though its authenticity could not for one moment be questioned; besides, an anecdote is somewhere upon record that in his advanced age, and when his faculties were upon the waver, he was heard to mutter to himself, while reading the book, "What a fine genius I had when I wrote this!" Moreover, so little doubt existed with the Ministers of the day, and at Court, of his being the author, that the fact obstructed his promotion to a vacant bishopric. It savours, therefore, of the bitterness of antipathy to take that from a man's literary fame which stood in the way of his worldly success. And as to the want of originality in the first thought of the "Gulliver"—that of making the agents of disproportioned size, to suit the purpose of his satire—there can be no serious ground taken for detraction on that score; for we must remember that this employment of the gigantic agency did not come from the corner-stone of Rabelais's satire, whereas it constitutes both the groundwork and the entire elevation of that of Swift; he has availed himself of a similar material, but he has made a totally different disposal of it. Is every one who writes an epic poem in twenty-four books, in the heroic stanza, with episode and simile interspersed, a copyist of Homer? And, lastly, and to dispose of the question of the "execution" of the "Gulliver's Travels", which Dr. Johnson pronounced to be so easy and mechanical—after he had wrenched the original invention from the author—it can only be said that we may look in vain for equal ease and propriety of action in the mechanism of the "Rasselas", or in the "Voyage of Life," in the *Idler;* and with no greater hope of success for any originality in the allegory, the design, or the satire of either. It was as unwise as it was invidious in Dr. Johnson (himself so exposed to detraction) to adopt such a course for lessening a great man's fame. The fact is, that the mere machinery of the "Gulliver" (easy of achievement as it was in Dr. Johnson's estimation) is so correct through all its proportions that this alone constitutes no small share of the merit of the work, and (united with the invention) it has become one of those effective levers that have pushed on the social world.

The poetry of Swift has been wholly—at all events, in a great degree—eclipsed by the predominant excellence of his prose inventions and dissertations. The same strong sense, however, the same natural, indigenous diction, and the same caustic humour characterise his poetical effusions as his satires and essays. There is an austere drollery and a most pure vein of irony in some of the poems of Swift that are extremely amusing: and now and then we come upon a golden thread of pathos (unpremeditated and unaffected) which appeals at once to the tribunal of sentiment and good feeling. Swift was the poet of sterling, downright sense, and not of speculative fancy, or of excursive imagination. So little congeniality, indeed, has he with that higher region of poetry, that it must have been interesting to have heard what his mathematical, utilitarian mind would have to say about the "Faerie Queene", or the "Midsummer Night's Dream". He would not have talked the amazing nonsense that Dr. Johnson did; but, with the same hard cynical faculty, he would have bound them to the Procrustes' bed of the French school of criticism, and by that code he might, perhaps (while he showed that they "*proved* nothing"), have missed the subtleties in that *mens divinior* which can "take the imprisoned soul and lap it in elysium." Even in his wit, Swift is serious and saturnine—not sportive and wanton. He did not *laugh* at the follies and vices of mankind—he was never seen to laugh; but he was impatient with them, and they made him angry. I know that there is an opinion prevailing with regard to the satires of Swift—most especially his prose ones—that they have an injurious tendency, inasmuch as they induce a degrading, and even desponding, sense of human nature. For my own part I do not feel this to be the case; and this feeling may arise from self-conceit, but more, I believe, from the sense I entertain of the dignity of the human creation. One exception I must allow, and that is, in the story of the Houynhyms and Yahoos; and that bitter satire, I suppose, was penned when the redeeming milk of hope and forbearance with regard to his species had all but dried up in his nature. . . .

If Swift wrote much that deserved to survive, and which will survive, to the latest posterity (for he is a British classic), he has also left a prodigious quantity that no mortal would care to look at twice. Few men perhaps, with equal grasp of mind, have written so much trumpery, and few so many ineffective, uninteresting, and nonsensical verses, as he. Fortunate for his executors and editors that he could not retrace his steps after quitting this world; since they would assuredly have felt the weight of his indignation due to their intemperate zeal in pouring out upon the public all the waifs and strays, scraps, odds and ends, tag-rag and bob-tail, scattered among his books and papers. If they had found a receipt for pickling cabbage, I verily believe that it would have been installed among his "works." Nevertheless, it is neither a fruitless nor a worthless employment to contemplate a mind like that of Swift during its carnival of negligence and frivolity. It is pleasant, in the first place, to notice the stern, unbending patriot, the haughty politician, who kept the Prime Minister, Oxford, at arm's length, and sent him to Coventry till he had apologised for an affront that that lord had passed upon him; for at the Queen's levee he no more noticed that principal officer of the Government than if he had been Silver or Gold Stick; and when alluding to the circumstance in his journal to Stella, he adds, in the spirit of an intellectual autocrat: "If we let these Ministers pretend too much, there will be no *governing* them." The man who bearded the Viceroy at his own levee in Dublin Castle, and made the roof ring with his indignant remonstrance at the unconstitutional acts of the English Parliament; who, by his own robust sense, unflinching and uncompromising firmness of purpose, and integrity of principle reconciled a bickering and unstable Ministry, and, for months, forcibly, and by his own unaided genius, kept them at the political helm—the eminent Bolingbroke being one of them—it is pleasant, I say, to see such a sturdy spirit bending to the relaxations of a drawing-room dilettante; writing Lilliputian odes, in lines of three syllables; Latin doggrels, puns and charades to Dr. Sheridan, and slip-shod verses from Mary the cook to the deaf old housekeeper. What pleasant humour in the poem, whether "Hamilton's bawn shall be converted into a barrack or a malt-house." What a spirited sketch of a militia captain, and how genuine (for that age) the soldiers' oaths, and rough handling of the canonical cloth. What excellent travesty upon rural poetry, in what he styles a "Town Eclogue; or, London in a Shower." . . .

So little concern did this remarkable man evince for his literary fame that, of all his works, not one was subscribed with his name, except the letter upon the English language, and that he addressed to the Earl of Oxford, the Prime Minister. Not one of his most intimate friends was aware of his being the author of the "Gulliver's Travels". Gay wrote over to him in Ireland, describing the sensation the book was producing in all circles, telling him that even the publisher was ignorant of its author, and adding, "If you are the man, as we suspect, your friends have reason to feel disobliged at your giving them no hint of the matter." Swift had none of the coquetry or pettiness of authorship; he could afford to wait till the world found him out; and he was even less regardful of the author's pecuniary emolument; for in one of his letters he declared that he never got a farthing for anything he had written, except once, and then he was indebted to the vigilance of Pope; and even this sum he abandoned to his friend. It is plausible to infer that the history of authorship does not furnish a parallel to the extent of this sacrifice. He never asked a favour (for himself) of king or statesman; still less would he condescend to dandle palms with the critics. Swift was the most stubbornly proud man of his age; and this bearing he supported in his tone of thought as well as action; for, in directing his genius, he followed no man as a model. In short, he was not only the most original, but, take him in all his phases of authorship, he was the most powerful and perhaps the most various writer of the century in which he flourished.

To sum up his character in few words, he was, as Sir Walter Scott says in his Life of him, a compound of anomaly and paradox. He was a strenuous believer, and yet was refused a diocese through the instrumentality of the Archbishop of York, who told Queen Anne that she ought to be certain that the man she was going to create a bishop was a Christian. This opposition arose from his irrepressible spirit of satirical levity, both in speaking and writing. The wonder is, that the Archbishop did not pronounce him a subtle Atheist.

In his politics he adhered to the Tory party—he was a sublime Tory. And yet no man has said or done stronger things in behalf of democratic freedom. Had he adhered to his first party and principles, he would have been as sublime a Whig. He entertained a rugged antipathy to his countrymen;

and yet he seized the first opportunity to vindicate their rights and liberties, and to rescue them from unjust oppression. And this he did after the most disgraceful outrages on their part offered to his own person. When he first went over to Dublin to occupy his living, the Whig party pursued him there; and such was the coarse political spirit of the age that he was not unfrequently pelted with mud as he walked the streets.

He lay all his life under the stigma of being penurious (this charge arose from his being orderly and *strict* in the employment of his revenue), and yet he was greatly and secretly bountiful.

He was avowedly the most classical writer of his day, and yet he could not take his degree at college.

He was the sole prop and stay of the Tory Administration; he had obtained promotion for numbers in the Church, and yet could not compass for himself the only place he desired.

He was actuated by strong impulses of kindness and affection—upon one occasion hurrying into a closet to weep when he saw the pictures taken down at his friend Sheridan's, who was removing from him; yet this friend he arrested for debt, and broke the hearts of two amiable women, whom there is little doubt he sincerely respected, if not loved; for all those poems to Stella, and that constant journal, proclaim him to have been—for the time, at all events, and for a long time, too—a sincere man; or, indeed, he was an astounding and gratuitous hypocrite, a charge that no one will be hardy enough to file against him. But, in fact, no man was more wilful, and less patient of dictation; and this, it may be, was the dormant seed in his nature, which in later life, fungus-like, overgrew and smothered his reason. We may feel for him in his secret thoughts—which at times must have been awful, since he evidently anticipated for years his own mental decay. He told Dr. Young—pointing to the blasted summit of a tree—that that was the way in which he himself should decline. With all his wilfulness and impatience, however, he would frequently, as an author, yield upon the tenderest points— that of deferring to the opinion of others. He struck out forty verses, and added the same number to one of his poems, in compliance with a suggestion of Addison's. Upon another occasion he altered two paragraphs in a pamphlet in opposition to his own judgment; and when, after the publication, his adviser became sensible that the changes were to its detriment, and expressed his regret and surprise that they had been adopted, Swift, with all the indifference of conscious power, answered, "I made them without hesitation, lest, had I stood up for their defence, you might have imputed it to the vanity of an author unwilling to hear of his errors, and by this ready compliance I hoped you would at all times hereafter be the more free in your remarks."

He constantly manifests in his works—more especially in the latter ones—a bitter misanthropy; and yet in his "heart of heart" he was an enduring friend, a firm and devoted patriot, a foot-to-foot partisan, a bountiful patron. The fund he appropriated in small loans to assist needy traders and even the poor basket-women in the streets, which consisted of the first £500 he himself had saved, is a proof that his misanthropy was little more than a skin-deep irritation; and as sympathy begets sympathy, no man, perhaps (not even excepting the famous "Agitator" of our own day—need I say Daniel O'Connell?), possessed so absolute a dominion over the affections of the commonalty. When the Archbishop of Dublin publicly charged Swift with inflaming the people against him—"I inflame them!" retorted the triumphant dictator; "had I but lifted my finger they would have torn you to pieces." Oh! truly, and indeed, we may parody Marc Antony's eulogy of the great Brutus, and say of Swift—"This was the noblest 'Tory' of them all"—

All the "party-mongers," save only he,
Did what they did in envy of "Whiggery";
He only, in a general honest thought,
And common good to all, made one of them.

I cannot pursue my parody, and say: "His life was *gentle*" (for it was anything but that); we may add, however:—

The elements
So mixed in him, that nature might stand up
And say to all the World: *This was a man.*

Truly may we exclaim with Hazlitt, "When shall we have another Rector of Laracor?"

—CHARLES COWDEN CLARKE,
"On the Comic Writers of England: VI. Swift,"
Gentleman's Magazine, September 1871,
pp. 436–456

JOHN NICHOL "JONATHAN SWIFT" (1880)

Dryden, then the veteran of our literature, sitting in the dictator's chair left vacant by Ben Jonson and waiting for Samuel Johnson, having perused an ode on the Athenian Society dating from Moor Park, February 14, 1691, hazarded the prediction, 'Cousin Swift, you will never be a poet.' The unforgiven criticism has received from the judgment of posterity an assent qualified by respect for the strongest satirist of England and for an ability which cannot help making itself here and there manifest even in his verse.

Swift's satire is of two kinds: the party polemic of his earlier years, which culminated in 1724 in the *Drapier's Letters,* and the expression of a misanthropy as genuine as that of Shakespeare's Timon, of a rage directed not against Dissent or Church or Whig or Tory, but mankind, finding mature vent in the most terrible libel that has ever been imagined—a libel on the whole of his race—the hideous immortal mockery of the closing voyage of Gulliver. Such a work could only have been written by one born a cynic, doubly soured by some mysterious affliction, and by having had

> To fawn, to crouch, to wait, to ride, to run,
> To spend, to give, to want, to be undone,

till he had lost any original capacity he may have had for becoming a poet. His genius, moreover, was from the first as far removed from that peculiar to poetry as it is possible for any genius of the first rank to be. The power of Swift's prose was the terror of his own, and remains the wonder of after times. With the exception of a few clumsy paragraphs thrown off in haste, he says what he means in the homeliest native English that can be conceived. Disdaining even those refinements or shades of expression to which most writers touching on delicate or dangerous subjects feel compelled to resort, he owes almost nothing to foreign influence. 'I am,' he wrote, 'for every man's working on his own materials, and producing only what he can find within himself:' he consistently carved everything he had to set before his readers out of the plain facts with which he professed to deal. In his masterpieces there is scarce a hint from any known source, rarely a quotation: his sentences are self-sufficient, and fit the occasion as a glove the hand. In the *Tale of a Tub* he anticipates Teufelsdrockh in his contempt for trappings of speech as of person; he regarded fine language as leather and prunella. Though Swift's Allegories are abundant, he disdained ordinary metaphor, in the spirit in which Bentham defined poetry as misrepresentation. But towards the close of the seventeenth and during the end of the eighteenth centuries, almost every English writer—apart from those purely scientific—had to pay toll to what he called the Muses. Bunyan seems to have written his bad lines to italicise the distinction between the most highly imaginative prose and poetry. In the next age no one who addressed the general public could escape the trial; and Swift's verses are at least as worthy of preservation as Addison's. In following a fashion he also gratified a talent,—nor Pope nor Byron had a greater,—for random rhyme. Generally careless, often harsh, his versification is seldom laboured: his pen may run till it wearies the reader; but we see no reason in fall of energy why Swift's Hudibrastic jingle should cease, any more than why the waves of Spenser's stanza should not roll for ever. The other merits of our author's verse are those of his prose—condensation, pith, always the effect, generally the reality, of sincere purpose, and, with few exceptions, simplicity and directness. The exceptions are in his unhappy Pindaric odes, and some of his later contributions to the pedantry of the age. The former could scarcely be worse, for they have almost the contortions of Cowley, without his occasional flow and elevation. Take the following lines from the 'Athenian Ode':

> Just so the mighty Nile has suffered in its fame
> Because 'tis said (and perhaps only said)
> We've found a little inconsiderable head
> That feeds the huge, unequal stream.

And again:

> And then how much and nothing is mankind,
> Whose reason is weighed down by popular air,
> Who by that vainly talks of baffling death:
> And hopes to lengthen life by a transfusion of breath,
> Which yet whoe'er examines right will find
> To be an art as vain as bottling up of wind.

As in Congreve's 'Address to Silence' the force of cacophony can no further go. It may be said that these lines were the products of 'green, unknowing youth,' but during the same years the same writer was maturing the *Tale of a Tub*. Swift had no ear save for the discords of the world, and in such cases a stiff regular measure, which is a sort of rhythmic policeman, is the only safe guard. Pindaric flights, unless under the guidance of the genius that makes music as it runs, invariably result in confusion worse confounded. Not least among our debts to Dryden may be ranked his fencing the ode from his cousin Swift. Of the pseudo-classic efforts of the latter, *Cadenus and Vanessa*, published in 1723, probably written about ten years earlier, may be taken as a type. No selection from his verses would be esteemed satisfactory that did not exhibit a sample of this once celebrated production: but, apart from the tragic interest of the personal warning it conveys, it is, as M. Taine says, 'a threadbare allegory in which the author's prosaic freaks tear his Greek frippery.' The same critic justly remarks that Swift 'wore his mythology like a wig: that his pleading before Venus is like a legal procedure,' and that he habitually 'turns his classic wine to vinegar.' The other writers of the time had turned it into milk and water, but Prior and the rest had a grace to which Swift was a stranger. Their laughter is genuine though light; his was funereal and sardonic. His pleasantry is rarely pleasant, and he is never at heart more gloomy than when he affects to be gay. Most of his occasional verses, written at intervals from 1690 till 1733, are either frigid compliments or thinly veiled invectives, many of which, like the epigrams that disfigure the otherwise exquisite pages of Herrick, have all the coarseness with only half the wit of Martial. His addresses to women are, as might be expected, singularly unfortunate. He says truly of himself that he

> could praise, esteem, approve,
> But understood not what it was to love.

He can never get out of his satiric pulpit, and while saluting his mistresses as nymphs, he lectures them as school-girls. His verses to Stella, whom he came as near to loving as was for him possible, and whose death certainly hastened his mental ruin, are as unimpassioned as those to Vanessa, with whose affections he merely trifled. Swift's tendency to dwell on the meaner, and even the revolting facts of life, pardonable in his prose, is unpardonable in those tributes to Venus Cloacina, in which he intrudes on a lady's boudoir with the eye of a surgeon fresh from a dissecting-room or an hospital. His society verses are like those of a man writing with his feet, for he delights to trample on what others caress. Often he seems, among singing birds, a vulture screeching over carrion.

Of Swift's graver satiric pieces, the *Rhapsody on Poetry* has the fatal drawback of suggesting a comparison with *The Dunciad*. In *The Beast's Confession*, vivid and trenchant though it be, the author appears occasionally to intrude on the gardens of Prior and Gay. Had he been an artist in verse, he might have written something in English more like the sixth satire of Juvenal than Churchill ever succeeded in doing. But Swift despised art: he rode rough-shod, on his ambling cynic steed, through bad double rhyme and halting rhythm, to his end. War with the cold steel of prose was his business: his poems are the mere side-lights and pastimes of a man too grim to join heartily in any game. Only here and there among them, as in the strange medley of pathos and humour on his own death, there is a flash from the eyes which Pope—good hater and good friend—said were azure as the heavens, a touch of the hand that was never weary of giving gifts to the poor and blows to the powerful, a reflection of the universal *condottiere*, misanthrope and sceptic, who has a claim to our forbearance in that he detested, as Johnson and as Byron detested, cowardice and cant.

—JOHN NICHOL, "Jonathan Swift," *The English Poets*,
ed. Thomas Humphry Ward, 1880, vol. 3, pp. 35–38

John Churton Collins
"Characteristics" (1893)

The chief peculiarity of Swift's temper lay in the coexistence not merely of opposite qualities but of opposite natures. The union of a hard, cold, logical intellect with a heart of almost feminine tenderness is no uncommon anomaly. But the anomaly which Swift presents is not an anomaly of this kind. In acute susceptibility to sensuous and emotional impression he resembled Rousseau and Shelley. His nervous organisation was quite as exquisite, his sensibility as keen, his perceptions as nice. He was as dependent on human sympathy and on human affection; he was as passionately moved by what men less finely tempered regard with composure. The sight of a fellow-creature in distress or pain, the spectacle of an unjust or cruel action, a fancied slight conveyed in a word or look, an offensive or disagreeable object, were to him, as to them, little less than torture. Thus on the sensuous and emotional side he had the temperament of the poet and the enthusiast. But Nature had not completed what she had begun. She had bestowed on him the *cor cordium;* she had endowed him with 'the love of love' and 'the hate of hate'; she had been lavish of the gifts which are the poet's most painful inheritance; but from all else, from all that constitutes the poet's solaces, the poet's charm, the poet's power, she had excluded him. Utterly devoid of a sense of the beautiful, of the beautiful in nature, in the human form, in morals, in art, in philosophy, he neither sought it nor recognised it when seen. Its representation in concrete form is always perverted by him into the grotesque and ugly. As a critic and philosopher he has only one criterion—plain good sense in the one case, practical utility in the other. Of any perception of the ideal, of any sympathy with effort or tendency to aspire to it, he was as destitute as Sancho Panza and Falstaff. On no class of people have the shafts of his contemptuous raillery fallen thicker than on those who would seek for finer bread than is made of flour, and on the originators of Utopian schemes. His own ideal of life began and ended, as he himself frankly admitted, with the attainment of worldly success.[1] Of transcendental imagination, nay, of the transcendental instinct, he had nothing. He never appears to have had even a glimpse of those truths which lie outside the scope of the senses and the reason, and which find their expression in poetry and in sentimental religion. He never refers to them as embodied in the first without ridicule and contempt, nor as embodied in the second without coldly resolving them into compulsory dogmas. 'Violent zeal for Truth,' he observes, 'has a hundred to one odds to be either petulancy, ambition, or pride.'[2] If he does not deny the divine element in man and in the world, it is only because it forms an article of the creed which for other reasons he thought it expedient to uphold. But what he did not deny he either ignored or obscured. A conception of human nature and of human life more inconsistent than his with any theory of divinity either within man or without it would be impossible to find, even in the writings of professed atheists. 'Miserable mortals!' he exclaims in his *Thoughts on Religion,* 'can we contribute to the honour and glory of God? I could wish that expression were struck out of our prayer-books.' His whole conception of religion appears to have been almost purely political. What Fielding puts into the mouth of Thwackum is literally descriptive of Swift's attitude: 'When I mention religion I mean the Christian religion; and not only the Christian religion, but the Protestant; and not only the Protestant, but the Church of England.' He makes no distinction between Deists and Nonconformists, between Roman Catholics and Infidels. They are all equally denounced, and regarded as equally excluded from the pale of what constitutes 'religion.' And what constitutes religion has been prescribed by the State. To that every man should be compelled to adhere. In relation to its essence and apart from its accidents he never contemplates it. 'Religion,' he insists, 'supposes Heaven and Hell, the Word of God, and Sacraments.'[3] He complains bitterly that men should be allowed a freedom in religious matters which they are not allowed in political; that a citizen who prefers a commonwealth to monarchy, and who should endeavour to establish one, would be punished with the utmost rigour of the law, but that a citizen who prefers Nonconformity to Episcopalianism is at perfect liberty to choose the one instead of the other.[4] So completely are the spiritual and essential elements of religion subordinated to its political and temporal utility, that he contends boldly that the truth or falsehood of the fundamental opinions on which the creed of the Christian rests are of comparatively little moment compared with the mischief involved in questioning them; that it is not requisite for a man to believe what he professes; and that it matters little what doubts and scruples he may have, provided he keeps them to himself.[5] A man may be allowed, he observes elsewhere in reference to this subject, to keep poisons in his closet, but not to vend them about for cordials.[6] If, as has been sometimes supposed, he depicts his ideal man in the King of Brobdingnag, and his ideal of human excellence in the Houyhnhnms, it is remarkable that religion has no place in the education and life of either. The virtues of the former are those of pure stoicism; the virtues of the latter are summed up in friendship, benevolence, temperance, industry, and cleanliness.

It is, of course, impossible to say, but it is very doubtful whether Swift's own opinions inclined certainly towards belief in the promises of Christianity, or even in a future state. The balance of probability is decidedly adverse to the first supposition, and wavers very uncertainly in favour of the second. His attitude towards the metaphysics of Christianity is always the same; he never dwells on them, and whenever it is possible he avoids them. In his sermon on the Trinity he speaks of his theme as 'a subject which probably I should not have chosen if I had not been invited to it.' Rigidly orthodox, he repeats over and over again that what the Church teaches is no matter for argument and question, but must be accepted implicitly and in its integrity. Episcopal Protestant Christianity supplies as a coercive moral agency what no system of morality apart from it is able to supply; it must, therefore, be retained, and if it is not retained with all its dogmas it ceases to be Christianity.[7] This is his note throughout in apology as in exegesis. Without unction, without fervour, without sentiment, he leaves us with the impression that he neither sought nor found in the Gospel which he accepted and delivered so faithfully anything that illuminated or anything that cheered. Of its power as a source of consolation in sorrow he was well aware. 'Take courage from Christianity,' he writes to Mrs. Whiteway, 'which will assist you when humanity fails.' But he took from it, or seems to have taken from it, little courage himself. It is mournfully apparent that no ray from the creed of faith and hope pierced the gloom of that long night which descended on the winter of his life. Assuming, as a churchman, the truth of Christianity, he was bound also, as a churchman, to assume the existence of a future state. But the evidence for supposing that it formed any article of his personal belief is very slight. In his *Thoughts on Religion* he makes no reference to it, but observes of death that a thing so natural, so necessary, and so universal could not have been designed by Providence as an evil to mankind. In his sermons he never dwells on it. In his letters of consolation in bereavement he wrote, of course, as propriety dictated that a clergyman should write. And yet even here his expressions are frequently very guarded and sometimes ambiguous. 'Religion regards life,' he writes to Mrs. Moore on the death of her daughter, 'only as a preparation for a better, which you are taught to be certain that so innocent a person is now in possession of.'[8] He would, he said to Pope, exchange youth for advanced old age, if he could be as secure of a better life as Mrs. Pope deemed herself.[9] 'If,' he remarked when his mother died, 'the way to Heaven be through piety, truth, justice and charity, she is there.' In his reflections on the death of Esther Johnson he makes no reference to immortality. In the prayers which he offered for her in her last illness he expresses a hope that she 'may be received into everlasting habitations,' but there is nothing to indicate that he felt the smallest confidence in the realisation of such hopes. His own epitaph is without a trace of Christian sentiment—that he had found in the grave a haven *ubi sæva indignatio ulterius cor lacerare nequit*—that he had left in his life an example which all who loved liberty would do well to imitate—this was the only assurance, this the only admonition, which he desired to proclaim from the tomb. It is possible, of course, that his reticence and reserve on religious subjects had its origin in the same cause which led him to conceal so studiously from guests in his house the fact that he daily read prayers to his servants—that it arose from his detestation of pretence and especially of pretentious piety. And this is by no means improbable, for there can be little doubt that, had he been as convinced of the truth of the Christian dogmas as St. Paul himself, he would have avoided ostentatious or enthusiastic profession.[10] But a distinction must be made between the avoidance of ostentatious or enthusiastic profession and such an attitude as Swift's. We must take into consideration the whole tenor of his character and writings, and the impression conveyed by them is that of a man who was endeavouring honestly to support a part. He was convinced of the absolute necessity of maintaining, in the interests of society as well as of particular individuals, the Christian religion with all its dogmas; he felt that the balance of what he could accept as sound and true in its teaching was more and much more than a counterpoise to what might be unsound and untrue; and he probably felt that what he could not accept he could not absolutely pronounce to be false. Applying the test of the politician, the magistrate, and the philanthropist, he was content to dispense with the test of the transcendental philosopher.[11] Hence his habit of avoiding all discussion of such subjects as the immortality of the soul and a future state, his guarded phrases, his plain unwillingness to commit himself to expressions of his personal opinions, his appeals to reason rather than to faith, the ethical as distinguished from the theological character of his teaching, the absence, in the stress of affliction, of any indication of faith and hope.

His deficiency on the side of what we commonly call sentiment is not less remarkable. Sentiment is never likely to be found in any great degree where the transcendental instinct is lacking. But the total atrophy, or rather non-existence, of both in a man of strong affections and of acute susceptibility to emotional impression is an anomaly rare indeed in the temper of men. Of sentiment Swift was so wholly devoid that it was unintelligible to him. Its expression in language he regarded as cant, its expression in action as affectation and folly. For him life had no illusions, man no mystery, nature no charm. He looked on woman's beauty with the eye of an anatomist, on earth's beauties with the eye of a chemist. In the passion which not unfrequently transforms even the grossest and most commonplace of human beings into poets he saw only brutal appetite, masquerading in fantastic frippery. And his delight was to strip it bare. All that fancy, all that imagination, all that sentiment had woven round it torn contemptuously away, he gloated with horrid glee over the naked shame of nature. For religious enthusiasm he could discern only physical causes; sometimes he refers it to hysterics or to sexual excitement taking a wrong turn, sometimes to a diseased and disordered brain. More generally he regards it as mere affectation assumed for the purpose of making money or of gratifying vanity by acquiring notoriety. His sole criterion as a critic and judge was unsublimated reason. In his estimate of men he made no allowance for impulse and passion except as indicating depravity or weakness. In his estimate of life and the world generally he saw everything in the clear cold light of the pure intellect. From no mind of which we have expression in record had the Spectres of the Tribe, the Den, the Forum, and the Theatre been so completely exorcised. But, as the eyes of the body may be blinded by excess of light, so the eyes of the mind may by excess of reason be blinded—by the very power which should give them sight. Of the truth by which men live, mere reason indeed obscures almost as much as she reveals. If life took its colour and its pattern from the philosophy of Swift as that philosophy finds embodiment in his ideal king and in his ideal creatures, how insipid would it become, how torpid, how inglorious! Swift's philosophy is indeed in essence precisely the philosophy of Falstaff in his soliloquy on honour:—

> "What need I be so forward with him that calls not on me? Well, 'tis no matter; honour pricks me on. Yea, but how if honour prick me off when I come on? how then? Can honour set to a leg? no: or an arm? no: or take away the grief of a wound? no. Honour hath no skill in surgery, then? no. What is honour? a word. What is in that word honour? what is that honour? air. A trim reckoning! Who hath it? he that died o' Wednesday. Doth he feel it? no. Doth he hear it? no. 'Tis insensible, then. Yea, to the dead. But will it not live with the living? no. Why? detraction will not suffer it. Therefore I'll none of it. Honour is a mere scutcheon: and so ends my catechism."

Now, apart from transcendental considerations, apart from sentiment, apart, in fine, from all that Swift ignores, how unanswerable is logic like this, how irrefutable the reasoning! But it is reasoning against which all that constitutes the true dignity and beauty of human life rises in revolt. It would paralyse the wings of the soul, dwarf and blight the heroic virtues, and degrade the whole level of action and aspiration. As Shakespeare's generous enthusiast so well says:—

> Manhood and honour
> Should have hare hearts, would they but fat their thoughts
> With this cramm'd reason: reason and respect
> Make livers pale, and lustihood deject.

Swift said himself that his favourite author was La Rochefoucauld, 'because 1 find my whole character in him.'[12] The remark is significant, and the resemblance in some respects between them unquestionable. But his true prototype was Hobbes. Hobbes had none of Swift's acute sensibility, none of his tense and vehement seriousness, nothing of his Titanism, nothing of his humour. But for the rest the analogy between them was complete. The intelligence of both moved only in the sphere of the senses and the pure reason. Pessimists and cynics by both temper and conviction, they were deficient in all those instincts and sympathies on which every true estimate and every true philosophy of humanity must be based. Both resolved mankind into mere animals, and the Yahoos of Swift are the 'natural men' of Hobbes. Both reduced all that ennobles, all that beautifies, all that consecrates life, to a *caput mortuum*. Both denied practically, and even ridiculed as metaphysical thinkers, what they asserted and maintained as ethical political legislators. Both, in effect, eliminated the element of supernaturalism, and defended religion on civil grounds. Hobbes based its sanction and authority on the will of the State, Swift practically on the will of the State Church. When Hobbes wrote 'It is with the mysteries of our religion as with wholesome pills for the sick, which, swallowed whole, have the virtue to cure, but chewed are for the most part cast up again without effect,'[13] he condensed what is in essence the argument of Swift. Both, by nature pure despots, regarded the mass of their fellow-men as fools and knaves, to be ruled with justice indeed, and, if possible, with clemency, but to be ruled with a rod of iron.

But it must not be forgotten that, if this anti-ideality and cynicism found its intensest and most powerful expression in Swift, it was essentially characteristic of the age into which he was born and in which he died. That age may be compared to a deep valley between two eminences. On the one side are the heights to which the enthusiasm of the Renaissance and the enthusiasm of Puritanism had elevated the national spirit; on the other side is the ascent sloping upwards to the equally lofty tablelands of the idealists of the New World. Between the year of Swift's birth and the first administration of Pitt, it may be safely said that in all that ennobles and in all that beautifies human life and human nature England had reached her lowest level. The morals and temper of the London of the Restoration would have disgusted the Romans of St. Paul, while much of its literature would hardly have been tolerated by the friends of Trimalchion. After the accession of Anne, it is generally supposed that the evil spirit of the preceding era was exorcised, and that a new and good spirit entered in. And this is to some extent true. The example set by the Queen herself, the decency and decorum observed at her Court, and the writings of Addison and his circle, undoubtedly exercised a salutary influence on society. But all that was touched was the surface. The change was more apparent than real. The filth, the cynicism, the inhumanity, the unbelief of the former age underlay—a foul substratum—the specious exterior. The accession of George I. rendered concealment no longer necessary, and with some slight modification all became as all had been before.[14] Wherever we turn we find variously diluted and variously coloured what we find condensed in Swift. What is Prior but the poet of disillusion? His most elaborate poem was written to show the nothingness of man and of the world, his *Alma* to ridicule metaphysics, his most successful tales to laugh romance to scorn; his best lyrics are but cynical trifles. What is Gay but an elegant fribble, who ordered a flippant jest to be inscribed as his epitaph?[15] Even the fine genius of Pope is without wings, and many of the passages which exhibit his powers in their highest perfection are directed to the ignoble purpose of degrading his species. Mandeville's *Fable of the Bees* is as shameless a libel on humanity as the *Voyage to the Houyhnhnms,* and his *Virgin Unmasked* would have disgraced Wycherley. In the *Richardsoniana* we have the very alcohol of cynicism. The greatest painter of the age devoted his talents to bringing into prominence all that is most humiliating and odious in man, and the pens of De Foe and Smollett vied with the pencil of Hogarth in depicting and heightening moral and physical ugliness and depravity. Nor is this spirit less apparent when it finds urbaner and more refined expression. The correspondence of Pope, of Bolingbroke, of Lady Mary Wortley Montagu, the conversations recorded by Spence, the Memoirs of Lord Hervey, and, indeed, the greater part of the polite literature and all the *ana* of the age, are the records of a society which, with *Que sçais-je?* for its motto, and *Nil admirari* for its creed, prided itself on its superiority to enthusiasm, to sentiment, to the ideal. If we turn to theology and philosophy, we find ourselves on the same low level. When Reid wrote, 'Philosophy has no other root but the principles of common sense; it grows out of them; it draws its nourishment from them; severed from this root its honours wither, its sap is dried up, it dies and rots;[16] and when Pope wrote

Good sense, which only is the gift of Heaven,
And, though no science, fairly worth the seven,

they merely expressed what has expression everywhere in the writings of their immediate predecessors and contemporaries. It was the age of the Deistic Controversy, of the sermons of Wake, Gibson, Sherlock, and Hare. The test of religious truth was social utility—its sanction, reason. 'I send my servants to church,' said Anthony Collins, 'that they may neither rob nor murder me'; and if he spoke as a freethinker he adduced what was practically the chief argument of the most orthodox theologians of that day in favour of supernaturalism. As the apostle of ideal truth not simply in the technical but in the comprehensive sense of the term, Berkeley stood absolutely alone. To eliminate as far as possible the transcendental element from religion, and to show how life may be sustained upon a minimum of moral and spiritual assumption, appears to have been the main object of the divines and moralists of those times.

But to return. Thackeray, in speaking of Swift's last days, has finely said: 'So great a man he seems to me, that thinking of him is like thinking of an empire falling.' The expression is not exaggerated. Swift is the one figure of colossal proportions in the age to which he belonged. Nay, we may go further. Among men whose fame depends mainly on their writings, there is, if we except Aristotle, Shakespeare, and perhaps Bacon, probably no man on record who impresses us with a sense of such enormous intellectual power. He has always the air of a giant sporting among pigmies, crushing or scrutinising, helping or thwarting them, as the mood takes him. Immense strength, immense energy, now frittering themselves away on trifles, now roused for a moment to concentrated action by passion, interest, or benevolence, but never assuming their true proportions, never developing into full activity—this is what we discern in Swift. We feel how miserably incommensurate was the part he played with the part which Nature had fitted him to play, how contracted was the stage, how mighty the capacities of the actor. In his pamphlets, in his two great satires, in his poems, in his correspondence, is the impression of a character which there is no mistaking. And it is not among philosophers, poets, and men of letters that we are to look for its prototype or its analogy, but among those who have made and unmade nations—among men like Caesar and men like Napoleon.

A comparison between Napoleon at St. Helena and Swift in Ireland has more than once been drawn. With two great distinctions between them, namely, that Napoleon was, morally speaking, an essentially bad man, and Swift an essentially good man, and that the one was without heart and the other with the heart of a woman, it would be possible to institute a parallel not simply between their relative position as exiles but between their temper and characteristics. Both scorned the homage which they punctiliously exacted, and the prizes for which they fought. Devouring ambition, finding in itself not merely the motive but the centre of action, and originating, if partly from the lust of dominion, partly also from the restless importunity of superabundant, nay almost preternatural energy, was the ruling passion of both.[17] Egotists, despots, and cynics, each owned no equal, each had no real confidant. The one towered over his kind on the sublime heights of power, the other in the proud solitude of his own consciousness. What was potential in the one found full and unimpeded expression; what was potential in the other perished undeveloped in embryo. But the genius which could indemnify itself for the lack of the material and conventional symbols of supremacy by writing *Gulliver's Travels* was in essence of the same superhuman type as the genius which half realised universal empire.

What Swift suffered in failing to attain the prizes which his haughty spirit coveted is only too plain from his diaries and correspondence. His pride amounted to disease. He was always on the watch for fancied slights. If a great man left a letter unanswered for a few days, or a friend let fall an ambiguous word, he was miserable. A man passing him in the streets without touching his hat or a woman failing to drop a curtsey seriously discomposed him.[18] To whatever degree of mere intimacy he admitted a person who could amuse or entertain him, he guarded his dignity with the most jealous care. 'He could not,' says Deane Swift, 'endure to be treated with any sort of familiarity, or that any man living, his three or four old acquaintances with whom he corresponded to the last only excepted, should rank himself in the number of his friends.'[19] His superiority to envy, of which he had not, we are told, the smallest tincture, his indifference to literary fame, and his scrupulous truthfulness in all that related to himself, had their origin in the same lofty consciousness of supereminence.

Such were the characteristics and temper of Swift. And it would seem as if Fortune, perceiving what opportunities Nature had given her for malicious sport, had in some spiteful mood resolved to make his life her cruel plaything. Everything that could depress, annoy, and irritate was his lot in youth. His early manhood, initiated by the fatal blunder he made in taking orders, miserable in itself, involved him in deeper miseries still. An

> abandon'd wretch, by hope forsook,
> Forsook by hopes, ill fortune's last relief,
> Assign'd for life to unremitting grief;
> For, let Heaven's wrath enlarge these weary days,
> If Hope e'er dawns the smallest of its rays[20]

—it was thus that he could write of himself at a time when most men are bounding blithely from the starting-post of life. Whenever a ray seemed to pierce the gloom it was always illusory. Hope after hope glimmered only to be extinguished. Even the paltry prizes he despised were beyond his reach, and his forty-third year found him eating out his heart in an obscure Irish vicarage. Then came power and eminence, without the glory and without the guerdon. A dictator and an underling, a despot and a tool, for nearly four years of his life, all that could pamper and flatter, and all that could gall and irritate his arrogant and sensitive spirit were his mingled portion. With exile as the reward of services great beyond any expression of gratitude, in that exile were accumulated tenfold all causes of irritation, till irritation became torture, till torture goaded passion into fury. And brooding over the life of this unhappy man, wretched alike in what he owed to Nature and in the spite of Fortune, hung a phantom horror. As there can be no doubt that Swift was never insane, and that the maladies from which he suffered had no connection with insanity, so there can equally be no doubt that he was himself convinced of the contrary—was convinced that he carried within him the gradually developing germs of madness, and that his terrible doom was inevitable.[21]

It has been sometimes supposed that Swift's rage for obscenity, so inconsistent with the austere purity of his morals and with his aversion to anything approaching indecency in conversation, had its origin in physical disease—that it was, as it so often is, a phase of insanity. But it is perfectly explicable without resorting to any such hypothesis. An observation of his own furnishes us with the true key—a nice man is a man of nasty ideas;[22] and he was one of the nicest and most fastidious of men. But its expression in its most offensive forms is to be attributed partly to misanthropy, intensifying this depraved sensibility, and partly to a desire to furnish dissuasives from vice. Of such poems as the 'Lady's Dressing Room' Delany observes, and probably with perfect justice, that they were 'the prescriptions of an able physician, who had the health of his patients at heart, but laboured to attain that end not only by strong emetics, but also by all the most offensive drugs and potions that could be administered.' He was, in truth, doing nothing more than the Saints and Fathers of the Church have habitually done, and with the same object. There are passages, for example, in St. Chrysostom and in St. Gregory, which are as nauseous and disgusting as anything that can be found in Swift. But this plea cannot be always, or indeed generally, urged in his defence; and how, in allowing himself such licence, he could see nothing incompatible with his position and behaviour as a clergyman, must remain a mystery.[23] Something is no doubt to be attributed to the age in which he lived, something to his constitution, and more to his rage against his kind. What is certain is that, as his misanthropy intensified, his imagination grew fouler and his filth became more noisome.

The writings of Swift are the exact reflection of his character, variously expressing itself on its various sides. Affectation and pretentiousness were his abhorrence; for literary fame he cared nothing, and he had therefore no inducement to aspire beyond the natural level of his powers. He wrote out of the fulness of his mind, as impulse or passion directed, practically, for the attainment of some immediate object, or idly, to amuse himself. To books he owed comparatively little. Butler was his model in verse. If he had any models in prose, they were the tracts of Father Parsons, and one of the most powerful political pieces extant in our language, Silas Titus' *Killing No Murder*. As a political pamphleteer, Swift is without a rival. Fenelon observed of Cicero, that when the Romans heard him they exclaimed, 'It is the voice of a God;' and of Demosthenes, that when the Athenians heard him they cried, 'Let us march against Philip.' The remark indicates the distinction between Swift's political pieces and the political pieces of such writers as Bolingbroke, Junius, and Burke. Compared with him, they appear to be but splendid sophists, maintaining with all the resources of rhetoric, and all the experience and skill of practised advocates, a case for the prosecution or a case for the defence. If the truth is of little moment to us, we concede to admiration what we ought to concede only to conviction. But the impression produced by Swift is the impression produced by a powerful and logical mind, with no object but the investigation of truth, amply furnished with the means of ascertaining it, and convinced itself before attempting to convince others. His profound knowledge of human nature and his experience of affairs enabled him to bring every point home, and to assume naturally, and with propriety, an air of authority such as in any mere man of letters would be affectation.

Swift is a poet only by courtesy. Good sense, humour, and wit are as a rule the distinguishing characteristics of his poetry, though, as Scott well observes, the intensity of his satire sometimes gives to his verses an emphatic violence which borders on grandeur, as in the *Rhapsody* and in the poem on the Last Day. But, if Apollo disowned him, he was not altogether deserted by the Graces, as *Cadenus and Vanessa* shows; and of the attributes of the poet a touch of fancy may certainly be claimed for him. It would, however, be doing him great injustice to deny his claim to a high place among masters of the *sermo pedestris*. As descriptive pieces his 'City Shower' and his 'Early Morning in London' are pictures worthy of Hogarth; his adaptations from Horace and Ovid are eminently felicitous and pleasing, while the verses on his own death and the 'Grand Question Debated' are among the best things of their kind. Some of his other trifles, particularly his Epistles, will always find delighted readers. His verse, though too mechanically monotonous, is unlaboured and flowing, his diction terse and yet easy and natural. In the art of rhyming, an accomplishment on which he especially prided himself, he has few superiors, and his rhymes are as exact and correct as they are ingenious and novel. Even the author of *Don Juan* spoke of himself as contemplating Swift's mastery over rhyme with admiring despair.

It is, of course, as a humorist and satirist that Swift is and will continue to be a power in literature. Models as his political pieces are—in their style nervous, simple, trenchant—in their method lucid, logical—in their tone masculine, vehement—few perhaps but historical students will turn to them, for to none but historical students will their ephemeral matter be intelligible. Two-thirds of his other writings have long ceased to be of interest to the many, but the *Battle of the Books*, the *Tale of a Tub*, the *Arguments against Abolishing Christianity*, the *Modest Proposal*, a dozen or two of his poems, and *Gulliver*, will keep his fame fresh in every generation. Here, then, are to be found the qualities upon which his claim to a place among classics must rest. They are easily distinguished. The first attribute of genius is originality, and Swift was essentially original. It is true that he was indebted to others for the hint of his three chief satires, but, as he has himself observed, if a man lights his candle at his neighbour's fire it does not affect his property in the candle which he lights.[24] Probably no other writer with the exception of Dickens has borrowed so little. His images and ideas are almost always his own; his humour is his own; his style is his own. In a well-known passage he claims to have been the first to introduce and teach the use of irony:—

> Arbuthnot is no more my friend,
> Who does to irony pretend,
> Which I was born to introduce,
> Refin'd it first, and taught its use.

This was not strictly true, as he had been anticipated by De Foe, whose *Shortest Way with the Dissenters* appeared nearly two years before the earliest of Swift's writings had been published. But a title to a place among classics depends not merely on originality—it depends also on quality, on the intrinsic value and interest of what is produced. Swift's serious reflections and remarks are the perfection of homely good sense—shrewd, trenchant, pointed, enriching life with new and useful truths. But his good sense is without refinement, without imagination, and without subtlety. The sphere in which his intelligence worked and within which his sympathy and insight were bounded was, comparatively speaking, a narrow one. He had the eye of a lynx for all that moves on the surface of life and for all that may be found on the beaten highway of commonplace experience, but the depths he neither explored nor perhaps even suspected. In his innumerable aphorisms, generalisations, and precepts it would be impossible to find one which either indicates delicate discrimination or reveals a glimpse of ideal truth.

His style has in itself little distinction and no charm, but for his purposes it is the more effective from the absence of distinction. A pure medium of expression, it owes nothing to art, for he disdained ornament and he disdained elaboration. To eloquence he makes no pretension. Proper words in proper places was his own ideal of a good style, and he was satisfied with attaining it.

As a master of irony he has few if any equals. It was his favourite weapon, tempered as finely as that with which the Platonic Socrates disarmed Protagoras and Hippias, and as that with which the author of the *Provincial Letters* lacerated the disciples of Le Moine and Father Annat. But the fineness of its temper constituted its chief resemblance to the irony of Plato and Pascal. It is without urbanity, without lightness, and without grace. Austere and saturnine, bitter and intense, it would seem strangely out of place as the ally of pleasantry; and yet seldom has pleasantry been so happily mated. Other humorists may move us to merriment and convulse us with laughter, but the irony of Swift is a source of more delicious enjoyment, of more exquisite pleasure. In its lighter forms it springs from a nice and subtle perception of the unbecoming and the ridiculous in their lighter and more trivial aspects, tempered with scorn and contempt; in its severer, from a similar perception of the same improprieties in their most impressive and most serious aspects, tempered not with scorn merely but with loathing, not with contempt merely but with horror and rage. The extremes are marked by the Dissertations in the *Tale of a Tub* and by the *Directions to Servants* on the one side, by the *Modest Proposal* and the *Voyage to the Houyhnhnms* on the other. And the mean is in the *Voyage to Brobdingnag*. It is in irony that Swift's humour most generally finds expression, and always finds its most characteristic expression. And naturally. Wherever intelligence of clairvoyant insight, however narrow its area, together with a calm or contemptuous consciousness of superiority, is united with acute sensibility and with the keenest perception of the difference between things as they seem and things as they are, irony will always be the note.

The attitude of Swift towards life and man is precisely that of Juvenal's deity—*ridet et odit*—he laughs and loathes. And his humour is the laughter. It is never good-natured. It is always sardonic, presenting a complete contrast to that of Cervantes and to that of Shakespeare. When we turn to the line which Shakespeare put into the mouth of Puck, 'Lord, what fools these mortals be!' and to the *Tempest,* and then to the *Voyage to the Houyhnhnms,* and to the poem in which the Deity dismisses his cowering creatures from the judgment bar, as too despicable to be damned—

I to such blockheads set my wit!
I damn such fools! Go go—*you're bit*—

we measure the difference between the humour 'which sees life steadily and sees it whole' and the humour of the mere Titan.

Swift forms one of an immortal trio. In the writings of Addison will be mirrored for all time the image of a beautiful human soul. Humour genial and kindly as it is exquisite, wit refined and polished as it is rich and abundant, and a style approaching as nearly to perfection as it is perhaps possible for style to do, will unite with the charm of his character in keeping his memory green. If the poetry of Pope has not the vogue it once had, the fame of the most brilliant of poets is secure. He may not have the homage of the multitude, but he will have in every generation, as long as our language lasts, the homage of all who can discern. He stands indeed with Horace, Juvenal, and Dryden at the head of a great department of poetry—the poetry of ethics and satire. But the third of the trio will as a name and as a power overshadow the other two. Before his vast proportions they seem indeed to dwindle into insignificance. And what figure in that eighteenth century of time is not dwarfed beside this Momus-Prometheus? Among men, but not of them, at war with himself, with the world, and with destiny, he set at naught the warning which Greek wisdom was never weary of repeating—

Born into life we are, and life must be our mould.

He was in temper all that Pindar symbolises in Typhon, and all that revolts Plato in the inharmonious and unmusical soul. And so, while his writings bear the impress of powers such as have rarely been conceded to man, they reflect and return with repulsive fidelity the ugliness and discord of the Titanism which inspired them. Without reverence and without reticence, he gloried in the licence which to the Greeks constituted the last offence against good taste and good sense, and out of the indulgence in which they have coined a synonym for shamelessness—the indiscriminate expression of what ought and what ought not to be said. A cynic and a misanthrope in principle, his philosophy of life is ignoble, base, and false, and his impious mockery extends even to the Deity. A large portion of his works exhibit, and in intense activity, all the worst attributes of our nature—revenge, spite, malignity, unclean-ness. His life, indeed, afforded a noble example of duty conscientiously fulfilled, of great services done to his kind, and of an active benevolence which knew no bounds. But it is not by these virtues that he will be remembered. He will live as one of the most commanding and fascinating figures which has ever appeared on the stage of life, and as the protagonist of a drama which can never cease to interest the student of human life and of human nature. In every generation his works will be read, but they will be read not so much for themselves as for their association. The fame of the man will preserve and support the fame of the author. For there is probably no writer of equal power and eminence in whose judgments and conclusions, in whose precepts and teaching, the instincts and experience of progressive humanity will find so little to corroborate.

Notes

1. 'All my endeavours, from a boy, to distinguish myself were only for the want of a great title and fortune, that I might be used like a lord by those who have an opinion of my parts, whether right or wrong it is no great matter; and so the reputation of wit and great learning does the office of a blue ribbon or of a coach and six horses.' (Letter to Bolingbroke, April 5, [1729])
2. *Thoughts on Religion* (*Works*, Bonn ed. viii. 173).
3. *Advice to a Young Poet* (*Works*, ix. 392).
4. *Thoughts on Religion* (*Id.* viii. 176).
5. *Thoughts on Religion* (*Works*, viii. 174).
6. *Gulliver's Travels—Voyage to Brobdingnag.*
7. See Sermons, *passim*, but particularly that on the Testimony of Conscience.
8. See his beautiful letter (*Works*, xvii. 197).
9. Letter to Pope, *Id.* p. 224.
10. 'There was no vice', says Delany, 'he so much abhorred as hypocrisy, and of consequence nothing he dreaded so much as to be suspected of it, and this made him often conceal his piety with more care than others take to conceal their vices.'—*Observations*, pp. 43–44.
11. Swift's opinions on religion probably differed little from those expressed so admirably by Polybius, vi. ch. 56, 57; by Strabo, i. ch. 2, 8; and by Cicero, *De Legibus*, ii. ch. 7.
12. Letter to Pope, Nov. 26, 1725.
13. *Leviathan,* ch. xxxii.
14. For the temper and tone of the England of Swift see particularly Hartley's *Observations on Man*, ii. 441, not published till 1749, but written many years before; Butler's *Preface to the Analogy*; Warburton's *Dedication to the Divine Legation*; Whiston's *Memoirs*, Part III. pp. 142–213; Voltaire, *Lettres sur les Anglais*; Montesquieu, *Notes on England*, where he says, 'Point de religion en Angleterre; si quelqu'un parle de religion, tout le monde se met a rire'; Hervey's *Memoirs*; the *Suffolk Papers*; Atterbury's *Representation*.
15. Life is a jest: and all things show it.
     I thought so once, and now I know it.

16. *Inquiry into the Human Mind.* Introduction, p. 4.
17. To this constitutional restlessness, to this morbid activity of mind, which was so striking a trait of Napoleon, Swift frequently refers. Thus in a letter to Kendall, dated February, 1691/2, he says, 'A person of great honour in Ireland used to tell me that my mind was like a conjured spirit that would do mischief if I did not give it employment. It is this humour which makes me so busy.' Again, in a letter recently printed by the Historical Manuscripts Commissioners, 'I myself was never very miserable while my thoughts were in a ferment, for I imagine a dead calm is the troublesomest of our voyage through the world.'
18. To confine illustrations to the diary at Holyhead—'The master of the pacquet boat hath not treated me with the least civility, altho' Watt gave him my name . . . yet my hat is worn to pieces by answering the civilities of the poor inhabitants as they pass by. I am as insignificant here as Parson Brooke is in Dublin. By my conscience, I believe Cæsar would be the same without his army at his back . . . Not a soul is yet come to Holyhead except a young fellow who smiles when he meets me and would fain be my companion, but it is not come to that yet . . . if I stay here much longer I am afraid all my pride and grandeur will truckle to comply with him.'
19. *Essay on Swift,* p. 361.
20. 'Verses on Sir W. Temple's Illness and Recovery,' written at Moor Park in 1693.
21. This is placed beyond doubt by the well-known incident recorded by Young in his *Conjectures on Original Composition.* The incident almost certainly occurred in or about 1717. See Scott, i. 443–44.
22. *Thoughts on Various Subjects.*
23. What is still more surprising is that, although these productions appeared anonymously, it was no secret that they were from the pen of the Dean of St. Patrick's; and how Swift, who in private life and in conversation never forgot and never allowed others to forget the respect due to his cloth, could expose himself to the derogatory retorts which his licence in this respect provoked is inexplicable. Yet so it was. See a ribald poem called 'The Dean's Provocation', which professes to account for the reason of his writing the 'Lady's Dressing Room'.
24. *Advice to a Young Poet.*

—John Churton Collins, "Characteristics,"
Jonathan Swift: A Biographical and Critical Study,
1893, pp. 241–268

HERBERT PAUL "THE PRINCE OF JOURNALISTS" (1900)

Journalists have acquired a habit of talking about each other. Twenty years, or even ten years, ago, they were as little inclined to blow the trumpet of their profession—occupation they would have called it then—as the permanent members of the Civil Service, who, as the late Lord Farrer so admirably said, prefer power to fame. Even their consciousness of one another's infirmities, always perhaps acute, was confined to private conversation. Journalism might have withstood all attacks upon its shrinking modesty but for the establishment of that excellent society, the Institute of Journalists. One form of self-assertion leads to another, and a presumptuous person ventured last summer to deliver at Oxford, in academic disguise, a lecture on Modern Journalism. In the course of it he expressed the opinion that the greatest journalist who ever lived was Jonathan Swift. As I think he was right on that point, however mistaken he may have been on others, I should like to support and develop the paradox. I use the word paradox in its proper sense of what is contrary to accepted belief, but is nevertheless true. If a paradox be not true, it is mere nonsense.

No one, or scarcely any one, thinks of Swift as connected with the press. As a satirist, as a poet, above all as a humourist, he is of course an English classic. Politicians, if they have read him, know that, in spite of his cloth, he was pre-eminently a statesman. But few of those who admire him the least have gone so far as to suggest that he was a journalist. Yet he wrote regularly, he wrote anonymously, he wrote on politics, and, if any further proof be needed, he wrote on both sides. He did not indeed write against time. His were days of leisure, not of morning and evening papers. Nor did he write ostensibly for money. But the Deanery of St. Patrick's was a reward for his political services, and may, I suppose, be reckoned as deferred pay. I doubt whether any great writer has put his name to so few productions as Swift. To the day of his death he never would acknowledge the work which prevented him from becoming a Bishop, the *Tale of a Tub*. The most famous of his controversial tracts were ascribed by a transparent fiction to a draper of Dublin. The one essay which appeared with Swift's name upon the title-page was the plea for setting up an English Academy of Letters, which, if it did not lower his reputation, has certainly not raised it. The robust common sense of Dr. Johnson, who knew the virtues and the foibles of Englishmen with a perfect knowledge, supplied in a single sentence the epitaph of that proposal. If such an academy were created, he said, most men would be willing, and many men would be proud, to disobey its decrees. With that solitary and perfunctory exception, Swift left his arguments and his illustrations, his invective and his sarcasm, to make their own mark upon the world. That that mark would be deep and ineffaceable, he must have known long before his mind sank into prematurely senile decay. No man was more fully conscious of his own tremendous powers. His genius burst, almost without an effort, the bonds of poverty and obscurity, of an uncontrollable temper and a sullen pride. He trampled on the insufferable patronage of the conventionally great with an arrogance more excessive than their own. He propitiated no one, he conciliated no one, and when he was doing the work of a Tory Ministry, he insisted upon a deference from Tory Ministers which in that ceremonious age must have seemed even stranger than it would now. After the death of Sir William Temple, upon whom he was dependent, and to whom in his way he was grateful, he called no man master. Indeed he called hardly any man equal. The force which he wielded without fear or pity, without mercy or scruple, was the force of sheer intellectual supremacy. Of his literary friends the only one who could be compared with him was Pope, and Swift came far nearer to Pope in verse than Pope came to Swift in prose. Among the public men with whom he associated there was none except Lord Oxford and Lord Carteret upon whom he did not look down. 'Send us back our boobies,' he exclaimed when Carteret came as Viceroy to Dublin. 'What do we want with men like you?' A characteristic compliment, characteristically worded.

Mr. Lecky has very properly included Swift among the leaders of Irish opinion. Yet there were few things which annoyed him so much as to be called an Irishman. That he was born in Ireland he could not deny. But he was ready with an answer. A man, he said, is not a horse because he was born in a stable. Much of his life, as everybody knows, was spent in Ireland, and the whole Cathedral of St. Patrick's, not otherwise interesting, is overshadowed by the awful inscription engraved by his own desire upon his tomb. The boast which he there somewhat inappropriately makes is a true one.[1] He did fight manfully and consistently for what he believed to be the liberties of Ireland. But by Ireland he meant Protestant Ireland, and her liberties were bound up for him in a Parliament where no Catholic could sit or be represented. Even upon the Irish House of Commons, when it presumed to touch the rights of the Protestant Church, he turned with a concentrated fury which makes the *Legion Club* almost terrifying to read after the lapse of more than a century and a half. Swift did not regard the Irish Catholics as citizens. He considered them, in Mr. Gladstone's picturesque phrase, to have nothing human about them except the form. In one respect only he was their friend. Despite his parsimonious habits, the indelible result of early indigence, he was generous to the poor. But his political sympathies and his political support were confined to the Protestants and to the Pale. Swift's politics are not, I think, difficult to understand. He was educated by Sir William Temple in loyalty to the Revolution of 1688, and he received some personal kindness from the King. He never became a Jacobite, or a thorough-going supporter of hereditary right. The Whigs did nothing for him after Temple's death, and he had a special grievance against Lord Somers. But his removal from one party to the other was not the mere consequence of personal disappointment. He had to choose between being a High Churchman and being a Whig. He chose not to be a Whig.

The position of a Whig clergyman has always been difficult. His politics are apt to make him ashamed of his profession. His profession is apt to make him afraid of his politics. The keen intellect and wholesome character of Sydney Smith raised him above shame or fear. He held that the Whig party and the Church of England were co-ordinate and providential instruments for the promotion of human happiness. Swift's intellect was as subtle as it was capacious, as clear as it was profound. But his character was warped and morbid, perverted by some insidious disease which has puzzled all his biographers, and will puzzle them till the end of time. While his logical powers were singularly acute and penetrating, his passions, and especially the passion of hatred, were altogether beyond the control of his will. If he hated the Whigs for not advancing him in the Church, he hated them also for making light of the holy orders which he had chosen to take. He used to say himself that while the Whigs detested the Church, they were mighty civil to parsons, whereas the Tory high-fliers, who exalted the Church above measure, treated the heirs of the apostolic succession as a kind of upper servants. If Swift had been a layman he would probably have remained a Whig. Why he took orders, except that there was no other visible opening for him, it is difficult to say. But having once put on the gown, he remained throughout his life as staunch to the Church of England and of Ireland as ever was soldier to his regiment or politician to his party. If he had been a student of Shakespeare, which he certainly was not, he might have said with Sir Oliver Martext, 'Not a fantastical fool of them all shall flout me out of my calling.' Sir Walter Scott, in his fascinating *Life of Swift* which can never be superseded until another man of genius undertakes the task, describes Swift as deeply and sincerely religious. It is presumptuous either to disagree with Sir Walter, or to probe the recesses of the human soul. We cannot follow Swift into his private chapel, or his secret devotions. We can only judge him by his works. There may be religion in the *Tale of a Tub*, though for my part I think that Queen Anne and Voltaire were right when from their different points of view they regarded it as casting ridicule upon all forms of the Christian faith.

It certainly did for Swift what *Tristram Shandy* did for Sterne. It cost him his chance of a bishopric. And much as one may be disposed to take the side of brilliant eccentricity against orthodox dulness, it is impossible to say that in these instances the royal objections were unfounded.

The man who can find religion in Swift's sermons must have a microscopic eye. Tried even by the standard of the eighteenth century, they are singularly secular. But perhaps the surest indication of his real creed is given in the striking verses on the Day of Judgment, which were not published till long after his death. They were privately sent by Chesterfield in a letter to Voltaire, but everybody now knows the vigorous lines:

> Ye who in diverse sects were shammed,
> And came to see each other damned;
> (For so folks told you, but they knew
> No more of Jove's designs than you).
> The world's mad business now is o'er,
> And Jove resents such pranks no more.
> I to such blockheads set my wit!
> I damn such fools! Go, go, you're bit.

The ingenious critic is at liberty to observe that Jove is an abbreviation of Jupiter, and that Jupiter was a heathen divinity not entitled to the respect of Christians. Such criticism would prove Montaigne to have believed in miracles.

It is of course true that in theological or ecclesiastical controversy Swift always took the orthodox side. He writes as one equally averse from the doctrines of Rome and the doctrines of Geneva. He was as 'sound on the goose' as Parson Thwackum himself. When he said religion he meant the Christian religion; when he said the Christian religion, he meant the Protestant religion; and by the Protestant religion he meant the religion of the Church of England. For the Deists of his time, such as Toland, Asgill, Collins, and Coward, he had a profound and a just contempt. He refers to 'that quality of their voluminous writings which the poverty of the English language compels me to call their style.' In his famous argument upon the inconveniences which would result from the immediate abolition of Christianity by law, he drenches them with vitriolic scorn. But it is all purely intellectual. 'As if Christianity wasn't good enough, and far too good, for such as you,' is the sentiment which underlies the invective. Professor Huxley was not an orthodox Christian. Yet he said that if Bishop Butler were alive, he would put to silence the shallow infidelity of the day. Swift showed no indignation against Bolingbroke, who was a notorious sceptic, nor against

Pope, who was certainly not a Protestant, and was a Catholic only in name. It was the material property, not the spiritual influence of the Church, for which he was most eager to fight. His clear strong mind was fretted by the pretentious cleverness of men who acquired a spurious reputation for wit and learning by their attacks upon established beliefs. If that is religion, then Swift was religious. But so far as religion is contained in the Sermon on the Mount, or the thirteenth chapter of the first epistle to the Corinthians, Swift had no more of it than Bolingbroke and a good deal less than Voltaire. He had the honesty to keep every vestige of it out of his own epitaph on himself.

Swift was by far the greatest writer who ever devoted himself to the service of the Tory party. Johnson's political pamphlets are worthless compared with Swift's, and when Burke thundered against the French Revolution he spoke for a large number of Whigs. Although I should not myself rate *The Conduct of the Allies* so high as *The Anatomy of an Equivalent,* or *Thoughts on the Causes of the Present Discontents,* I know of no other English pamphleteer who could be put on a level with Halifax, Swift and Burke. But whereas Halifax was for years what we should call a Cabinet Minister, and Burke the greatest orator in the House of Commons, Swift was disqualified from even entering Parliament. Nor was he really trusted by the Ministers whom he served. As Mr. Morley says, he was the dupe of his great friends. They called him Jonathan; they treated him with every external mark of confidence and attention. If they had not, he would have turned upon them with the utmost ferocity. But they did not tell him that they were Jacobites at heart, and in communication with the King over the water. It was not special knowledge that gave Swift the mastery, but the fact that he had a statesman's mind. Macaulay has written in the margin of the letter to the October Club that a man must have been behind the scenes in politics to understand the excellence of this pamphlet. It might, he says, have been written in defence of the Whig Government from 1835 to 1841. It might, I add, have been an apology for the Liberal Government from 1892 to 1895. It is the old dilatory plea against expecting everything at once, wanting the millennium, as Mr. Anthony Hope says, in a Pickford van, but expressed with a plausible and persuasive subtlety that takes in almost everyone, except the author. Yet even then when his object was to conciliate the country and allay dissatisfaction with Lord Oxford, Swift cannot refrain from irony. Eminent statesmen, he remarked, had sometimes told him that politics were only common sense. It was the one thing they told him that was true, and the one thing they wished him not to believe. More delicate, and not less deadly, is the account of the Minister who, because he can judge better than the public when he knows more than they, thinks that he must be wiser than the rest of the world when their information is the same as his own. In practical sagacity Swift may be compared with the favourite object of his aversion, Sir Robert Walpole. He had one of those intellects which no sophistry can delude, and which are incapable of deviating from the path of reason. When the nation was mad over the South Sea Bubble, Swift, in a few simple stanzas, exposed the whole fabric of deception in a manner intelligible to a child.

What they do in heaven, said Swift, we know not; what they do not we know. They neither marry, nor are given in marriage. *Chatter about Harriet* was the late Professor Freeman's epigrammatic summary of recent literature on Shelley. There is nothing new to be said about the relations between Swift and Stella. Sir Henry Craik, in his exhaustive biography, has collected the evidence in favour of the marriage. Mr. Churton Collins, one of the few people who write too little, has argued with great ability the negative case. Every detail of Swift's career is interesting. But as the alleged marriage was a nominal, and not a real one, it is possible to exaggerate the importance of this particular incident. Upon the general subject of Swift's conduct to women Sir Walter Scott has said the last, or the last profitable, word. With exquisite delicacy, and with true insight, he has shown that Swift's passions were of another kind, and that he was incapable of falling in love. Unfortunately he could inspire feelings which he could not return. But that is a subject which Thackeray has made his own for ever. It is, of course, to Swift's friendship for Stella, whatever its precise nature may have been, that we owe the celebrated *Journal,* with its 'baby language,' its unflinching revelation of character, and its great historical value. I cannot see the tenderness which some have found or thought they found in it. It was written at the happiest, or least unhappy, period of his life, and yet it is full of gloomy pride, of obstinate isolation, of implacable revenge. For acute observation of men and manners, for lurid insight into hidden motives, for a haughtiness of temper which no despot could have surpassed, it is singular in the documents of autobiography. It was Swift's curse that nothing mean or vile or low or nasty ever escaped the pitiless keenness of his penetrating eye. He employed his unrivalled powers of ridicule and invective on the side of religion and virtue, but of decency he did not know the meaning. Even the 'troughs of Zolaism' contain nothing fouler than some of Swift's so-called poems. These are only fit to be burned by the common hangman, and it is wonderful that they should have been preserved. Some of his best and gravest work contains expressions from which most laymen would have shrunk, and of which any clergyman should have been ashamed. But Swift was ashamed of nothing. He was exempt from moral and apparently even from physical nausea. No idea was too disgusting for his imagination, no image too loathsome for his pen. The *Journal to Stella* owes, I cannot help thinking, some of its charm to its freedom from this disfiguring grossness. For this must be said of Swift, whether it be against him or in his favour, he neither conceals what is repulsive nor varnishes what is foul. Filthy he often is, prurient never. He cannot have made vice attractive to man or woman.

He was, in sober truth and earnest, a real cynic and misanthrope. Born with a temper which was a greater misfortune than any corporal defect, he nursed and cherished the *sæva indignatio* of which he boasts on his tomb until it subdued his will, overpowered his reason, and left him to expire a driveller and a show. He is the only great writer who did actually hate his fellow-men. The ordinary characteristics of human nature were to him odious in themselves. And when they appeared most fair, his terrible fancy transformed them. He could not see a beautiful woman without fancying how coarse her skin would look under a microscope. *Gulliver's Travels* has been called a political satire. It is a satire and a libel on humanity. More and more savage does the author grow with the progress of his work, until in the last part he is like the demoniac raging among the tombs. Critics have praised the verisimilitude of *Gulliver,* and told the story of the Irish Bishop who said he did not believe a word of it. There is a humorous exactness of detail in the wildest extravagances of the fiction, no doubt. But Swift had not the peculiar gift of Defoe. He does not inspire belief in everything he says, like that most imaginative and unscrupulous of romancers. To do so a man must have his prejudices and passions under control. Swift could govern himself well enough when he was writing on politics or upon any abstract question. It is in dealing with mankind that his fury carries him away.

Only such an intellect could have been proof so long against such a temper. Only such a temper could in the end have ruined such an intellect. It was said of a former Speaker that he always flew into a passion in Parliamentary English. Swift's irritability, to use a mild word, did no injury to his style. Of Swift's prose it seems to me almost impossible to speak too highly. It has not the splendour of Milton's, or Dryden's, or Burke's. But as a method of conveying thought it is perfect. Nothing once said by Swift could ever be said again without being spoiled in the saying. Absolute and utter simplicity is the distinguishing mark of his style. No doubt this simplicity is a highly artificial product. It is the result of pruning, of trimming, of cutting down. The result and the object of these processes is to leave the reader face to face with the precise idea which the writer wished to convey. There is no veil, however thin, between the mind of the author and the mind of the public. Clearness and force could not be more harmoniously combined. Swift's reasoning faculty, when he used it at all, worked with consummate accuracy and without the slightest friction. There were very few things he could not understand, and whatever he could understand he could explain to the humblest capacity. His mind supplied him with an endless succession of ludicrous images, but he used them only when they assisted the point he wished to drive home. Tricks and mannerisms he discarded and abhorred. After the lapse of nearly two hundred years his best work shows little or no trace of obsolete phrases and idioms. It was the choicest English then, it is the choicest English now. The *Drapier's Letters* deal with the coinage of Wood's halfpence. Nobody except an historical student cares any longer for Wood, and the copper coins he introduced into Ireland under contract with the Government. But the *Drapier's Letters* can be read with delight by all who enjoy masculine reasoning, simple eloquence, and racy humour.

Swift's prose masterpiece is now, I think, commonly admitted to be the *Argument against the Abolition of Christianity*. The *Mechanical Operation of the Spirit* is almost equal to it. The *Drapier's Letters* are as much superior to Junius as Junius is superior to Wilkes. The Dean's own judgment upon the *Tale of a Tub* is well known. 'What a genius I had when I wrote that book!' he said in his clouded and declining years. The *Tale of a Tub* has passed beyond criticism and become a standard of satirical excellence. It is from no affectation of singularity that I prefer the later produce of that 'savage and unholy genius' to this early effort. There is genius in the *Tale,* of course. Swift was right in that. It is an exuberant genius, bursting all bounds of taste and congruity, with all Voltaire's license and none of Voltaire's tact. As one grows older one comes back to Horace:

Est modus in rebus, sunt certi denique fines.

With all Swift's admiration for the *Tale of a Tub,* he did not repeat the experiment. He had, in a literary sense, sown his wild oats. He began to curb not his irony, but his fancy, and the soberer he grew the more deadly he became. Under the frown or smile of that irony everything pretentious shrivelled up and disappeared. The Dean detested hypocrisy so bitterly that he railed even against ordinary devotion. The tears of a widow weeping for her husband were to him a cloak for her wish to find another. He could not believe in purity of motive or unselfishness of aim. Yet he was not without virtues of his own. He gave away money to the needy, though no professional miser loved money more. He risked the loss of his own liberty in order to fight, if not for the liberties of Irishmen, at least for the liberties of Ireland. His patriotism was genuine and incorruptible. If he sometimes trampled on the weak, he never stooped to flatter the strong. Although his early opinions were liberal, there is no reason to doubt the sincerity of his later Toryism. The truth is that as Burke bowed down and worshipped the British Constitution, so Swift bent the knee to the Established Church. Both may have been wrong, but one was as honest as the other.

Swift taught by example, and not by precept. It may be doubted whether he had any theories of style. He was a sound classical scholar, though, like most men of his time, especially Pope and Addison, he studied Latin rather than Greek. Ignorance of the Greek language accounts for Sir William Temple's belief that the *Letters of Phalaris* were genuine, and Bentley's monumental treatise was out of Swift's depth altogether. But he knew Horace and Virgil a good deal better than he knew Shakespeare or Milton. He had the classical standard of taste, with a rooted dislike of anything tawdry, showy, or 'flash.' His criticisms on Bishop Burnet exhibit an equal abhorrence of the Bishop's politics, which were Whiggery of the purest water, and the Bishop's English, which was anything but pure. He was the master, not the servant, of language, and he could always make it do exactly what he wanted. For slovenly writing, as for slovenly knowledge, he had an irrepressible contempt.

"The most accomplished way (he says in the *Tale of the Tub*), the most accomplished way of using books at present is two-fold: either, first, as some men do Lords, learn their titles exactly, and then brag of their acquaintance. Or secondly, which is indeed the choicer, the profounder and polite method, to get a thorough insight into the index, by which the whole book is governed and turned, like fishes by the tail. For to enter the palace of learning by the great gate requires an expense of time and forms. Therefore men of much taste and little ceremony are content to get in by the back door."

One is reminded of the well-known couplet:

For index-learning turns no student pale,
Yet holds the eel of science by the tail.

'As some men do Lords' cannot, I suppose, be grammatically defended. Like other masters of English, such as Newman and Froude in our own day, Swift is occasionally careless of minute accuracy, and his dullest editors have an obvious satisfaction in pointing out these trivial defects. A mistake showing real ignorance is not to be found in Swift.

It was from the *Battle of the Books,* not one of Swift's happiest efforts, that Matthew Arnold took one of his most successful and popular phrases. The *Battle of the Books* is, we may be thankful to reflect, all that remains of the foolish controversy over the rival merits of ancient and modern literature. The disputants might as profitably have employed themselves in comparing the relative excellence of Virgil and Dryden, or of Homer and Pope. Swift, in gratitude to Temple, who oddly took the side of authors he could not read, came forward as their champion.

> "As for us, the ancients (he wrote,) we are content with the bee to pretend to nothing of our own beyond our wings and our voice; that is to say, our flights and our language. For the rest, whatever we have got, has been by infinite labour and search, and ranging through every corner of nature. The difference is that instead of dirt and poison we have rather chose to fill our hives with honey and wax, thus furnishing mankind with the two noblest things, which are sweetness and light."

There is an imaginative beauty in this passage to which Swift seldom attains. His habitual vein was irony, which came as surely and as naturally to him as the rhymed couplet came to Pope. There is scarcely a better specimen of this, his favourite weapon, to be found in all his works than the final sentences of the strange and sinister *Argument,* to which I have so often referred. He had already asked what young men of wit and fashion would have for the object of their raillery if the Christian religion were abolished; how Freethinkers could gain a reputation for learning; and what could hinder Popery from being put in the place of religion. Then comes the climax:—

> "To conclude, whatever some may think of the great advantage to trade by this favourite scheme, I do very much apprehend that in six months time after the Act is passed for the extirpation of the Gospel the Bank and East India Stock may fall at least 1 per cent. And since that is fifty times more than ever the wisdom of our age thought fit to venture for the preservation of Christianity, there is no reason why we should be at so great a loss merely for the sake of destroying it."

That seems to me finer than anything in Voltaire. Voltaire always seems to be conscious of his own cleverness, to be showing what he can do. Very wonderful his performances are. But in Swift's best work, this *Argument* for example, the strokes descend upon the victims with the grim, relentless force of circumstance or fate. It is not so much Swift as the naked truth of things, stripped of all subterfuge and disguise, speaking through Swift's mouth, while upon Swift's face there is never the flicker of a smile.

In his *Thoughts on Various Subjects* Swift displays a lighter and, if such a word may be used of such a man, a more genial mood. The sarcasm is there, as indeed it is everywhere. But it is of a less cruel and more human sort. 'The reason why so few marriages are happy is because young ladies spend their time in making nets, not in making cages.' For exquisite felicity of diction that little apophthegm is unapproached and unapproachable. Like all the best verbal wit, it is not merely verbal. It is worth, to my mind, half a dozen essays from the *Spectator*. Somewhat grimmer is the following:—

> "Venus, a beautiful, good-natured lady, was the goddess of love; Juno, a terrible shrew, the goddess of marriage; and they were always mortal enemies."

But, after all, this was the last subject on which Swift could pose as an authority. Here is a judgment more in his line:—

> "As universal a practice as lying is, and as easy a one as it seems, I do not remember to have heard three good lies in all my conversation, even from those who were most celebrated in that faculty."

From the friend of Pope this is much. But we could wish that the Dean had given us the two.

> True genuine dulness moved his pity,
> Unless it offered to be witty.

So wrote Swift with truth and sincerity, in the most celebrated of all his poems. The Dean's most shining merit was his hatred of cant. Carlyle attacked the cant of philanthropy, forgetting that there was a cant of misanthropy as well, and that malevolence may be quite as sentimental as its opposite. But Swift detested shams in general, not merely the shams obnoxious to himself in particular. His loathing of his own kind was not affectation. It was an awful reality. In more wholesome ways, and from more manly motives, he despised from the bottom of his soul all who pretended to gifts or virtues which they did not possess. Intellectual contempt was at the root of his animosity against superficial deism and against the false wit which would amuse no one if it were not profane. His *Letter to a Young Clergyman* shows that he applied the same principle with strict impartiality to those of his own cloth. Swift indeed felt for the clergy as Johnson felt for Garrick. He would not suffer any one else to criticise them without rushing to their defence, and yet no one criticised them more severely than himself. His advice to this young man might have been read and pondered with advantage by the contemporary school of divines, whose sermons Archbishop Tait once described as like essays from the *Spectator* without the Addisonian eloquence.

> "I cannot forbear warning you in the most earnest manner against endeavouring at wit in your sermons, because by the strictest

computation it is very near a million to one that you have none;
and because too many of your calling have made themselves
everlastingly ridiculous by attempting it. I remember several
young men in the town who could never leave the pulpit under
half a dozen conceits; and the faculty adhered to those gentlemen
a longer or shorter time, exactly in proportion to their several
degrees of dulness. Accordingly I am told that some of them retain
it to this day. I heartily wish the brood was at an end."

About Swift's own sermons there is some uncertainty. There are not many
of them extant, and it is doubtful whether they were preached. The religious
or spiritual element is as conspicuously absent from most of them as it is from
Sterne's. With all his staunch Protestantism, and his not less resolute High
Churchmanship, in which may be traced a curious resemblance between him
and Archbishop Laud, Swift could be coarser than Rabelais, and profaner than
Voltaire. Men have been convicted and imprisoned in this country for treating
sacred subjects less offensively than Swift treats the Holy Communion in the
Tale of a Tub. The only distinction which could have been drawn by the most
ingenious counsel for the defence is that the ostensible object of Swift's satire
was not the Christian religion, but the Church of Rome, and the essence of
blasphemy is not so much its objects as the methods by which those objects
are attempted or achieved. The following passage from Swift's sermon on the
fate of Eutychus, though it may be unsuitable to the pulpit, is not unfit for
publication, and is certainly neither 'conceited' nor dull:—

"The accident which happened to this young man in the text hath
not been sufficient to discourage his successors; but because the
preachers now in the world, however they may exceed St. Paul in
the art of setting men to sleep, do extremely fall short of him in the
working of miracles, therefore men are become so cautious as to
choose more safe and convenient stations and postures for taking
their repose without hazard of their persons; and upon the whole
matter choose rather to entrust their destruction to a miracle than
their safety."

That has all the best qualities of Swift's humour without any of the faults
which sometimes disfigure it. The ideas are intensely ludicrous, and the
images by which they are conveyed excessively comical. And yet there is
all the appearance of grave reasoning, of flawless logic, and of an obvious
reflection which almost apologises for being a platitude. The little phrase
'upon the whole matter' is inserted with admirable artifice. It suggests the

imperturbable demeanour of a dignified judge, calmly weighing the reasons on both sides, and concluding that it was better to sit in church upon a bench from which there was no possibility of falling.

Swift was not only a statesman and a satirist. He was also the father of what is now called Society Verse. It is curious that before he hit upon the form which best suited him, and in which the inimitable stanzas on his own death were composed, he should have perpetrated some of those crazy Pindarics which were fashionable when he was young. The 'Odes' to Archbishop Sancroft and to Sir William Temple, particularly the latter, are not to be matched for badness among the worst imitations of Cowley. It was a strange theory that because Pindar wrote Greek poetry of the highest excellence in a rather difficult and complicated metre, therefore English poetry could be written in no metre at all. Fortunately the error came to a speedy and ignominious death at the hands of Swift himself. Well might Dryden, who died in 1700, say, 'Cousin Swift, you will never be a poet.' Swift never forgave the insult, and he says, in the *Tale of a Tub*, with a malignity which for once was stupid, that Dryden would never have been taken for a great poet if he had not in his own Prefaces so often made the assertion. But he profited by the condemnation, and wrote no more Pindarics. In 1698 he produced the first of the poems, if poems they are to be termed, which will be read with pleasure and copied with freedom so long as English verse remains a vehicle of thought. I mean of course the famous lines, *Written in a Lady's Ivory Table-Book*.

> Here you may read, 'Dear charming saint;'
> Beneath, 'A new receipt for paint;'
> Here, in beau spelling, 'Tru tel deth,'
> There, in her own, 'For an el breth;'
> Here, 'Lovely nymph pronounce my doom!'
> There, 'A safe way to use perfume;'
> Here, a page filled with billet-doux;
> On t'other side, 'Laid out for shoes;'
> 'Madam, I die without your grace,'
> 'Item, for half a yard of lace.'

Two years afterwards, when chaplain to Lord Berkeley in Ireland, Swift wrote *Mrs. Harris's Petition*, which as a bit of low comedy is unsurpassed in literature. Has Dryden's prophecy been fulfilled? That depends upon the definition of poetry, which has never yet, and perhaps never will be, authoritatively defined. But those who deny the title of poet to Swift must deny it also to Pope. They stand and fall together. Pope was Swift's avowed model. He never, he said, could read a line of Pope's without wishing it were his own. Is there such a thing as the poetry of common sense? Horace thought there was, and by his judgment I am content to abide. Swift, like Pope, creeps on the ground. He does not strike the stars. He has no height of imagination, no depth of passion, and, even in his verses to Stella, no store of tenderness. Few lines of his are more characteristic than his playful exposure of the South Sea Bubble:—

> A shilling in the bath you fling;
>   The silver takes a nobler hue
> By magic virtue in the spring,
>   And seems a guinea to your view.
> But as a guinea will not pass
>   At market for a farthing more,
> Shown through a multiplying glass
>   Than what it always did before.
> So cast it in the Southern Seas,
>   And view it through a Jobber's Bill,
> Put on what spectacles you please,
>   Your guinea's but a guinea still.

This is quite conclusive and entirely prosaic. Swift became with practice a perfect master of form in verse, and the lines on his own death are flawless from beginning to end. In this respect he far excelled his contemporary Prior, and has not been outdone by his successor Praed. Cowper was his admiring student, and Johnson's birthday odes to Mrs. Thrale were modelled on Swift's to Mrs. Johnson. The consummate mastery which Swift gradually obtained over his instrument, and the perfect ease with which he wielded it, are perhaps the secret of its permanent charm. The satiric humour, which in his prose is apt to be savage, and in the *Legion Club* is ferocious, is mellowed and chastened with social playfulness in *Cadenus and Vanessa*, or *Baucis and Philemon*.

> As Rochefoucauld from nature drew
> His maxims, I believe them true;
> They argue no corrupted mind
> In him, the fault is in mankind.

Swift's estimate of the illustrious Frenchman is sound and just. The cynicism of La Rochefoucauld was the cynicism of an outraged sentimentalist. He expected too much of men and women. Because they were not angels, because their lives did not square with their theories, he believed the mass of them to be utterly base. But he always recognised that there was a noble remnant. He stopped far short of Swift's universal misanthropy. *Il y a peu d'honnêtes femmes,* he says, in the bitterest of all his maxims, *qui ne soient lasses de leur métier.* There were a few, and to La Rochefoucauld it was the minority that made the world fit for human habitation. It was not a high standard of morals, nor a small capacity for belief, that drove Swift into cursing and railing. It was constitutional distemper and despair. If Archbishop King knew the secret of his misery, he kept it like a gentleman and carried it to the grave. The death of Stella, as Thackeray says, extinguished his last ray of hope, and almost his last gleam of reason. 'After that darkness and utter night fell upon him.' If one cannot truly say 'What a noble mind was here o'erthrown,' one may at least feel that a gigantic intellect sank suddenly into the abyss. There was no warning. Until Swift became a lunatic, his mind cut like a diamond through the hardest substances in its way. No sophistry ever deceived him. No difficulty ever puzzled him. There was nothing he thought which he could not express. The pellucid simplicity of his style, both in prose and in verse, came of clear thinking and sound reasoning, assisted by the habit of daily explanation to unlettered women. It is easy to understand him, because he understood so easily himself. A great deal of time is wasted by the 'general reader' in guessing at the meaning of authors who did not mean anything in particular. Uncertainty is the fruitful parent of obscurity, and many people write obscurely in the hope that they will be thought profound. Like the subaltern who would not form his letters distinctly lest his correspondents should find out how he spelt, there is a class of writers who will not be plain lest the poverty of their thoughts should be exposed. Swift, it must in fairness be admitted, did not treat of questions which transcend the powers of human language. His prose is never metaphorical, and his poetry could always be translated into prose. He had what the French call an *esprit positif.* Philosophical speculation did not attract him, and if he inwardly cultivated any religious mysticism, he kept it entirely to himself. Eloquent he was not. He seldom rises and seldom falls. What made him the prince of journalists was his mental tact. He had the public ear. He knew precisely when the anvil was hot, and when he ought to strike it. To say that he never took a bad point would be to exaggerate, though there are not many controversialists who took so few. When he turned Bishop Burnet's fears of a Jacobite restoration into ridicule, he merely showed that the worthy Bishop knew the danger, and that he did not. That any one should ever have thought Harley a greater minister than Walpole seems incomprehensible to us, and though it may have been true friendship, it was false judgment. But Swift's particular errors are quite unimportant now. His value to posterity lies in his matchless humour, his statesmanlike wisdom, his hatred of pretence and sham, his intellectual integrity, and above all the sustained perfection of his English style.

Notes

1. Hie depositum est corpus
   Jonathan Swift, S.T.P.,
   Hujus Ecclesiae Cathedralis
   Decani:
   Ubi sæva indignatio
   Ulterius cor lacerare nequit.
   Abi Viator,
   Et imitare, si poteris,
   Strenuum pro virili libertatis vindicem.
   Obiit anno (1745)
   Mensis Octobris die (19)
   Aetatis anno (78).
   (Here lies the body of Jonathan Swift, Doctor of Divinity, Dean of this Cathedral Church, where fierce rage can tear the heart no more. Go, traveller, and imitate, if you can, an earnest, manly champion of freedom. He died on the 19th of October, 1745, in the 78th year of his age.)

   The dates were of course left blank by Swift. No alteration was made in the epitaph, except to fill them in.

—HERBERT PAUL, "The Prince of Journalists,"
Nineteenth Century, January 1900, pp. 73–87

Chronology

1667	Jonathan Swift is born in Dublin, Ireland, to English parents; father dies.
1674–82	Studies at Kilkenny School.
1682–88	Trinity College, Dublin; B.A. *speciali gratia* in 1684; work toward an M.A. interrupted by the Glorious Revolution.
1689–94	Secretary to Sir William Temple, Moor Park; meets Stella (Esther) Johnson; first outbreak of Ménière's disease probably in 1690.
1694	Takes Anglican deacon's orders.
1695	Ordained priest in the Church of Ireland; moves to Kilroot parish.
1697–98	He most likely writes *A Tale of a Tub* at this time.
1699–1710	Appointments and livings in the Church of Ireland. As domestic chaplain to the Earl of Berkeley, Lord Justice of Ireland, Swift begins his career as defender of the rights of the Church of Ireland, working with the Whigs.
1704	*A Tale of a Tub* and *The Battle of the Books* are published.
1707	Meets Vanessa (Hester) Vanhomrigh.
1708–09	*The Bickerstaff Papers*.
1709	With Steele, founds the *Tatler*.
1710	Goes over to the Tories.
1713	Appointed dean of St. Patrick's Cathedral, Dublin; from this time, he lives mostly in Ireland.
1724–25	*The Drapier's Letters*.
1726	*Gulliver's Travels*.
1729	*A Modest Proposal*.
1742	He is declared insane.
1745	Swift dies and is buried in St. Patrick's Cathedral.

Index

PR
3727
.J6265
2009